ASPECTS OF GREEK AND ROMAN LIFE

General Editor: the late H. H. Scullard

★　★　★

THE LAW

IN CLASSICAL ATHENS

Douglas M. MacDowell

THE LAW IN CLASSICAL ATHENS

Douglas M. MacDowell

CORNELL UNIVERSITY PRESS

ITHACA, NEW YORK

First published 1978 by Cornell University Press.
First printing, Cornell Paperbacks, 1986.

Library of Congress Cataloging in Publication Data
(For library cataloging purposes only)

MacDowell, Douglas Maurice.
  The law in classical Athens.

  (Aspects of Greek and Roman life)
  Includes bibliographical references and index.
  1. Law, Greek. 2. Law—Greece—Athens.
I. Title.   II. Series.
LAW   340.5′5′3′85   78-54141
ISBN 0–8014–1198–x (cloth)
ISBN 0–8014–9365–x (paper)

Printed in the United States of America

CONTENTS

PREFACE

Ancient Greek law is a fragmented and elusive subject for study. Every city-state had its own laws; no doubt there were similarities and some states copied laws from others, but we should never assume without evidence that any particular rule was shared by two different states. And often the evidence is lacking. Even for Athens, the state about which we know most, we have only a limited number of texts of actual laws. Our chief source of information is the texts of about a hundred law-court speeches, in all of which the speakers are arguing on one side of a case, so that their statements about the law are tendentious and incomplete. These have to be supplemented by allusions in comedy, history, philosophy, and other literature, which have their own difficulties of interpretation.

Yet the attempt to understand the subject is worth making. Law is the formal expression of a people's beliefs about right and wrong conduct, and no people in the world has had more interesting and original beliefs about conduct than the ancient Greeks. Besides, the Athenians' legal system, though less coherent than the Romans' a few centuries later, was probably the most comprehensive that any people had yet devised, and was certainly the first to be established on a democratic basis. So it has a special importance for students of society and morality as well as for readers of Greek literature.

Many specialized books exist in which topics of Greek law are discussed in detail, most often in German, but it is hard to find any book in English which gives a satisfactory introduction to the subject. This is what I have tried to provide: a book which can be read by anyone interested in the Greeks, even if he has no previous knowledge of their law. Such a book cannot include everything, and my principles of selection and arrangement are practical rather than logical. I have concentrated on Athens in the period from Perikles to Demosthenes (approximately 435 to 322 BC) because that is the period about which the Attic orators tell us; but I have also included an opening chapter on trial procedures in Homer and Hesiod, because those poets are read by most students of Greek literature and they offer a base from which to measure the Athenian achievement; and I have occasionally used evidence from authors such as Menander who wrote in and about a period slightly later than Demosthenes. Constitutional law, sacred law, and the rules of hereditary and local groups, such as phratries and demes, are largely or entirely omitted; so also are jurisprudence and philosophical discussion of law. The first part of the book is mainly about the chronological development of the legal system, the second about the kinds of conduct regulated by law, and the third about legal procedures in the fourth century. But such a division cannot always be maintained; and my aim has been not to construct a strictly logical scheme, but to produce a book which can be read straight through and understood by a reader to whom the subject is new.

By profession I am a classicist, not a lawyer, and any lawyers who read this book may find my discussion of law unsophisticated. But I do not regard this as a serious handicap, since the Athenians themselves were not professional law-makers and had no knowledge of Roman or modern jurisprudence. More serious, perhaps, is the fact that, although I have read a good deal of modern work on Athenian law, I cannot claim familiarity with everything which has been written on it. Nevertheless I doubt whether I have missed anything of major importance; and the references in the notes at the end of the book, though very selective, should give a sufficient lead to those readers who wish to investigate a particular topic further. Even for specialists, I hope that the book will be of some use as a summary of the present state of knowledge of the subject; and they will find that it also incorporates some new suggestions of my own. It was completed in the summer of 1977, and does not take account of any publication which had not reached me by then.

All three-figure dates in the book are BC; a date with a diagonal stroke, such as 403/2, means one Athenian year, from midsummer to midsummer. I refer to Attic speeches by the names of the orators to whom they are traditionally attributed; that should not be taken as implying necessarily that I think the attribution correct in any particular instance. Finally I should like to record here my thanks to my colleague Dr R. A. Knox, whose constructive comments have helped me to make a number of corrections and improvements.

Glasgow   D. M. MacDowell

Part One: The Growth of a Legal System

1 JUDGEMENTS IN EARLY GREECE

INTRODUCTION

Quarrels and disputes are as old as mankind, or older. Two men may each claim to possess some desirable object or property, or a man may complain at another's behaviour and demand compensation or atonement.

The most primitive method of settling a dispute is for one of the disputants to overpower the other by force or intimidation. The civilized method is to refer the dispute to a third party, whose decision both disputants are required to accept. In some cases they do this willingly: both agree to submit the dispute to a judge (or judges) and undertake to accept his decision. In other cases one of the disputants is unwilling: he wishes to stay as he is, or to keep what he has, and only under compulsion will he submit to judgement.

Therefore, if judgement is to be effective in all cases, and not only in cases where both disputants accept it willingly, it must be backed up by power which extends over them both; that is, by the authority of the state or community to which they both belong. The simplest means of achieving this is for the judge and the ruler to be the same person. In an elementary society one man rules the others, and he also judges their disputes. Just as two squabbling children appeal to an adult to decide who shall have the toy train to play with, so in a simple society a man who believes himself wronged appeals to the king, and the king, like a fair but firm father, decides.

But some kings are not firm, and some are not fair; and who is to judge the king? A difference (some might say, the difference) between a simple and an advanced society is that in an advanced society judgements on individuals are not just made by another individual but are the judgements of the community, to which every individual is subject. The problem then is to select judges who can be taken to represent the whole population, and whose judgement may be regarded as that of the community.

The Athenians in the sixth, fifth, and fourth centuries BC developed for this purpose an elaborate system of trial by jury. It was one of the most democratic systems which have ever existed, and it was one of their greatest achievements in the organization of society. But, in order to appreciate the significance of what the Athenians did to improve methods of settling disputes, we need to know what methods were already in use before they got to work.

The evidence for judicial procedures in Greece before the end of the seventh century BC is not very satisfactory; for it consists simply of the poems of Homer and Hesiod. It is no use expecting to find in these poems a systematic account of judicial procedures. They are intended to be tales of gods and heroes (or, in the case of Hesiod's *Works and Days*, fraternal advice about farming and other matters), not legal or sociological treatises. Nevertheless, they do reveal incidentally a great deal of information about early Greek society and institutions, and they do contain allusions to disputes of various kinds. So it is reasonable to enquire what happens in Homer or Hesiod when a dispute arises: how is it conducted and resolved?

The answers are not consistent throughout the *Iliad* and *Odyssey*, the *Theogony* and *Works and Days*; in various disputes the characters conduct themselves in different ways. This may be because different poems (or even different parts of the same poem) were composed by different poets, at different times or in different places; but it is also possible for one person to observe and describe different procedures which are all in contemporary use. This is not the occasion to discuss how the Homeric poems were composed. Probably everyone would agree that the various kinds of dispute-procedure mentioned in the Homeric and Hesiodic poems all existed in early Greece, even if not all in the same place at the same time; and that is enough for the present purpose.

PRIMITIVE DISPUTES

In what different ways, then, are disputes settled in Homer? One method is for the two men who quarrel just to fight until one of them wins. In one passage in the *Odyssey* it is regarded as normal and acceptable for a man to get hit while fighting to keep possession of his cattle.

'Indeed, there is no sorrow or grief in a man's heart when he is hit while fighting for his own possessions, for cattle or white sheep; whereas ...' (*Odyssey* 17. 470–3)

And in the *Iliad* two men fighting to decide the boundary between their allotments of land are such a common sight that they are used in a simile to illustrate the fighting of soldiers at Troy.

'Just as two men contend about boundaries, with measuring-rods in their hands, in a common field, and fight about equal shares in a small piece of ground, so . . .' (*Iliad* 12. 421–4)

The matter-of-fact manner in which these fights are mentioned incidentally in order to provide a comparison or contrast implies that fighting is a regular way of settling a dispute.

A fight sometimes involves a whole family; for in the ancient world the family (in the wider sense of the word, including cousins) long retained great solidarity, and injury to the property or person of one of its members might be resented by them all. Thus in the *Odyssey*, if Telemakhos had had brothers, they could have been expected to help him in a fight against the wooers who were ruining the household. Above all, if a man is killed, his family is expected to exact vengeance from the killer. So Orestes kills his father's murderer Aigisthos, and this action is regarded as highly meritorious and honourable.[1]

But not everyone likes fighting, even in Homer. Some people prefer talking. In particular, talking may seem a better way of settling a dispute if one's opponent is stronger than oneself – though in this case the opponent may prefer fighting. So Iphitos found when Herakles took his mares; he went to Herakles's house, and Herakles entertained him as a guest, but when he asked for the mares Herakles killed him and kept the mares. But in other cases verbal negotiation may have been more successful; perhaps it proved so when Odysseus in his youth went to Messene to claim compensation for three hundred sheep.[2] The cases in which talk would be most likely to lead to a settlement would be those in which each of the parties was willing to compromise to some extent: 'Look here: if you'll agree to . . ., I'll agree to . . .' Although no instance of this kind of bargaining is described in detail in Homer, probably this was the procedure which led to the acceptance of payment (in property or precious metal) for homicide: the killed man's relatives, instead of killing the killer or chasing him into exile, agree to accept recompense (*poine*) in settlement of the dispute. In the *Iliad* Aias son of Telamon alludes to this when criticizing the stubbornness of Achilles.

'A man accepts recompense from the killer for his brother or his son who is dead; and so the one remains in his own country after paying a great amount, and the other's spirit and pride are appeased when he has received recompense. But *you* . . .' (*Iliad* 9. 632–6)

This means that the killer agrees to make a substantial payment, and the killed man's relative agrees not to seek further vengeance. Verbal negotiation leads to a bargain. Aias clearly regards this as a right and proper way to settle a dispute, since he contrasts it with Achilles's obstinate refusal to make a concession.

KINGS

In the examples mentioned so far the settlement of the dispute, whether by blows or by words, is conducted entirely by the disputants themselves, without any participation by outsiders. But of course it often happens that disputants, who do not wish to fight, are yet unable to reach agreement by talking to each other; and so they appeal to some other person to judge between them. This appeal to an outsider, thought to be impartial, is the origin of judicial procedure.

During the chariot-race in the *Iliad*, held at the funeral games in honour of Patroklos, two of the spectators watching from a distance disagree about which chariot is in the lead. Idomeneus maintains that Diomedes is leading, Aias son of Oileus that Eumelos is. Idomeneus proposes a bet.

'Come on, let us wager a tripod or a cauldron, and let us both make Agamemnon son of Atreus the judge of which mares are leading, so that you may learn and pay up.' (*Iliad* 23. 485–7)

The word *istor*, which I have here translated 'judge', literally means 'knower'; it means a man who knows better than others what is true, or what is right. Idomeneus's proposal for settling the dispute is that he and Aias should both agree to accept the decision of a man who knows better than they do. In this particular case the proposal is probably stupid, since to see the distant chariots what is required is keen eyesight rather than good judgement, and there is no reason to suppose that Agamemnon's eyes are any better than those of Idomeneus or Aias; and in fact Aias sensibly refuses to take the bet. But for our purpose it is most significant that Idomeneus suggests Agamemnon as the judge.

Agamemnon is the Greeks' leader, the chief of the kings. Idomeneus's assumption is that the right person to judge any dispute is the king.

This is a regular assumption in Homer. A number of passages show that judging disputes is regarded as one of the functions of a king. In the *Odyssey* Nestor 'knows judgements' more than other men because he has been king for three generations, and in the *Iliad* it is twice said that Zeus gives to a king the sceptre and the rules of judgement (*themistes*).[3] This probably means that a king was believed to enjoy divine inspiration; that is what would make him better than other men as a 'knower' of what is right. But it is not the only possible reason why a king was regarded as a good person to judge disputes. Another likely reason is his power. A disputant whose claim was rejected by a judge might just ignore the decision if the judge was merely an ordinary person, one of his own equals, but he would be afraid to ignore the king. So a king's judgement would be effective.

Hesiod's *Theogony* begins with an elaborate hymn to the nine Muses, daughters of Zeus, who among other activities watch over good kings.

'Whenever the daughters of great Zeus honour and watch over at birth one of the god-fostered kings, on his tongue they pour sweet dew, and out of his mouth flow gentle words. All the people look to him as he decides rights by straight judgements. Speaking surely, he skilfully ends at once even a grave dispute. This is the function of prudent kings: for people who are harmed in their dealings, they bring about restitution easily, talking men over with soft words.'

(*Theogony* 81–90)

This is the ideal of the king in a simple society, treating his subjects as a kindly father treats his children. When they quarrel, they appeal to him, and he decides what is fair. His decisions command instant assent, not just because he is the king, but also because he is a skilful and persuasive speaker, whose honeyed words reconcile his quarrelling subjects.

The picture is too good to be generally true, as Hesiod himself discovered. In his later poem *Works and Days* he urges his brother Perses to reach agreement with him privately and not seek justice from kings; disputes waste time which should be devoted to farming.

'When you have plenty of that [sc. agricultural produce], you can raise up disputes and strife for other men's property. But in your case, you will have no second chance to behave in this way; but let

us decide our dispute here and now, by straight judgements, the best
that Zeus sends. Previously we divided our inheritance, and you
seized a great deal else and tried to carry it off by great flattery of
gift-devouring kings, who are willing to give this kind of judgement.'

(*Works and Days* 33–9)

Further on in the poem he describes how the gods, and especially the
virgin daughter of Zeus named Dike (which should be translated
'judgement' or 'law' rather than 'justice'),[4] observe the behaviour of
men, to reward the just and punish the unjust.

'And whenever anyone scorns and thwarts her crookedly, at once
she sits by her father Zeus, son of Kronos, and relates the lawless
men's intent, that the people may pay for the wickedness of the kings,
who with evil intent turn judgements aside by stating them crookedly. Beware of this, O gift-devouring kings; make your speeches
straight, and forget crooked judgements altogether!' (*Works and Days*
258–64)

Since the *Theogony*, Hesiod's view of kings has turned sour; he has
found that they may be unfair as well as fair. Probably this was the
result of his quarrel with Perses over their inheritance from their father.
Perhaps what happened was that Perses claimed that Hesiod had taken
more than his share, appealed to the king, and persuaded the king (by
flattery or bribery, Hesiod suggests; but we should bear in mind that it
may have been generally regarded as normal and proper for kings to
receive gifts)[5] to decide in favour of Perses; and now, when a further
dispute had arisen, Perses wished to appeal to the king again. Since we
have only Hesiod's prejudiced statements, we cannot tell who was in
the right in this particular case. But we can accept the picture which it
gives of the judicial procedure in Boiotia around 700 BC. The procedure is as simple as it could be: a man who considers himself un-
fairly treated by another can appeal to the king, and the king gives his
decision.

The 'king' in Hesiod's case will be the local ruler; this probably
means the ruler of Thespiai, the Boiotian city in whose territory
Hesiod's village of Askra lay. The plural 'gift-devouring kings' in the
Works and Days passages might seem to imply that several rulers ruled
and judged jointly; but in the *Theogony* passage judgements are given
by one king, and so the plural in *Works and Days* may be just scornful

rhetoric, and it may be incautious to rely on it, as some modern scholars do, as evidence that more than one king ruled at a time. The king had sole authority and responsibility. Clearly Hesiod was reluctant to accept the king's first decision, and reluctant to have the second dispute submitted to the king; yet there is no suggestion that he might refuse to accept the king's judgement. If Perses appealed to the king, Hesiod could not stop him; if the king decided against Hesiod, Hesiod could not ignore the decision. This shows that the king had authority over Hesiod and Perses. But it does not mean that there was a legal rule (still less a written law) establishing the king's jurisdiction; his actual power would be enough to cause his decisions to be accepted.[6]

ELDERS AND PEOPLE

But kings are not the only persons to judge disputes in Homer. True, in discussing judges other than kings one might be tempted to discount queen Arete, who settles disputes among the Phaiakians, since she is stated to be quite exceptional; and when Telemakhos is called 'a giver of judgements' (*dikaspolos*) in Ithaka, that might possibly mean that he deputizes for the absent king Odysseus, although he certainly is not regarded as actually being king.[7] But when Achilles before Troy swears an oath by the sceptre which 'the sons of the Akhaians hold in their hands, the givers of judgements, who guard the rules of justice received from Zeus' (*Iliad* 1. 237–9), then it seems quite clear that judgements are given not by one king alone but by a number of leading men; and in a scene represented on the shield of Achilles 'the elders' are said to be giving judgement (see page 19). So we must accept that in a Homeric community others besides the monarch might be 'givers of judgements', and in other passages where a judge is mentioned we need not insist that a king is meant. The man who 'rises from the assembly for his supper, who decides many disputes of young men who seek judgement' (*Odyssey* 12. 439–40) is probably not a king but one of a number of elders or leading men who have spent a large part of the day in session to judge disputes.

This last passage suggests that more or less regular sittings of the chiefs or elders might be held to judge, in the course of a day, whatever disputes were brought before them.[8] It also shows that the place where such sittings were held was the assembly place (the Agora). Several other passages also mention the assembly place as the place where judgements are given.[9] Judgement may be given by one man or by a small number of men, but it is given in the presence of the people.

The presence of the people is not, I think, just incidental; it is an essential concomitant of judicial procedure in Homer. Some light is thrown on its purpose by another episode in the funeral games in the *Iliad*. Before the chariot-race begins Achilles sets out the various prizes, and at the end of the race each competitor claims the prize which is his due. Antilokhos claims the second prize, a mare, but then Menelaos indignantly objects that Antilokhos beat him by unfair means.

'Menelaos stood up in great vexation, implacably angry with Antilokhos. The herald put the staff in his hand and ordered the Argives to be silent, and then the godlike man spoke among them.

' "Antilokhos, you used to be wise; now what have you done! You spoiled my reputation and obstructed my horses by thrusting your own, which were far inferior, in front. Come, leaders and rulers of the Argives; judge between the two of us impartially, so that no Akhaian soldier may ever say, 'Menelaos overcame Antilokhos by lies and went off with the mare, because, though his horses were far inferior, he himself was superior in rank and power.' Well, I myself will give a judgement; and I declare no other Danaan will find fault with me, for it shall be fair. Noble Antilokhos, stand here, as is right, before your horses and chariot, hold in your hands the pliant whip, which you have driven with before, put your hand on the horses, and swear by the god who moves and shakes the earth that you did not intentionally hinder my chariot by a trick."

'The wise Antilokhos replied, "Be patient now; I am much younger than you, king Menelaos, and you are my superior. You know how a young man transgresses. His mind is hasty and his prudence slight. So be forbearing, and I will myself give you the mare which I have taken. And if you should also ask for something more from my house, I should be willing to give it to you at once, rather than fall for ever from your favour and be a sinner against the gods." ' (*Iliad* 23. 566–95)

So Antilokhos hands over the mare to Menelaos, and Menelaos is so pleased that he forgives Antilokhos and gives the mare back to him.

This argument is not only a contest of honour but also a dispute over the ownership of a piece of property.[10] Menelaos's method of settling it is to make a speech in the hearing of the other Greeks; he suggests that the leaders and rulers should judge the dispute, but then instead, before they have a chance to do so, he challenges Antilokhos to swear an oath that he raced fairly. The idea is that Antilokhos will be afraid to perjure himself, for fear of punishment by the gods; so if he swears everyone will believe him, and if he refuses to swear everyone will conclude that he did commit a foul. If the onlookers are thus convinced that Menelaos is telling the truth, presumably they will compel Antilokhos to hand over the mare. Menelaos's whole speech, though addressed to Antilokhos, is not intended merely to convince Antilokhos (who already knows whether he committed a foul or not); it is intended to convince the bystanders. He is trying to bring to bear on Antilokhos the pressure of public opinion.

Appealing to public opinion is something different from appealing to the king. A king may have special expertise as a judge, from talent or experience or divine inspiration. The general public can hardly be said to have special expertise. But what they do have, if they care to use it, is power. It is hard for an individual to defy the king, but it is even harder to defy the whole population. Judgement by the people, therefore, may be even more effective than judgement by the king or the elders. But the trouble is, in Homeric society, that the people are often inarticulate and an assembly indecisive.

There is one clear example in the *Odyssey* of a dispute being brought before the assembly of the people of Ithaka in the king's absence (besides one or two others where the possibility of such a complaint is suggested but it is not actually carried out). It occupies much of the second book, before Odysseus's return home. His son Telemakhos wishes to complain about the behaviour of the wooers and their spoliation of his property. He would defend himself and the household by force if he could, but he is too weak to do so. He cannot appeal to the king, because Odysseus is away; so what he does is to call an assembly of the people and lay his complaint before them. Speeches are made for and against, but in the end the meeting breaks up without making any decision.

THE TRIAL ON THE SHIELD OF ACHILLES

Thus a Homeric assembly is sometimes ineffective without leadership. The most effective decision is one in which public opinion is crystallized and expressed by the king or elders. The reason why judgements are given in the Agora is that they are given in accordance with the sentiments of the people assembled there. This is confirmed by the most important of all the Homeric passages referring to judicial proceedings.

This passage is not easy to interpret in detail, and some points in it remain doubtful and disputed. It occurs in the eighteenth book of the *Iliad*, where there is a long description of the marvellous shield of Achilles and the elaborate scenes pictured on it. Among the rest there is a city at peace, in which the following activity is in progress in the Agora.

'In the assembly place were people gathered. There a dispute had arisen: two men were disputing about the recompense for a dead man. The one was claiming to have paid it in full, making his statement to the people, but the other was refusing to receive anything; both wished to obtain trial at the hands of a judge. The people were cheering them both on, supporting both sides; and heralds quietened the people. The elders sat on polished stones in a sacred circle, and held in their hands sceptres from the loud-voiced heralds; with these they were then hurrying forward and giving their judgements in turn. And in the middle lay two talents of gold, to give to the one who delivered judgement most rightly among them.'

(*Iliad* 18. 497–508)

This passage has been discussed at great length by specialists in ancient law,[11] and it would be out of place to discuss here every controversial detail. It is clear that the object of dispute is the payment of recompense (*poine*) for the killing of a man. In early times, if a man was killed, the usual consequence was that his family thought it their duty to kill the killer in revenge. The killer would be unlikely to escape death unless he left the country and became an exile; and, if he was in fact killed, his family in turn would seek to kill his killer, so that an unending blood-feud between the two families resulted. To avoid this, a killed man's family might accept an amount of gold or other property as recompense for the killing, after which the affair was closed. In our passage the wording of the third sentence is ambiguous, and it could be translated: 'The one was claiming to have paid it in full . . ., but the other was denying that he had received anything.' Some scholars therefore take the view that the dispute is simply about the factual question whether the killer has already paid recompense or not. But the alternative view is preferable: the question is whether recompense is to be accepted or a blood-feud to continue. The killer, who admits that he committed the homicide, has publicly put down some payment and claims that nothing more is required of him, but the killed man's relative refuses to take it and insists that the feud between them shall continue. The dispute is not just about payment of a debt, but about the lengths to which revenge may be taken – a question closely related to the basic theme of the *Iliad*.

But the most important problem in this passage is: who will actually decide the case? It is clear that opinions are delivered by an unspecified number of elders. Each of them holds a sceptre as a symbol of his judicial function (the words 'they held sceptres in their hands' are clearly plural, so that it is not the case here, as elsewhere in the *Iliad*, that there is only one sceptre, held by each man in turn as he speaks), and each in turn gives his judgement. But their judgements may not all be identical; how will it be decided which one shall be accepted? The poet says that the disputants 'both wished to obtain trial at the hands of a judge'. The word for 'judge' (*istor*, 'knower') is singular. Who is this judge who will settle the dispute?

Various solutions have been proposed, among which three seem to deserve particular consideration.

(*a*) The judge is the chairman of the proceedings: either the king, or an elder who presides over the others. The other elders are just assessors; after hearing their opinions, he alone makes the final decision.

(*b*) The judge is the elder whose opinion is considered by the people to be the best. After each elder speaks the crowd, if it approves, applauds or cheers; the opinion which receives the most applause is the one which is accepted.

(*c*) 'At the hands of a judge' just means 'by arbitration' and refers to all the elders. The view of the majority of the elders prevails.

Each of these solutions is, in my opinion, possible; none can be definitely disproved. The trouble is that the poet describes the trial in progress, and simply does not tell us what will happen at the end of it. Nevertheless several considerations seem to tell in favour of *b*. With *c*, the use of the singular 'judge' for all the elders is really very awkward. It is also doubtful whether the notion of counting votes and accepting a numerical majority as decisive existed in Homeric times. With *a*, it is somewhat surprising that the king or chairman is not mentioned with a description of his activity, as the disputants, people, heralds, and elders all are. In favour of *b* it has been argued that the two gold talents mentioned in the last sentence of the passage (one talent contributed by each disputant) are a reward for the elder who gives the best judgement, so that some procedure for selecting the best individual judgement must have been followed. (The alternative translation of this sentence 'to give to the one who pleaded his case most rightly among them', meaning that the two talents were to be awarded to the successful disputant, is probably wrong, because there are only two disputants but 'most rightly' is superlative, not comparative.) Another argument in favour of *b* may be drawn from the sentence about the disputants' speeches, 'The one was claiming to have paid it in full, making his statement to the people . . .'; with *b* the speakers naturally address the people because it is the people who will decide which elder's judgement is to be accepted, whereas with *a* and *c* there is no particular reason why they should address the people rather than the elders.

If *b* is right, the most significant feature of this trial is the participation of the people. The two disputants come to the assembly, and each makes his speech to the people. As they speak, the crowd (or various individuals or groups within it) cheer or boo to show which statements they find convincing. When the two speeches are finished, the heralds quieten the crowd and call on the elders to give their judgements. The elders are men who are supposed to be good 'knowers' because of their age and experience. Each elder tries in turn to express in words the view of the case which he thinks the people take, or ought to take. The people cheer or applaud a judgement which they think good, and the heralds (presumably) have to decide which elder's judgement has received the most applause. This elder is the 'knower' whose verdict decides the case, and he receives the award of two talents for giving the best judgement. But the decision is, effectively, the people's.

PUBLIC OPINION

So in Homer the origin of democratic judgements can already be seen. Though verdicts may be delivered by a king or by elders, they are influenced and guided by public opinion. The speakers haranguing the crowd on the shield of Achilles, and Menelaos publicly challenging Antilokhos to an oath, are forerunners of the orators who addressed Athenian juries. The trial on the shield is far more civilized, and marks a far more advanced stage of judicial development, than the fights and arguments in some of the other passages from Homer which I have quoted.

But how typical is it? The case is an imaginary one, which a poet describes as being pictured by a god on a hero's shield. But similar trials must have been held in historical fact. Clearly the procedure is not imaginary, but one which the poet has actually seen in operation;

and it is not a special procedure devised for a single case, but a settled and regular one. But this does not mean (as modern readers sometimes assume) that it was the normal procedure in every Greek city at the time of the composition of the *Iliad*. All that we can legitimately infer is that this procedure was employed in at least one Greek community at a date not later than the time when this particular passage of the *Iliad* was composed. Some scholars believe the description of the shield of Achilles to have been composed at a later period than other parts of the *Iliad*, and in any case it cannot be dated with any precision.

Even in the place or places in which this procedure was established, it was probably not used for every dispute. The disputants on the shield come to trial voluntarily: 'both wished to obtain trial at the hands of a judge'. What would have happened if one of them had not so wished? There is nothing to show that he would have been compelled to attend the trial or to accept the judgement. Even when a formal judicial procedure was available, some men might prefer a fight. Still, if one disputant appealed to the king or elders and to the assembly, it would not be easy for his opponent to ignore their decision; and the more organized the community became, the harder it would be for an individual to defy formal public judgements. It was clearly in the public interest that disputes should be settled by judicial procedure rather than by fighting. No doubt there were some occasions when the king took the initiative, stepping in to break up a fight and impose his judgement even though neither disputant had asked him to do so. But 'When did the use of judicial procedure become obligatory?' is a bad question; the change must have been gradual, and some places in Greece doubtless lagged far behind others.

Almost no clear and precise conclusions can be drawn from the evidence which has been surveyed in this chapter. In individual passages of Homer and Hesiod it is hard to distinguish historical fact from poetic colouring or idealization. Even where we feel confident that the poetic narrative does indicate that some particular type of judicial procedure was used in real life, we usually cannot tell in what part of Greece it was used, or at what date. For any specific place in Greece at any date before the seventh century BC (with the sole possible exception of Hesiod's district of Boiotia) our answer to the question 'What kind of judicial procedure was used in this place at this date?' must be, on our present evidence, that we do not know. Nevertheless, the evidence does show that there were three features of the judging of disputes which did exist somewhere in the Greek world in this early period, so that we must beware of saying that any of these originated in classical Athens. They are:

(1) Judging by an individual man, who has authority to decide a dispute because of the office which he holds (e.g. as king).

(2) Judging by a group of men, who because of birth or experience or other qualifications are considered to be particularly well fitted to perform this function.

(3) Influencing of a verdict by a crowd of ordinary men, who have no special qualifications for judging, but whose opinion must still be taken into account by the man or men who are to pronounce the verdict.

Monarchy, aristocracy, democracy: these are the three approaches to the problem of judging, as to other problems of society. The next chapter will indicate the part played by each of them in judicial procedures in classical Athens, and the way in which the third came to dominate the other two.

II MAGISTRATES AND JURIES

According to legend Athens was once ruled by kings, such as Aigeus and Theseus. By the seventh century BC the hereditary monarchy had already ceased to exist; yet there remained throughout the classical period an official called 'the king'. To distinguish him from kings in the ordinary English sense, it is convenient to use the Greek word 'basileus'. His duties were largely, though not entirely, confined to religious matters. Some of them were just ceremony and formality. Little is recorded of the transition from the hereditary absolute monarchs of the legendary period to the officials of the same title in the historical period. The fullest account is given in the third chapter of the *Athenaion Politeia* (the book on the Athenian constitution doubtfully attributed to Aristotle, which I shall refer to as *AP*), but some modern scholars reject much of it, on the ground that no adequate evidence about prehistoric Athens can have been available in Aristotle's time, so that the account must be largely guesswork.[12] But in any case it is fair to conjecture that the kings gradually lost various functions, when they had performed those functions unsatisfactorily and agreed or were compelled to hand them over to other men; and that the kingship ceased to be hereditary at some date when a king died leaving either no son at all or no son fit to rule; so that the title and functions of the basileus in classical Athens were, more or less, what the king had left when everything else had been taken away from him.

The most significant diminution in the powers of the king may well have occurred at the time (whenever it was) when the official called 'arkhon' was first created; for in classical times the arkhon seems to have been regarded as superior to the basileus, and the word itself, which just means 'leader' or 'ruler', implies that this official was intended to take precedence over all others. But some of the king's powers were doubtless transferred at different times to other officials whom we know to have existed later. There was the polemarch, whose name means 'commanding in war'; and there were the thesmothetai, whose name means something like 'laying down law' or 'stating rules'.[13]

The arkhon, the basileus, the polemarch, and the six thesmothetai came to be known as 'the nine arkhons', but by the fifth century many other types of official also existed, any of which could be called an *arkhe* ('rule' or 'office' or 'magistracy'): generals, market controllers, and so on.

At an early period the arkhon, the basileus, and the polemarch are said to have held office for ten years, and at an even earlier period for life; but some modern scholars reject this statement, perhaps rightly. Anyway, from 682 onwards they held office for one year only, and so did the holders of almost all the other offices created subsequently. Until 487 the normal method of appointment seems to have been election. In 487/6 the system of appointing the nine arkhons was changed, and they were picked by lot out of a number of candidates previously selected; and at some later date (not earlier than 457) the system was changed again, and they were henceforth appointed entirely by lot. Lot was also used for appointment to most other offices in classical Athens; the only important exceptions were the strategoi (generals) and other military officials, who continued to be elected. The widespread use of lot meant that in democratic Athens an arkhon could not be expected to have any particular ability, knowledge, or other qualifications; he was a layman, not a specialist. A fourth-century speaker remarks that when one Theogenes became basileus he was 'inexperienced in affairs' (Demosthenes 59. 72).

If we had only the names to go by, we should probably think that among these numerous officials the thesmothetai were the ones responsible for giving rulings in disputes. In fact, though the thesmothetai dealt with more legal cases than the other officials, many of the others had responsibility for legal cases too. An account is given in *AP* 56–9 of the duties of the nine arkhons in the fourth century: the arkhon introduced into court various kinds of case concerning property and family matters (inheritance, guardianship, and so on), the basileus introduced cases connected with religion (impiety, disputes about the duty to perform a sacrifice or the right to claim a priesthood) and also cases of homicide and deliberate wounding, and the polemarch introduced various kinds of case involving persons who were not Athenian citizens. There is then a long list of different types of case for the thesmothetai. But this does not mean that the thesmothetai had all cases which were not the responsibility of the arkhon, the basileus, or the polemarch; for we know from individual references elsewhere that other officials introduced certain types of case connected with their spheres of activity. For example, military officers (strategoi, taxiarchs, and hip-parchs) introduced cases of desertion and evasion of military service, and market officials (agoranomoi and sitophylakes) introduced cases of overcharging and other misconduct in the market.

In the fourth century, introducing a case usually (for details and exceptions see chapter XVI) meant arranging for a trial by jury. But in the seventh century the popular juries of Aristotle's time did not yet exist. How then did a seventh-century arkhon proceed when a dispute was brought to him? The obvious presumption is that he simply decided the case himself; and indeed AP 3.5 says this was so, though it is doubtful whether the statement is based on evidence or is no more than a presumption. The arkhons had replaced the king of legendary times. Judging was probably a function of the king in early Athens as in Hesiod's Boiotia, and when the hereditary monarchy ceased the arkhons took over this function. One may imagine the following sequence of development (but it must be remembered that it is almost entirely conjectural):

(1) The king was the sole ruler and judge. When two Athenians had a dispute which they could not settle between themselves, they (or one of them) appealed to the king and he decided it.

(2) The office of arkhon was created to take over various functions from the king. It became the rule that certain types of dispute (about property and family matters, and perhaps others) should now be decided by the arkhon. Other types (disputes about religious matters, accusations of homicide, and perhaps others) continued to be decided by the king. It may have been at the same time or later that the king (basileus) ceased to be hereditary.

(3) The office of polemarch was created (not necessarily later than the office of arkhon) to take over the function of commanding military expeditions. It was when Athenians left Athens for military expeditions that they were most liable to come into contact and dispute with individual non-Athenians; and so it became the rule that the polemarch, rather than the arkhon or basileus, was the official to whom an Athen-ian appealed in any dispute with a non-Athenian, even when the dis-pute arose in Athens.

(4) Disputes became too numerous for the arkhon, the basileus, and the polemarch to deal with all of them. So the office of thesmothetes was created to relieve the other officials of some judicial functions. Certain types of dispute were reserved for the arkhon, the basileus, or the polemarch; all the rest were decided by the six thesmothetai.

(5) From time to time other officials were created to supervise particular matters; and, at least in some cases, such officials had authority to decide disputes within the fields of activity of which they had charge. (6) The onset of democratic ideas and feelings caused various kinds of limitations and checks to be placed on the individual official's power of decision. The two main kinds were written laws, to which the official's judgements had to conform, and juries, whose verdicts the official had to accept. The result was that officials' freedom of judgement eventually dwindled almost to nothing. This change, which occurred gradually between the seventh and the fourth century, forms the main theme of the rest of this chapter.

THE AREOPAGOS

The Areopagos was a council so called because it met on the hill of Ares, west of the Akropolis. There is no reliable evidence about its origin and early history (Aiskhylos in *Eumenides* has Athena institute it), but it is reasonable to guess that it began as a group of leading men who advised the king about important or difficult decisions, either at his request or (more likely) because they were strong enough to compel him to attend to their views. Membership may well have been hereditary, like the kingship; thus the council would represent the aristocracy.

AP conveys the impression that in the seventh century the judicial powers of the Areopagos were virtually unlimited: 'The council of the Areopagites had the function of guarding the laws, and it managed the most numerous and important affairs in the state, with authority to punish and fine all offenders' (*AP* 3.6). However, this should not be taken as meaning that the Areopagos ever did in practice try all offenders. Many disputes must have been decided by the arkhons without reference to it. But evidently the Areopagos held trials for certain particularly serious offences.

What offences were these? They surely must have included those offences for which the Areopagos held trials under the presidency of the basileus in later times (when it was not hereditary, but consisted of ex-arkhons). Those were intentional homicide and wounding, arson, and destruction of sacred olive trees.[14] Other cases of homicide were tried in later times by the ephetai, who in the fifth and fourth centuries were fifty-one men chosen by lot (see page 117). But Polydeukes (often called by the Latin form of his name, Pollux), writing in the second century AD, says that Drakon instituted them and that they were appointed according to rank.[15] It is doubtful whether Polydeukes had reliable evidence about Drakon. But it is quite credible that the ephetai existed in the seventh century BC, and that they were originally chosen according to rank, which would probably mean that they were all members of the Areopagos. If this is right, all kinds of homicide cases were judged at this period by members of the aristocratic council.

Another offence which appears to have been allocated to the Areopagos for trial in early times was 'tyranny'. In the 630s or 620s a man named Kylon attempted with some supporters to make himself ruler of Athens. They occupied the Akropolis, but were besieged there; and, after Kylon and his brother had escaped, the rest gave in and were persuaded to leave sanctuary on the Akropolis on the understanding that their lives would be spared but they would submit to a trial, which was to be held (according to an Aristophanic scholiast) by the Areopagos. But Megakles, who was the arkhon, put them to death. Some years later the family of Megakles (the Alkmeonids; he himself was dead by then) were accused of being 'accursed' or 'polluted' by this sacrilege, and were tried by three hundred men appointed according to rank. They were condemned, those alive were exiled, and the bones of those dead were dug up and cast out of Attika.[16]

Each of these two cases was unique. The trial of Kylon's supporters by the Areopagos for attempting to set up a tyranny did not in the event take place at all. The trial of the Alkmeonids appears to have been a trial by the aristocracy of one of its own leading families. The jury of three hundred may perhaps be regarded as a special meeting of the Areopagos, strengthened for the occasion by some aristocrats who were not regular members, to try a special case of homicide. But there may have been other cases besides these. Plutarch quotes a law of Solon extending amnesty to men who had been outlawed before Solon became arkhon 'except those condemned by the Areopagos or by the ephetai or at the Prytaneion for homicide or bloodshed or for tyranny'. This is good evidence that before 594 the Areopagos held trials for tyranny and imposed outlawry (atimia) on those found guilty. AP states that Solon made a law under which the Areopagos judged men conspiring 'for subversion of the people', and in another passage that there was a lenient law imposing atimia on anyone setting up a tyranny.[17] There are errors of anachronism here, since in Solon's time, when democracy did not yet exist, the expression 'subversion of the people' is unlikely to have been used, and atimia still had its severe sense of 'outlawry' and had not yet come to mean the more lenient penalty of disfranchisement (see page 73). But we can accept that in the late seventh and early sixth century anyone accused of setting up a tyranny was subject to trial by the Areopagos.

This, then, was an early limitation of the judicial power of the king or the arkhons in Athens: certain offenders, most notably those accused of homicide or of attempting to seize control of the state, were referred to the aristocratic council.

THE ELIAIA

It is likely that the arkhons and the Areopagos in the seventh century took some account of popular opinion informally when giving their verdicts, but it was not until the sixth century that formal authority to judge was for the first time extended to non-aristocrats. Solon is traditionally supposed to have introduced his reforms in the year 594/3 when he was arkhon. Several scholars have argued that a later date is more likely, but anyway it cannot be later than the middle of the sixth century. The accounts which we have (especially those in *AP* and Plutarch) concentrate mainly on his economic reforms, above all on his relief of poor farmers from debt and consequent enslavement. The economic and political reforms are outside the scope of this book; yet they are not altogether separate from his legal innovations, for the same principal motive prompted them. The ordinary people of Athens had come to resent the rule of the aristocracy, whom they thought selfish and oppressive. Economically, aristocrats controlled the land; politically, aristocrats were the governing officials and council; judicially, aristocrats administered justice. The non-aristocrats demanded a fairer share in all three fields, and the aristocrats, presumably in fear of revolution, agreed to accept reforms proposed by Solon.

'The most democratic parts of Solon's constitution seem to be these three: first and most important, stopping loans on the person; secondly, enabling the volunteer to avenge the wronged; and thirdly, the thing which they say has most strengthened the masses, appeal to the law-court. For when the people controls the vote, it controls the constitution; besides, because the laws are not worded simply and clearly, but like the one about inheritances and heiresses, it is inevitable that many disputes occur, and the law-court adjudicates everything, both public and private.' (*AP* 9)

With regard to the third item in this list, 'appeal to the law-court', it is clear that *AP* is telling us that in some way Solon gave the people authority to make judicial decisions. This phrase is the record of the most decisive single step towards democratic justice. Unfortunately, it is so compressed that modern scholars are not agreed about its interpretation.

What is 'the law-court'? Athens later had many law-courts, but it seems unlikely that Solon set up a whole lot of courts. It may be significant that another word for 'law-court', known to have been used in an archaic Athenian law,[18] is Eliaia (often written *heliaia*, but inscriptions[19] indicate that the form without *h* is correct), which seems etymologically to mean 'assembly'. On this (admittedly tenuous) ground it is now generally assumed that Solon's law-court was simply the assembly of Athenian citizens, the Ekklesia; for some reason not known to us it was conventional to call the assembly the Eliaia instead of the Ekklesia when the purpose of its meeting was judicial.[20]

'Appeal' is the usual translation of the Greek word *ephesis*, but not all scholars are agreed that it is correct here. Two fundamentally different interpretations have been offered.

(a) If a disputant was dissatisfied with the magistrate's judgement, he could appeal against it to the Eliaia. The Eliaia heard the case afresh and gave its own judgement, which overrode the magistrate's.[21]

(b) Solon limited by law the penalties which a magistrate could impose on his own authority. As long as the magistrate kept within this limit, his judgement was final; but if he wished to exceed it he had to refer the case to the Eliaia, which could confirm or reject the higher penalty.[22]

One fact which might be regarded as evidence in favour of *b* is that in the fourth century there existed several laws which gave a magistrate authority, for a specified offence, to impose a fine up to a certain limit, but required him to refer to a court cases in which he thought a severer penalty was required (see pages 235–7). The wording of these laws implies that, as long as the magistrate kept the penalty within the limit, no appeal was allowed against it. Since the power of magistrates to make decisions on their own authority diminished as Athens became more democratic, especially after most of them came to be appointed by lot, it is most unlikely that the authority to impose penalties without appeal would have been restored to them later if Solon had deprived them of it. It should therefore be accepted (even though *AP* does not mention exceptions) that Solon did not make all judgements by magistrates subject to appeal; there were at least some minor kinds of case in which the magistrate's judgement was final.

But this does not yet enable us to choose between *a* and *b*. Granted that in certain minor cases the magistrate's judgement was final, the question still remains about all other cases: were cases heard by the Eliaia only if one of the disputants objected to the magistrate's judgement, or was the magistrate required to refer cases to the Eliaia even if neither disputant objected?

Some scholars have maintained that this question is decided in favour of *a* by the usage of the word *ephesis*. It is alleged that in judicial contexts this noun and its related verb and adjective are used only when the initiative for a second hearing is taken by a dissatisfied party in the case; that is, that they can only mean 'appeal'.[23] But it is not certain that this is correct. There is an instance in a fifth-century Attic inscription (the well-known decree regulating relations between Athens and Khalkis) where the word *ephesis* appears, on the more natural interpretation, to be used for compulsory reference of cases to another court when serious penalties were involved, not depending on objection by a dissatisfied party.[24] Therefore, so far as linguistic usage is concerned, is seems possible that *ephesis* might mean either *a* or *b*.

But there is one other piece of evidence which tells in favour of *a*. Plutarch's account of Solon's work includes the sentence: 'Even in the case of matters which he allotted to the officials to judge, he likewise granted appeals (*epheseis*) to the law-court about them to those who wished' (*Solon* 18.3). The last words of this sentence show beyond doubt that Plutarch thought *a*, not *b*, was what Solon did; reference of a case to the Eliaia took place only when one of the disputants wished it. Can we trust this account, written nearly seven centuries after Solon's time? A good deal in this chapter of Plutarch's *Solon* closely resembles the very chapter of *AP* which I have been trying to interpret; and it has been suggested that Plutarch has simply read this chapter of *AP* and added his own comments, so that anything which is in Plutarch and not in *AP* would have to be regarded just as a conjecture, not as independent evidence. But I think that is too sceptical. Plutarch's account does contain several points of detail which are not in *AP*, and we know that he did make considerable use of a number of fourth-century historical works which have not survived for us to read. So the probability is, I think, that his phrase 'to those who wished' does come from a good source, and it should be believed as long as no better evidence is found which contradicts it.

My conclusion, then, is that *a* is essentially correct: Solon laid down that the Eliaia should judge a case if, but only if, one of the disputants wished to appeal against the judgement already given by a magistrate. But with this I would incorporate from *b* the proviso that there were some kinds of case in which the magistrate's judgement remained final, not open to appeal, as long as the penalty was kept within a specified limit. Despite these exceptions it is obvious that Solon's innovation gave the Athenian people a degree of control such as they had never had before over the judicial actions of the aristocratic arkhons.

It may well be that at first some people were diffident about exercising their right of appeal to the Eliaia, and the magistrates' verdicts continued to be accepted in many cases. But in the course of time such diffidence would naturally diminish. It is obvious that in nearly all disputes the disputant against whom the magistrate decided would be dissatisfied with the magistrate's verdict, and would welcome any opportunity to get the case reopened, unless he was inhibited by some other consideration. In archaic Athens men may have been inhibited by awe of the aristocracy from objecting to the verdicts of aristocratic officials, but this kind of inhibition must have waned as Athens became more democratic. In modern times people are inhibited from legal appeals chiefly by the financial expense, but no expense was involved in appealing to the Eliaia. So before long Athenians must have come to realize that, if a magistrate decided against one, one had nothing to lose by appealing.

The result in the end was that (except in the cases involving penalties below certain limits, in which the magistrate's verdict was final and no appeal was allowed) magistrates ceased bothering to give verdicts at all. Before the end of the fifth century we find that a magistrate's hearing (*anakrisis:* see pages 240-2) was just an occasion when the disputants explained to him what their dispute was about; as soon as he was satisfied that the dispute was a serious one, in which he could not give a final verdict himself, he did not waste time trying to reach a decision (to which one or other of the disputants would be sure to object), but proceeded to make arrangements for a trial by the Eliaia – or rather (since a number of courts had by then succeeded the Eliaia) by the court appropriate to the type of case. He presided over the trial, but he made no attempt to influence the verdict; and when he 'gave judgement' (the Greek verb is *dikazein*) at the end of the trial, that means only that he formally stated the verdict which the jury had reached. This is the logical conclusion of the practice which we saw in a more primitive form in Homer, where the disputants make their speeches in front of a crowd of onlookers, and the king or other judges try to give a decision in accord with the applause or other indications of popular opinion (pages 16–23).

There is no evidence to show exactly when magistrates ceased to give their own verdicts in such cases. An attempt has been made to show that they still gave verdicts in the 490s, on the basis of a story in Plutarch that Themistokles said he would use his powers as arkhon to help his friends; but, even if the story is true, the attempt fails, because at that date an unscrupulous arkhon would anyway have had other ways of helping his friends, quite apart from judicial verdicts.[25] The attempt to show that they still gave verdicts in the 460s, on the basis of certain words in the decree regulating Athenian relations with Phaselis, also fails, because those words may mean merely that the magistrate presided at the trial and formally announced the verdict, not that he decided the verdict.[26]

Many scholars have, nevertheless, assumed that there must have been a particular occasion when magistrates were formally forbidden by law to give verdicts. Although it is possible that this was done, there is no evidence for it and no special reason to believe it. It is equally possible, perhaps likelier, that the practice of giving a verdict at the magistrate's hearing simply fell into disuse, because it was pointless when appeal to the Eliaia was sure to follow. One might compare the royal assent given to British acts of parliament. It is well known that in practice the monarch no longer has power to reject bills. But if one asks 'On what occasion did the monarch lose this power?' the question is unanswerable, the power never having been abolished by law. One can say that the last monarch who actually vetoed a bill was Queen Anne, but who can say which later monarchs might have used the veto successfully if they had tried? Likewise, some Athenian magistrate must have been the last to give a verdict (in a type of case in which reference to the Eliaia or to a jury was allowed); but there may have been no specific occasion which was the last time a magistrate could have given a verdict if he had wanted to. All we can say is that by the end of the fifth century none still did.

DEMOCRATIC JURIES

As it became more and more usual to appeal to the Eliaia against magistrates' verdicts, it must have become necessary for the Eliaia to meet more often to hear the appeals. Other factors also will have caused the number of trials to increase: the population of Athens was growing, and ordinary Athenians were becoming readier to stand up and speak up for what they believed to be their rights. Yet the amount of time which the assembly of citizens could spend hearing cases was not unlimited; they had to make a living too. How could the right of appeal to the people be preserved without bringing the work and other activities of the people to a standstill?

The solution found to this problem was brilliant, one of the greatest contributions ever made to democracy and the administration of justice. It was to regard a limited number of ordinary citizens as representing all the citizens: a part of the community stood for the whole, and the decisions of the part counted as decisions of the whole. The right to trial by a jury of ordinary citizens (not persons having any special position or expertise) is commonly regarded in modern states as a fundamental part of democracy. It was in Athens that it was invented.

It is a pity that we do not know who was the man who first thought of it, or when. The earliest time at which there is firm evidence that democratic juries existed is in the middle of the fifth century, when, on the proposal of Perikles, pay for jurors was introduced.[27] But there is no particular reason to believe that this was when juries were first instituted.

To be a juror a man had to be aged thirty or more and in possession of full citizen rights. From those who volunteered, 6000 were chosen by lot to be jurors for the year (possibly 600 from each of the ten tribes, though there is no proof of this).[28] Juries for the various courts were made up out of this list of 6000. The courts did not all sit every day, and no courts sat on festival days and days when the Ekklesia met; so not all the jurors were needed every day, and each juror received pay only on a day when he actually sat to try a case.[29] For some time the pay was two obols a day; it was raised to three obols a day on the proposal of Kleon, probably in 425.[30]

The principal purpose of introducing pay may have been to obtain a fair representation of the poorer classes on the juries. Without pay a poor man would be unlikely to volunteer for jury service, since he could not afford to lose the money or produce which he would otherwise make by his normal work. However, two or three obols a day was not a high rate. An able-bodied man would normally be able to earn more by work of other kinds. Probably it was never intended that judging cases should be regarded as work, or the office of juror as a full-time occupation; perhaps it was expected that many men would be glad to perform this service for the community, provided only that they did not have to starve while doing it. But what happened in practice was that relatively few able-bodied men volunteered; many of the volunteers were old men who were no longer fit for ordinary work and could not earn money by other means. Thus the juror's pay could serve the purpose of an old age pension; and although the device of paying jurors succeeded in producing a fair (perhaps more than fair) representation of poor citizens, it did not produce fair representation of different age-groups. This is the state of affairs which Aristophanes presents comically in his *Wasps* (performed in 422). The chorus of that play consists of destitute old men whose only livelihood is the pay they get as jurors. Their poverty is shown in a half-comic, half-pathetic song by the chorus-leader and his young son who is escorting him to the court in the early morning.

Boy: Will you give me something, father, if I ask you?
Father: Certainly, my boy. Tell me, what nice thing do you want me to buy? You'll say knucklebones [a cheap toy], I expect!
Boy: No, dried figs, daddy. It's nicer –
Father: Hang me if I will!
Boy: Well, I'm not coming with you any more, then!
Father: Out of this measly pay I have to get meal and firewood and meat for three of us – and you ask me for figs!
Boy: Tell me, father: if the court doesn't sit today, how shall we buy lunch? Have you got any good prospect for us . . .?
Father: I really don't know where our dinner will come from.
(Aristophanes Wasps 291–311)

THE ALLOTMENT OF JURORS TO COURTS

Each of the magistrates responsible for introducing cases sat always in the same court.[31] The court mentioned most often is 'the Eliaia of the thesmothetai'. This was the court for many important types of case, some of which required particularly large juries (1000 jurors or more), and it must have had a larger building than the other courts (perhaps the building known as the Metiokheion).[32] That may be why this court took over the title 'Eliaia', which in earlier times had meant the full Athenian assembly (see page 30). The Odeion, a building originally erected for musical performances (as the name indicates), was also used as a law-court, and so was the Stoa Poikile.[33] Other courts used in the fifth or fourth century were called the New Court, the Inserted Court, the Court at Lykos, the Kallion, the Triangular Court, the Greater Court, and the Middle Court.[34] Attempts have been made to identify the remains of various courts in the Agora excavations, but most of the identifications are uncertain.[35]

In the fifth century each juror was allocated to one court for the year,[36] but it is not known how many jurors were allocated to each court, nor whether every court had the same number. We know of occasions when the Ekklesia voted for the setting up of a special court with 1000, 1500 or 2000 jurors.[37] The regular courts may well have had fewer jurors than these special ones, but it is not known whether 500, a usual number in the fourth century, was already usual in the fifth. The prosecution (*graphe paranomon*) of Speusippos by Leogoras in 415 is said (in Andokides I. 17) to have been tried by 6000 jurors. If the figure there is right (and it has been doubted), this must have been a very unusual case; the Ekklesia, because of its alarm over the profanation of the Eleusinian Mysteries and the mutilation of the Hermai, must have set up a special court in which the jurors from all the ordinary courts came together to try an exceptionally important case. Otherwise there is only one fifth-century case for which the number of jurors is recorded: a case mentioned in a speech of Isokrates, which was tried by 700 jurors. Some editors emend the figure to 500, but we know so little about the sizes of fifth-century juries that we cannot be sure that 700 is not correct. The date of the case is not known; it cannot be later than the date of the speech in which it is mentioned (which is probably 400), but it could be some years earlier.[38]

Towards the end of the fifth century there seems to have been some trouble with corruption of juries: Anytos, the man who later accused Sokrates, is alleged to have invented a method of bribery called *dekazein*.[39] That is probably why we find that early in the fourth century a different system of allocating jurors to courts was in operation. The best evidence for it is a passage of comic parody in Aristophanes's *Ekklesiazousai*. Praxagora and the other women in Athens are instituting a 'communist' state in which there will be no private property. Meals will be provided for everyone by the state. When everyone owns everything there will be no theft, so that the law-courts can be abolished and their equipment put to better uses.

Blepyros: And what will you do with the allotment machines?
Praxagora: I'll put them in the Agora. I'll set them up beside Harmodios and draw the lots for everyone, so that the man whose lot comes

out will go off happily knowing what letter he's dining in. The herald will proclaim that the men from *beta* are to proceed to the Stoa Basileios for dinner, *theta* to the Stoa next to it, and the men from *kappa* are to go to the Stoa Alphitopolis.
Blepyros: With a hearty kappetite?
Praxagora: No, no, but to dine there.
Blepyros: And anyone whose letter for dining isn't drawn out will be sent away by the rest?
Praxagora: No, that won't happen with us. We'll provide plenty of everything for everyone. (Aristophanes *Ekklesiazousai* 681-90)

From this parody the actual procedure for the allocation of jurors at this period can be inferred. At the beginning of the year, instead of being allocated to courts for the year, the jurors were divided into a number of panels of equal size, each denoted by a letter of the alphabet. Perhaps there were ten panels, lettered from *alpha* to *kappa* (as we know was the case later in the fourth century). Each morning all the jurors, except those absent for illness or other reasons, assembled in one place. A letter of the alphabet (perhaps from *lambda* onwards, as later) was allocated to each court which was to be used that day. Then lots were drawn from two containers (one for the panels of jurors, one for the courts); the first panel of jurors to be drawn went to sit in the first court to be drawn, and so on. If the number of courts to be used on a particular day was fewer than ten, there would be some panels of jurors left without courts; they would have to go home without pay that day. (In Aristophanes's *Wealth* 1166-7 there is an allusion to jurors who try to get themselves registered in several 'letters', so as to reduce their chances of getting left out; this of course must have been illegal.)

Praxagora's words make clear that all jurors who had the same letter (*beta*, for example) went to the same court; so the later system by which lots were drawn for individual jurors was not yet in use at the time of *Ekklesiazousai*, and lots were drawn only for complete panels. The panels, to be interchangeable, must all have been the same size. If there were 6000 jurors altogether (as in the fifth century; but there is no evidence for this total later than the year 415) and ten panels (as later in the fourth century),[40] then each jury had 600 jurors or (if two or more panels were put together for an important case) 1200 or 1800 or a higher multiple. But in fact the only jury whose size we happen to know at about this date was 500.[41] So either the total number of jurors was now 5000 (not 6000), or there were twelve panels (not ten), or else a jury formed from a panel of 600 was called 'five hundred' because each panel was likely to have up to 100 absentees on any one day: there is no way of telling which of these alternatives is right.

There is also no information about the exact date when this system was introduced. Aristophanes's references show simply that it was in use at the time of *Ekklesiazousai* (performed in 393 or 392) and *Wealth* (388). Its purpose must have been to prevent bribery by making it impossible to know before the day of the trial which panel of jurors would try a particular case. Yet it must have been found unsatisfactory in some way, for soon afterwards the system was changed again.

The new system was extremely complicated. It is described in detail in *AP* 63–5; here a summary must suffice. Each man registered as a juror for the year was issued with a *pinakion*, which was a bronze or wooden 'ticket' or 'name-plate' inscribed with his name and one of the first ten letters of the alphabet (*alpha* to *kappa*); within each of the ten tribes (*phylai*) there was approximately the same number of jurors with each letter. Every morning the jurors of each tribe assembled separately, beside one of the ten entrances to an enclosure which gave access to all the courts. The nine arkhons and the secretary of the thesmothetai were in charge of the allotment, one of these officials for each tribe. Each juror on arrival put his *pinakion* into a box marked with his letter. The arkhon (or secretary) picked one name at random out of each box; the juror so picked became for that day the 'plugger' for the jurors with that letter. He plugged the other *pinakia* from his box into one of the vertical rows (columns) of slots on the front of one of the allotment machines (*kleroteria*). There were two allotment machines for the tribe, each having five vertical rows of slots for *pinakia*, making ten vertical rows in all; one vertical row would contain all the *pinakia* marked *alpha*, one those marked *beta*, and so on, so that each horizontal row contained *pinakia* all marked with different letters. Into the allotment machines the arkhon (or secretary) next put some small white and black cubes (or balls), a white one for each five jurors required from that tribe that day, a black one for each five men who would be left over; for example, if 300 jurors were required from the tribe and there were 400 applicants, he would put thirty white cubes and ten black cubes into each of the two allotment machines. He then drew the cubes out one by one. If the first cube was white, the five men whose *pinakia* were in the top horizontal row of slots on that allotment machine were picked for jury service that day; if it was black, they were not. The second cube decided the fate of the second row, and so on. Each juror picked for service in this way then drew from an urn an 'acorn' or ball marked with a letter (from *lambda* onwards; these letters were allocated by lot earlier in the morning to the courts which were to be used that day) to decide which court he was to go to. He was then given a coloured stick which entitled him to enter that court (each court had a different colour), and immediately (before anyone had a chance to bribe him) entered the enclosure leading to the courts. That is a condensed summary of the procedure; readers who wish to know more details should turn to *AP*'s account and Sterling Dow's meticulous interpretation of it, with J. H. Kroll's definitive study of the surviving *pinakia*.[42]

When *AP* was written, jurors' *pinakia* were made of box-wood, but many bronze *pinakia* have been found, which, as Dow and Kroll have shown, belong to the second quarter of the fourth century; Kroll believes 378/7 to be the most likely year for their introduction. (Jurors' bronze *pinakia* are stamped with the facing owl design of the reverse of a triobol coin, symbolizing their entitlement to the daily pay of three obols. They are distinct from bronze *pinakia* without this stamp, which were used by citizens not registered as jurors, from about 370 to 322 according to Kroll's dating, for the annual allotment of arkhonships and other offices.) So these *pinakia* show that this system of allotment had been introduced well before the middle of the century. Other evidence pointing the same way is a reference in the Demosthenic speech *Against Timokrates* (belonging probably to the year 353) to a decree ordering a trial by 'two jury-panels (*dikasteria*), amounting to 1001 men'.[43] The purpose of the odd number is to avoid a tie in the voting; but there would be no point in specifying an odd number unless the attendance of the exact number specified could be ensured. Now, under the previous system of allotment, whether the size of a panel of jurors was 600 or 500, a panel would seldom or never be complete, for on any one day there were likely to be some absentees. So, when a decree was passed requiring a jury of 1001, the system of allotment then in use must have been one in which a jury was not composed of a whole panel *en bloc*, but was made up out of the individuals known to be present on the day of the trial. So the system of allotment of jurors individually, as described in *AP*, must have been introduced before the date of *Against Timokrates*, and the desire to have a precise number of jurors for each case may have been the reason, or one of the reasons, for introducing it.[44]

The reference to 'two jury-panels, amounting to 1001 men' implies that 500 or 501 jurors were regarded as one panel or section. There are a few other allusions in the second half of the fourth century to juries of 1000 or 1500 or 2500; these may be loose allusions to juries which really numbered 1001 or 1501 or 2501 and consisted of two or three or five panels.[45] But there are also mentions of juries of 201 (loosely called 200) and 401;[46] so juries were not necessarily multiples of 500. Possibly, for a jury of 201 or 401, 500 jurors were first picked by the usual allotment procedure, and then the surplus was excluded by a further drawing of lots.[47] But we have not enough evidence to be certain about such details. Nor do we know how, when a jury of (say) 500 was made up by picking five jurors from each of the ten 'letters' in each of the ten tribes, one further juror was selected to give a total of 501.

One more refinement was added to the system in the second half of the fourth century. Until then each magistrate responsible for bringing a certain type of case to court had always used the same court. This was still true around 340, when there is a reference in the speech *Against Neaira* to a type of case tried always in the Odeion. But soon afterwards, before *AP* was written, the practice began of allocating courts to magistrates by lot each day.[48]

The whole system of allotment of jurors, as it was developed in the fourth century, shows the Athenians' quite exceptional faith in lottery as a means of ensuring fairness and preventing corruption. The lengthiness of the allotment procedure and the huge numbers of men included in each jury (in the fifth century as well as the fourth) also show that they thought it worth while to devote an enormous amount of time to jury service. In proportion to their population, the Athenians must have spent more man-hours in judging than any other people in history. Not for nothing did the juror become a symbol of Athens in comic crosstalk. In Aristophanes's *Clouds*, for example: 'Look, this is Athens.' 'What? I don't believe it; I can't see any jurors sitting.' And in *Birds*: 'What country are you from?' 'From the country of the fine ships.' 'You're not jurors, are you?'[49] And so on.

All this made it easy to identify a jury with the whole population. An Athenian jury *was* the Athenian people. When a speaker addressing a jury wishes to refer to the Athenian state, his word for it is the pronoun 'you'.[50] And since in democratic Athens the people was supreme, a decision by a jury was final. There could be no appeal.

III THE CODE OF LAWS

In a primitive society, when a dispute was taken to the king or any other judge, he would simply use his discretion in making his judgement. Of course he would usually be guided by the ideas current in the community about right and wrong, and by previous decisions in similar cases; and expressions of opinion by other people present at the hearing, including the crowd of spectators (as in the scene on the shield of Achilles), would help him to assess the disputants' claims. But public opinion can be discordant or vague. A conscientious judge would often find its guidance inadequate. A selfish judge would often have scope to make a judgement favourable to himself. An individual citizen too would sometimes find it hard to know whether he could take some particular action without fear of punishment.

One function of rules or laws is to reduce such doubts. If it is agreed and authoritatively stated that a certain kind of behaviour is wrong, and perhaps that it will incur a specified punishment, that gives guidance to individuals about their conduct. It also helps the community to control its judges, since each judgement has to conform to the law previously laid down. Even in an absolute monarchy, where the king who made the laws could also change them or break them virtually with impunity, a king who laid down a law and then gave judgements which did not conform to it would at least incur resentment. Another function of laws is to help a government to insist that disputes should be submitted to judgement by duly appointed judges, not decided by the private use of force. A man who has suffered wrong at another's hands is more likely to be willing to refrain from retaliation, and to refer the case to a judge and accept his verdict, if he knows that the judge will give a verdict according to a stated rule.

The earliest laws were oral. But oral laws are generally unsatisfactory: when a dispute arises, people can too easily disagree about what the law is. So all civilized communities put their laws in writing. Nowadays copies are printed for all who wish to read them. In ancient Greece, though people might make copies of it, a law itself was a single document, kept in an official archive or (especially in democratic Athens) exhibited in a public place for all to see, inscribed usually on wood or stone to make surreptitious alteration difficult. A classical Greek could think of a law as a physical object.

In Athens the first written laws were Drakon's. The traditional date of Drakon's legislation is 621/0 BC; the evidence for this date is thin, but still no evidence proves it wrong. It is not known what office he held, if any, nor what circumstances caused the rulers of Athens to wish, or at least to accept, that laws should be put in writing at this particular time.[51] Plutarch preserves the tradition, which has given rise to our word 'draconian', that the penalties laid down in them were very severe.

'One penalty was specified for nearly all offenders, death; so that those convicted of idleness were put to death, and those who stole vegetables or fruit were punished in the same way as temple-robbers or killers. Consequently Demades in later times was a hit when he said that Drakon wrote his laws in blood, not in ink. Drakon himself, they say, when asked why he fixed death as the penalty for most offences, answered that he thought small offences deserved it, and he knew no greater penalty for great ones.'   (Plutarch *Solon* 17. 2–4)

We have no reliable account of Drakon's laws. (The account in *AP* 4 is generally regarded as spurious.) There are scattered allusions to various individual laws, especially those on theft and idleness, which evidently were notorious in later times (as Plutarch's passage indicates); but some of these allusions are probably inaccurate, for they were written two centuries or more after Drakon's laws were repealed by Solon, when it is unlikely that the authentic texts still existed.[52]

But there may be an important exception. Drakon's laws on homicide are said not to have been altered by Solon, and the Athenians of the fifth and fourth centuries believed that the law on homicide then in force was Drakon's and had remained unaltered since his time.[53] This law was reinscribed on stone in 409/8. Much of the inscription is now in the Epigraphical Museum in Athens, and R. S. Stroud has recently studied it afresh and published a better text than was previously available.[54] Some scholars, including Stroud, are prepared to accept it as an accurate and unaltered copy of the seventh-century law. But it is doubtful whether the Athenians in 409 would have had any means of knowing if the old text, from which the new inscription was made, incorporated amendments made in the sixth or early fifth century; and it may be safer to admit that they did not really know (and consequently we do not know either) whether it was an unaltered text of Drakon's law or not.

Still, it can at any rate be taken as certain that Drakon did put in writing laws about homicide and other offences, and that this was a very important step forward towards two objectives: it helped the government in Athens to check killing and other violent behaviour (especially killing in revenge for killing) by specifying a judicial procedure which must be followed; and it helped to check the arkhons and the Areopagos from making wayward or inconsistent judgements, or imposing inadequate penalties.

Solon, we are told, abolished all Drakon's laws except those on homicide, and made new ones. These laws, like Drakon's, were inscribed on four-faced wooden blocks called *axones*, which were set in frames and could be turned round on axles to enable the four sides to be read, and on *kyrbeis*, which were blocks with pointed tops and may have contained mainly religious laws.[55] Henceforth the laws of Drakon on homicide and of Solon on other matters were the laws of Athens. Of course additions and amendments had to be made from time to time, and the wooden *axones* were eventually superseded by stone inscriptions. But the name stuck: orators in the fourth century often refer to a law existing in their day as 'the law of Solon', even when there is actually no doubt that it does not go back to Solon's time. Consequently it is very hard for us to pick out genuine laws of Solon from the laws we know to have been in force later. An attempt has been made by E. Ruschenbusch to assemble what can be known of the texts of Solon's laws, but in many instances it remains uncertain whether a particular law is really Solon's.[56] No attempt will be made here to list Solon's laws, but some account of his innovations in legal procedure is given on pages 29-32 and 53-4, and individual laws attributed to him are mentioned in later chapters where they are relevant.

LAWS AND DECREES

Once Drakon and Solon had provided Athens with a written code of laws, magistrates were expected to conform to it; and so were juries, when they were instituted. Although the decisions of juries were not subject to any control or appeal, that does not mean that it was considered proper for jurors to give whatever verdicts they liked: the juror should vote to condemn a person who had contravened the law, and to acquit a person who had obeyed it. In the fourth century each juror swore an oath at the beginning of the year (not at the start of each trial); and, although the text of the oath as given in Demosthenes's speech *Against Timokrates* has been thought by modern scholars to include a number of misquotations and spurious clauses,[57] at any rate it certainly included some such words as 'I will judge according to the laws and decrees of Athens, and matters about which there are no laws I will decide by the justest opinion.'[58] So the juror was not free to decide for himself what kind of action should be regarded as right or wrong; he had to decide in accordance with the law or the decree, if a relevant one existed. What, for this purpose, constituted a valid law, and what was the difference between a law and a decree?

The Greek word *nomos* has actually a wider meaning than the English word 'law'. It can mean 'custom' or 'way of life', besides having other meanings which may be found in a lexicon and are not relevant here; it is the term for a norm of action recognized by a society, what is agreed to be the right thing to do.[59] So the use of this word does not necessarily mean that a particular rule has been written down. Nevertheless, by the fourth century *nomos* was the normal word for a statute, a law published in writing and validated by a political process.

In the days of Drakon and Solon, the word generally used for any of their laws seems to have been not *nomos* but *thesmos*. *Thesmos* is a word for a rule laid down or imposed by authority, whether by a king, or by a law-maker such as Drakon, or by a council or assembly. It is therefore subtly different from *nomos*: a generally accepted rule of behaviour (*nomos*) may have been originally laid down by some authority, but not necessarily so; and a rule laid down by authority (*thesmos*) may not invariably be generally accepted. So, when we find that the usual Athenian word for a law was *thesmos* in the seventh and sixth centuries but *nomos* in the fifth and fourth, that is significant. It marks the change to a democratic attitude, and implies that the validity of a law depends rather on its acceptance by the community than on the power of a ruler. This change in terminology has been studied in detail by Martin Ostwald. He suggests that the substitution of *nomos* for *thesmos* as the official term for a statute was a deliberate act of policy by Kleisthenes as part of the establishment of democracy in 507. This is a plausible suggestion, though it cannot be proved.[60]

Once democracy was established, new laws were made by vote of the Ekklesia, the assembly of all citizens. Business for a meeting of the

Ekklesia was considered beforehand by the Boule (council); but any citizen could submit a proposal to the Boule, and if the Boule approved it and brought it before the Ekklesia it could be passed, with or without amendment, by a majority vote of the citizens present at the meeting, and so become law. Thus another word came into regular use, *psephisma*. This word, usually translated 'decree', is more literally 'a voting', and is used for a rule or decision made by the voting of the Ekklesia. (In origin the word must have referred to voting by pebble, *psephos*, but it came to be used also for decisions reached by show of hands. Its use was not confined to decisions of the Ekklesia, but of course a *psephisma* of some other meeting did not have the force of law.) In the fifth century *nomos* and *psephisma* were overlapping terms: any new law was made by vote of the Ekklesia and so could be called either a *nomos* or a *psephisma*, though any law of Drakon or Solon still in force had not been made by vote and so could only be called a *nomos* or, if the speaker preferred to use an old term for an old law, a *thesmos*. But, perhaps partly because the surviving laws of Drakon and Solon, to which the term *psephisma* was not applied, were the oldest and most firmly established of Athenian laws, it was normally assumed that a law (*nomos*) was something more fundamental and more permanent than a decree (*psephisma*). A law made a general rule about some activity, a decree specified action to be taken in a particular case.[61] But this distinction was not a sharp one, and there was not, before the late fifth century, any distinction at all between a law and a decree in the method of enactment.

A new law intended to have permanent validity was inscribed on wood or stone and set up in a public place for all to see. Such laws were put in various places where it seemed likely that people might want to refer to them. For example, the laws of Ephialtes and Arkhestratos about the council of the Areopagos were placed on the Areopagos; a law about the Eleusinion was placed in that temple; a law about a ritual in honour of Dionysos was placed in the temple of Dionysos in the Marshes.[62] These, it must be remembered, were not merely copies of the laws; they were the laws themselves, the official texts. It is doubtful whether there existed, at any time before the last decade of the fifth century, any central collection of laws. The most that seems likely is that each arkhon may have had an official set of copies of the laws relevant to his office.[63] If any other Athenian wanted to know the law about some matter, he would normally have had to find out where that law was, and walk there.

A further complication was that a speaker in a court would sometimes invoke an 'unwritten law', a rule or principle which, it could be
maintained, was generally accepted by the community, or was ordained
by the gods, even though it had never been put down in writing by
Solon or anyone else ('Everyone knows it's wrong to . . .'). The
authority of Perikles could be quoted in court for the importance of
unwritten laws.[64] All this made it increasingly difficult for an Athenian
to know what law a jury would, or should, apply in a particular case.

THE REINSCRIPTION OF THE LAWS

Towards the end of the fifth century substantial efforts were made to
improve this state of affairs. In 410 officials were appointed with the
title 'anagrapheis' (meaning 'inscribers'). Their duty was to collect
copies of all 'the laws of Solon' and have them inscribed afresh on
stone. One of them was a man named Nikomakhos, who is attacked
in a speech of Lysias composed some years later.

'When he was instructed to inscribe the laws of Solon in four
months, instead of Solon he appointed himself as law-maker, and
instead of four months he made the office last six years. While
getting paid by the day, he inserted some laws and deleted others.'
(Lysias 30. 2)

That is a prejudiced account of Nikomakhos's activities. Since, as
Lysias goes on to say, he underwent the normal examination of his
conduct in office when he gave up his appointment in 404 and there is
no suggestion that he was found guilty of misconduct, we need not
believe that his activities were as improper as Lysias suggests. Probably
it was thought in 410 that four months would be long enough for
reinscribing 'the laws of Solon', but when the anagrapheis actually got
to work collecting the laws they discovered obscurities and inconsistencies. So their term of office was extended and they revised the
texts of the laws to remove these difficulties, though 'inserted some
laws and deleted others' is no doubt a gross exaggeration. In 409/8
they were also given the task of inscribing 'the law of Drakon on
homicide' on stone and setting it up in front of the Stoa Basileios (see
page 42). Besides the surviving parts of that inscription, fragments have
been found of stones which seem to have formed three walls at the
Stoa Basileios. They are inscribed on one side in the old Attic letters

used before 403 and on the other side in the Ionic letters used after that date; and, though the fragments are too scanty to make certainty possible, it is generally thought that the inscription in Attic letters is the one which Nikomakhos and the other anagrapheis made in 410–404 of 'the laws of Solon'.[65]

If, as seems likely, the anagrapheis in 404 had completed their new inscription of 'the laws of Solon and Drakon', the Athenian legal code was then in a more coherent and accessible state than it had been for a century. Unfortunately a further disturbance occurred immediately: in the same year the Athenians suffered final defeat in the Peloponnesian War, the democratic constitution was suspended, and the oligarchic regime of the Thirty assumed control. In 403, after a period of civil war, democracy was restored, but the Athenians evidently felt that they could not simply go on as if nothing had happened; the events of 404/3 had shown that the old legal code was somehow inadequate, and some kind of fresh start must be made. At one meeting of the Ekklesia, perhaps the first of the restored democracy, there was talk of making new laws to replace 'the laws of Solon and Drakon'. But at a further meeting it was agreed, more sensibly, that the existing legal code need not be abandoned; all that was needed was some additions to it. On the proposal of a man named Teisamenos a decree was passed, of which we have the text, laying down a procedure by which 'the laws of Solon and Drakon' were reviewed to see which of them needed supplementation, and any additions thought necessary were prepared and scrutinized by two boards of men called 'nomothetai' (meaning 'law-makers'), together with the Boule. These additions, if approved, were then inscribed on the stone wall with the existing laws.[66]

When this had been done, the Athenians declared this year, 403/2, that of the arkhonship of Eukleides, to be the start of a new era, as far as the legal code was concerned. No law passed before 403/2 was valid henceforth unless it was included in the new inscriptions made in the years from 410 to 403; no uninscribed law was to be enforced; no decree could override a law; and no prosecution could be brought henceforth for offences committed before 403/2.[67]

Several other changes were made at the same time or soon afterwards. One was the adoption of the Ionic alphabet for the inscription of laws and other official documents; this change had no legal significance, but it symbolized the determination to make a fresh start. Another was the reinscription on stone of the official religious calendar of sacrifices.

Nikomakhos, doubtless with other anagrapheis, was responsible for this in the years 403–399, and the sacrificial calendar was inscribed on the back of the same stone walls at the Stoa Basileios which had 'the laws of Solon' on the front. It was not exactly part of the legal code, but the decision to reinscribe it was evidently another result of the general desire to have a clear and accessible statement of all official rules.[68] Another innovation was the establishment of a central record office: when a new chamber was constructed for the Boule ('the New Bouleuterion'), the old one became the Mother Goddess's precinct (Metroon) and was used for keeping laws, decrees, and other official documents, written on papyrus instead of stone.[69] This must have made a vast improvement in the use of public documents; for example, it would now be easier to have the official text of a law brought into court and read out to the jury.

LEGISLATION BY NOMOTHETAI

The other important change made in 403/2 or soon afterwards was a change in the procedure for making or amending laws (*nomoi*). Presumably it was felt that the old method, by which a simple majority vote at one meeting of the Boule and one meeting of the Ekklesia was enough to abolish any existing law, however fundamental, or to make any new one, however drastic, was one of the things which had made revolution easy in 404. What was needed was a more careful check on legal changes before they took effect. This was arranged henceforth by the device of having every proposed change in the laws submitted to a meeting of nomothetai.

Details of the system are not entirely clear.[70] At first, it seems, legal changes could be proposed only at certain times of year. Anyone wishing to propose a new law or an amendment of an existing law had to submit his proposal in writing, and it was read out at several (probably three) meetings of the Ekklesia and also displayed in public for people to read it for themselves. This gave people time to think about it before it came to a vote. If, after this, the Ekklesia voted in favour of it, it did not become law immediately, but was referred to a meeting of nomothetai, some of the year's jurors. Like the jury at a trial, they were equivalent to the whole Athenian people. We know little about their proceedings (except that they voted by show of hands, not by ballot like a jury), but evidently they considered the proposed legal change in detail, and especially whether it conflicted with other laws already in force. If the nomothetai voted in favour of the proposal it became valid law.[71]

After a few years the procedure was streamlined in some respects, presumably because it was found to be unnecessarily cumbersome and time-consuming. By the middle of the fourth century it was permitted to propose legal changes at any time of year, and the public reading and display of proposals before the Ekklesia voted on them was waived. But after the Ekklesia's vote they still had to be submitted to a meeting of the nomothetai, whose decision was the final one. Nomothetai were now appointed afresh for each occasion by the Ekklesia and no longer had necessarily to be jurors.[72]

There were also regular procedures for bringing to the attention of nomothetai any inconsistencies or other faults which were found in the existing laws. At the beginning of each year there was a review procedure called 'voting on the laws' in the Ekklesia; if the Ekklesia voted that any of the four groups in which the laws were arranged was unsatisfactory, that group was referred to nomothetai for correction.[73] For a while special commissioners of some sort were elected to sort out contradictions in the laws; from about the middle of the fourth century, the thesmothetai were given the task of inspecting the laws every year for inconsistencies and redundancies, which, if they were considered sufficiently serious by the Ekklesia, were passed on to nomothetai to be put right. [74]

All this shows that there was much more concern in the fourth century than in the fifth to ensure that the code of laws remained coherent and consistent and was not subjected to ill-considered changes. Some modern scholars have been surprised at the extent to which control of legislation was handed over by the Ekklesia to nomothetai. But it may seem less surprising if three important features of the system are kept in mind. One is that the nomothetai did not take the initiative in proposing any new laws themselves; proposals could be made by any Athenian, as previously, and the nomothetai merely pronounced for or against the proposals which were laid before them. A second is that no proposal went to nomothetai unless the Ekklesia voted that it should: the Ekklesia could always stop any proposed change. A third is that the nomothetic system applied only to laws, intended to be permanent, not to decrees. In practice most of the Athenians' decisions were of a more temporary or specific kind, and so were made by decree, which meant a simple majority vote of the citizens present at one meeting of the Ekklesia.

'GRAPHE PARANOMON'

Whether a new proposal was for a law or for a decree, the proposer himself had a responsibility to make sure that it did not contravene any existing law, either in form or in content. If it did, he could be prosecuted. As soon as the prosecutor made a sworn statement (*hypomosia*) that he intended to bring a *graphe paranomon* ('prosecution for illegalities'), the proposed law or decree, whether the Ekklesia had already voted on it or not, was suspended until the trial had been held. If the defendant was found guilty, he was punished, usually by a fine, and his law or decree was annulled. If a man was convicted three times of this type of offence, he suffered disfranchisement (*atimia*) in addition.[75]

The earliest known cases of a *graphe paranomon* are the prosecution of Speusippos by Leogoras in 415 and a case involving Antiphon and Demosthenes (the general, not the orator) at about the same time.[76] How long before that the procedure was instituted, and who suggested it, are unknown, and in the absence of evidence the various guesses made by modern scholars need not be recounted; whoever suggested it was no doubt a man who believed in the maintenance of law and the existing constitution. Its constitutional significance lies outside the scope of this book; readers interested in that topic should turn to recent books by H. J. Wolff and M. H. Hansen.[77]

In the fourth century it was also possible to prosecute by *graphe* for 'making an unsuitable law' (*nomon me epitedeion theinai*). This charge was in one way narrower than that of a *graphe paranomon*, since it was concerned only with new laws, not with new decrees; in another way it was wider, because 'unsuitable' is a vague term which might cover other faults besides contravention of an existing law. There was a time-limit: if proceedings were not instituted within one year, the proposer of a new law could no longer be punished, but it was still possible to proceed by *graphe* against his law, which was annulled if the prosecution was successful; and this in fact was the position when Demosthenes composed the surviving speech *Against Leptines* in 355/4 for a *graphe* against Leptines's law.[78] On the other hand the speech *Against Timokrates* (Demosthenes 24) was within the time-limit and demanded punishment for Timokrates. The penalty in this kind of *graphe* was assessed by the jury, and could be very severe; in 382/1 a man named Eudemos was actually put to death.[79]

No fifth-century cases of prosecution for 'making an unsuitable law' are known, and the fact that this procedure applied only to laws suggests that it may have been instituted in the period after 403, when the distinction between laws and decrees was precisely defined. Like the system of legislation through nomothetai, it may have resulted from the special anxiety at that period to preserve the code of laws from undesirable changes. But decrees continued to be attacked by *graphe paranomon*, which seems to have been much the commoner of the two charges. It became a popular method of accusing prominent politicians who made frequent proposals in the Ekklesia. Kephalos, a politician at the beginning of the fourth century, boasted that, though he had proposed many decrees, he had never had a *graphe paranomon* brought against him; but the boast of Aristophon, who died in the 330s, was that he had been acquitted in *graphai paranomon* seventy-five times.[80]

The best known of all *graphai paranomon* was a politically motivated one, the case of Demosthenes's crown. In 336 Ktesiphon proposed a decree that the people of Athens should confer a gold crown on Demosthenes, and the herald proclaim it in the theatre at the Dionysiac festival, in honour of his merit and virtue and 'because he continues saying and doing what is best for the people'.[81] Aiskhines, Demosthenes's old political rival, stopped the decree by bringing a *graphe paranomon* against Ktesiphon. The case came to trial in 330 (we do not know why it was delayed for six years, but the reasons must have been political, not legal), and Aiskhines's speech *Against Ktesiphon* and Demosthenes's *On the Crown*, delivered in support of Ktesiphon, both survive, two of the longest and most admired examples of ancient oratory. Aiskhines gives three reasons for saying that Ktesiphon's decree was illegal. First, there was a law forbidding conferment of a crown on any office-holder who had not yet undergone the examination of his conduct in office (*euthyna*), and Demosthenes did hold office as a teikhopoios (in charge of building and repair of the city walls) and as an official in charge of the theoric fund at the time when Ktesiphon made his proposal. Secondly, he says, there was a law that a crown conferred by the people should be proclaimed at a meeting of the Ekklesia and nowhere else, whereas Ktesiphon's proposal was for a proclamation in the theatre at the Dionysia. Thirdly, it was illegal to include a false statement in a decree, and it was false, according to Aiskhines, to say that Demosthenes's speeches and policies were good for Athens. The third of these arguments is the one in which Aiskhines is really interested, and the greater part of his speech consists of criticism of Demosthenes's whole political career; and Demosthenes in his reply gives a detailed account of the political events, especially of the years 346–338, with justification of his policy of resistance to Philip of Macedon. These speeches are two of our most important sources of information about the political history of Greece in that period, and they mark the culmination of the fourth-century tendency to use a *graphe paranomon* as a field for a political battle. Ktesiphon was acquitted, because of Demosthenes's popularity and rhetorical skill, despite the fact that some at least of Aiskhines's arguments seem to have been legally sound. It was hard to persuade an Athenian jury to give more weight to the rules of law than to the personalities involved in a case.

IV PROSECUTORS AND CASES

For an offender to be tried and punished, it was necessary that someone should tell a magistrate and court what he had done wrong. In early times there were two ways in which that might happen. One was that the person (or family) who was the victim of the offence or wrong could accuse the offender. The other was that a magistrate who noticed an offence, or had it drawn to his attention, might investigate it on his own initiative. But eventually it was realized that these two ways were not sufficient to bring all offenders to justice. Some kinds of wrong affected an individual victim who was unable to proceed against the offender; for example, an orphan deprived by relatives of property which he ought to inherit. And, much commoner than that, there was the kind of offence which was bad for the community generally rather than for any individual in particular; for example, a citizen who avoided his duty to perform military service when required. The arkhons could not be expected to investigate every such offence for themselves.

This was presumably what Solon had in mind when he introduced the second of what are called in *AP* (quoted on page 29) the most democratic parts of his constitution: 'enabling the volunteer to avenge the wronged'. This phrase implies that until Solon's time a prosecution for an offence could be brought only by a person (or family) who was the victim of it. In making it possible for any volunteer (*ho boulomenos*, 'he who wishes') to prosecute if he thought something wrong had been done, Solon showed awareness that some wrong-doing was harmful to the community as a whole. He said that it ought to be everyone's concern to see that the laws were obeyed and that people behaved rightly.[82] This is how a fourth-century orator emphasizes the importance of prosecutors in the legal system:

'There are three things above all which protect and preserve democracy and the prosperity of the state: first the code of laws, second the vote of jurors, and third the trial which delivers offences over to them. The law exists to state what should not be done, the prosecu-

tor to report those who are liable to penalties under the laws, and
the juror to punish those brought to his attention by both of these;
so that neither the law nor the vote of the jurors can take effect
without someone to deliver offenders over to them.' (Lykourgos
Against Leokrates 3–4)

Of course it must always have been possible for anyone to draw a
magistrate's attention informally to (for example) an evader of military
service, leaving it to the magistrate to decide whether to look into the
matter and do something about it; the novelty introduced by Solon
must have lain in allowing the informer to state the case for the prosecution at a trial. Moreover, we know that in the fourth century the
right of a volunteer to prosecute did not extend to all offences; and
since it is most unlikely that this right was reduced between the sixth
century and the fourth (a period in which the rights of ordinary Athenians to participate in public affairs grew greater, not less), it is virtually
certain that Solon too limited it to certain types of offence. The reason
why the limitation is not mentioned in *AP* is that the account there is a
short summary of democratic features which were new when Solon
introduced them. It was a novelty that volunteers were allowed to
bring prosecutions, whereas there was nothing new in the fact that
there were prosecutions which volunteers could not bring. Presumably
the range of offences which Solon opened to volunteer prosecutors
was similar to the range which was dealt with in the fourth century by
public cases (as indicated later in this chapter). But the Athenian distinction between public and private cases was by no means the same as
the modern distinction between criminal and civil cases, and it is
probably more misleading than helpful to regard Solon as the founder
of criminal law in Athens, as G. M. Calhoun did in his book on the
subject.[83]

WHAT THE LAWS SPECIFIED

A would-be prosecutor needed to know what type of case he could
bring for the offence with which he was concerned, and to which
magistrate he should apply. This information was discoverable from
the law about that particular offence. But how specific were the laws
on these matters?

We have the texts of a number of laws (though only a small proportion of the total which must have existed), either in the original
stone inscriptions or in quotations in surviving forensic speeches. Very

few of these texts are complete. Most of the stones are fragmentary; most of the quotations in speeches extend only to the clauses which are more or less relevant to the orator's case. And some of the quotations are not genuine at all, but merely attempts by later students or forgers to compose suitable-looking legal texts for insertion where they seemed to be needed. Nevertheless, although so many individual laws are lost, there is quite enough evidence to show what kind of thing was normally, or sometimes, included in the text of a law.

By the end of the fifth century (though this will not have been true of earlier laws such as Solon's) a law always began with a record of the date and procedure by which it was made, known to modern scholars as 'the prescript'. This consisted of a number of set phrases or formulas, naming the official bodies by whom the law was passed (the Boule and the people in the fifth century, the nomothetai in the fourth), the arkhon (whose name marked the year), the man who proposed the law, and sometimes other particulars.

Apart from the prescript, there was no regular form of words or order of topics. Athenian laws were not composed by professional draftsmen, and it was up to the individual proposing a law to express his proposal in the way he thought best. In these circumstances it is not surprising that the main point of a law tended to come first, immediately after the prescript, whether or not that was the most logical place for it. Commonly this was an instruction to do or not to do something (expressed by a jussive infinitive or a third person imperative); or it might be a conditional clause ('If anyone . . .') specifying some activity or behaviour which was to incur a penalty; or it might be a ruling that something was to have legal effect or validity. It was usually stated very briefly and baldly, with no definition of terms or description of circumstances. One law (as we should call it) might list a number of activities which were prescribed or banned; the Athenians would then commonly call it 'laws' in the plural.

When the purpose of the law was to specify duties or functions of arkhons or other officials, or the rules of business in the Ekklesia or Boule or courts (which it was the responsibility of the officials presiding over those bodies to observe), nothing else needed to be in the text. It could be assumed without being stated that an official who contravened the law was liable to accusation and penalty at the regular examination of his conduct in office (*euthyna*: see page 170). Sometimes, however, such a law did specify a penalty, such as a fine of a certain amount, which was to be imposed on an official who contravened it.

But when a law was about the activities of other people, who were not officials subject to regular examination, the question naturally arose what action was to be taken if the law was broken. So some laws, at least, specified the magistrate to whom a complaint or prosecution should be made, the category of person entitled to make it (for example, any Athenian citizen who wished, or any person entitled to take legal proceedings), the procedure by which it was to be made (for example, *graphe* or *phasis*), and either the penalty incurred by the offender if he was found guilty or a statement that the penalty was to be decided by the jury in each case. Here is an example of a law containing all these four items:

'And if anyone gives away an alien woman in marriage to an Athenian man, as if she were related to him, let him be disfranchised, and let his property be forfeited to the state, and let a third part of it belong to the successful prosecutor. Let a *graphe* be submitted to the thesmothetai by those who are entitled, in the same way as for simulating citizenship.' (Law quoted by Demosthenes 59. 52)

In many of the surviving texts of laws some or all of these items are missing, but it seems unlikely that any of them was left vague in fact. In some cases, where the surviving text is incomplete, they may actually have been stated in a part of the text which we do not have. In other cases, where they were not explicitly stated, we should assume that they were clear by implication.

That assumption is easy enough to make about the penalty: if the law did not specify a penalty for some offence, it could be taken for granted that the penalty was to be assessed by the jury. Likewise with the persons entitled to prosecute: a private case could be initiated only by a person who claimed that he personally had suffered some injury or deprivation, whereas a public case could be initiated by any man (except slaves and disfranchised citizens) unless explicitly restricted. Thus, if the correct procedure of prosecution for a particular offence was known, the category of person entitled to prosecute could be deduced from that and did not need to be stated in the law (though this was sometimes done all the same). The identity of the magistrate to whom a prosecution should be brought may also, even when not explicitly stated, have been clear from the context in which a law was placed. There is some evidence that, at least in the fourth century, laws were arranged in order according to the magistrates responsible for administering them.[84] Thus an Athenian finding a law among (say) the laws of the thesmothetai would know that the thesmothetai were the magistrates to whom any prosecution for infringing it should be brought, even if the thesmothetai were not mentioned in the text of that particular law.

What is less easy for us to make out is whether every law prescribed a specific legal procedure for use against persons who contravened it. This raises the question whether legal procedure was restricted to defined and named 'actions'. How detailed was the classification of cases?

TYPES OF CASE

Athenian cases are generally classified according to the procedure by which they were initiated and brought to the stage of trial. The word for a case is *dike*, and the broadest distinction is between a private case (*dike idia*) and a public case (*dike demosia*).

A public case concerned an offence or dispute which was regarded as affecting the community as a whole, and consequently anyone who wished was entitled to prosecute. The volunteer could be any free adult male, except that some kinds of case could not be brought by a non-citizen and none could be brought by a disfranchised citizen. The offences for which public cases could be brought included those which obviously affected the whole community equally, such as treason or desertion from the army or embezzlement of public funds. But also some offences against individuals came into this category, either because the individual victim of such an offence might be incapable of taking legal action for himself, or just because such behaviour was regarded as so serious that it was offensive even to those who did not suffer by it personally; among them were maltreatment of an orphan, seduction of a free woman, certain kinds of theft, and *hybris*.

The most ordinary type of public case was *graphe* (meaning 'writing'), so called presumably because it had originally been the only type of case in which the charge had to be put in writing, though by the fourth century written charges had become the rule in other cases too. Because Solon introduced prosecution by volunteers, it is commonly assumed that it was he who introduced the name and procedure of *graphe*, though there is no explicit evidence for that.

Different names were given to public cases having various distinctive features. All these varieties will be mentioned in later chapters in connection with the kinds of offence for which they were used, but it may be convenient to have a list of them here in summary form. All were open to volunteer prosecutors, who in the fourth century spoke for the prosecution in court; but most of them probably grew out of older and more informal procedures (earlier than Solon's reforms and the introduction of *graphe*), in which someone had brought an offender to a magistrate's attention and the magistrate had exercised his own powers to enforce the law.[85] The distinctive feature of *apagoge* was that the prosecutor began by arresting the defendant and taking him to the public prison. In *ephegesis* the first step was that the accuser led a magistrate to where the defendant was and told the magistrate to arrest him. In *endeixis* the prosecutor, having delivered his charge to the magistrate, could arrest the defendant if he wished but was not required to do so.[86] In *apographe* the prosecutor submitted a list of property which, he claimed, the defendant retained in his possession although it ought to have been forfeited to the state; if he won the case, the prosecutor was rewarded with three-quarters of the value of the property. In *phasis* a successful prosecutor received half the amount which the defendant was condemned to pay; whether there were other procedural differences between *phasis* and *graphe* is uncertain. The name *eisangelia* was used for several distinct kinds of case: a case initiated by a denunciation to the Ekklesia or Boule, a case for maltreatment of an orphan or heiress, and a case in which a public arbitrator was accused of misconducting an arbitration. Possibly the only distinguishing feature shared by the various kinds of *eisangelia* was that a prosecutor suffered no penalty if he dropped the case before trial or obtained only a few of the jury's votes (see page 64). In *probole* the case had a preliminary hearing in the Ekklesia before going for trial in a court. The procedures of *dokimasia*, for checking that a man was not disqualified to be a citizen or to hold an office or to speak in the Ekklesia, and *euthyna*, to check that a man had performed the duties of an office rightly, can also be regarded as types of public case.

A private case, properly *dike idia*, was often called just *dike*. It concerned a matter which was regarded as not affecting the community as a whole but only the individuals involved. Only the person who claimed that he suffered some wrong or deprivation could be the prosecutor. A special kind of private case was *diadikasia*, used when a right (for example, to claim an inheritance) or an obligation (for example, to perform a trierarchy) was disputed between two or more persons. Its distinctive feature was that there was no prosecutor or defendant; all the claimants were on equal terms.

A homicide case (*dike phonou*) was anomalous. Since a man could not be prosecuted for homicide by the person he had killed, the case could not be a private one in the strict sense. The prosecutor would usually be a relative of the dead person; whether a non-relative was allowed to be the prosecutor is disputed (see page 111). Yet *graphe* and the other terms for public cases were not used for homicide, probably because the Athenians retained for homicide cases throughout the classical period the procedure believed to have been instituted by Drakon or earlier, before *graphe* was invented.

It is clear that many laws on various subjects specified the types of case which were to be brought against anyone who infringed them. Some kinds of offence could be regarded as coming under more than one law, making more than one type of case possible. Examples are given in the speech *Against Androtion* (Demosthenes 22. 26-7), where we are told that for theft the laws permit four different procedures: *apagoge*, *ephegesis*, *graphe*, or a private case (*dike klopes*). But the implication of this and other texts is clearly that it was not permitted to use any other procedures than those specified in the relevant laws. Indeed many modern scholars have believed that what is implied is something still more precise and systematic. The Athenian orators and later writers quite often refer to a case by combining the name of the procedure with a genitive noun denoting the offence: *dike aikeias* (for battery), *graphe lipotaxiou* (for desertion from the army), and so on. It has been inferred that these phrases are the names of a comprehensive set of 'actions', something like the *actiones* of Roman law, and that no case could be brought unless it was a *dike aikeias* or a *graphe lipotaxiou* or some other of the individually named 'actions' (possibly as many as a hundred of them) prescribed by law.

But this goes too far. The Athenians knew nothing of Roman law, and they were not so systematic. In the surviving texts of their laws these two-word phrases, each consisting of the name of a procedure with an offence in the genitive, are very seldom found; both the offence and the procedure are often expressed by verbs. Even in the orators some offences seem to have no suitable nouns for putting in the genitive and so are expressed by long phrases ('*graphe* that he was wrongly imprisoned as a seducer' and the like). If a man prosecuted another for hitting him, in contravention of the law which forbade hitting, it was sometimes convenient to call that a case for battery (*dike aikeias*), but we should not assume that the law gave it that name, nor that if the name had not existed the case could not have been brought.[87]

On the other hand we must not, in avoiding that error, fall into the opposite error of believing that a case could be brought concerning a sphere of conduct on which there was no law at all. We must not be misled by the clause in the jurors' oath which ran 'I will judge according to the laws and decrees of Athens, and matters about which there are no laws I will decide by the justest opinion' (see page 44). The 'matters about which there are no laws' need be nothing more than specific questions within the fields of activity covered by laws. For instance, when Euthyphron's father, according to Plato's *Euthyphron*, left a man bound in a ditch and death resulted, Euthyphron proposed to accuse him of homicide. There was, we can assume, no law saying whether leaving someone bound in a ditch did or did not count as homicide; so the jury would have to decide that question 'by the justest opinion'. But that does not mean that there was no law forbidding homicide and specifying a legal procedure for homicide cases.

A crucial example is the case of the first speech *Against Boiotos* (Demosthenes 39). The speaker, Mantitheos, is accusing his own half-brother. The ground of his complaint is that the brother, although given the name Boiotos by their father (now deceased), has adopted the name Mantitheos, with the result that the two of them are constantly confused. Now it is certain that there was no law saying that a man could not change his name, or that he must keep the name given him by his father, or that he must not have the same name as his brother; for, if there had been, Mantitheos would have quoted it. Was there then no law on the matter at all? On the contrary:

'Now, if he can point to a law which gives children authority over their own names, you would be right to vote in favour of what he is saying now. But if the law, which you all know as well as I do, gives parents authority not only to give the name in the first place, but also, if they wish, to annul it again and disown the child, and if I have shown that our father, who had authority according to the law, named him Boiotos and me Mantitheos, how can you vote in favour of anything except what I say?'   (Demosthenes 39. 39)

Since Mantitheos avoids quoting the law to which he refers, we do not know exactly what it said. Probably it was a law about minors, and did not in truth say whether an adult was permitted to adopt a new name or not. But it is not necessary to decide here whether Mantitheos's interpretation of the law was correct. The fact which is relevant here is that a law about naming children did exist. Neither Mantitheos's case nor any other is known to have concerned a subject about which there was no law at all. Nor would it have been practicable for anyone to bring a case concerning a subject about which there was no law: he would not have known which was the right magistrate to apply to, nor whether the procedure should be a private *dike* or *graphe* or *apagoge* or something else. Nor would the magistrates themselves have been able to answer these questions; they did not have (as the Roman praetor had) power to create new forms or causes of action.

The conclusion should therefore be that, although a law did not specify a named 'action' like *dike aikeias* or *graphe lipotaxiou*, it did always indicate which procedure, *dike* or *graphe* or another, was the right one to use against anyone who contravened it, unless that was clear without being stated (as in the case of laws about the functions of officials who were subject to *euthyna*). And if no law existed on some subject, so that no procedure was specified, then no legal proceedings on that subject were possible. That may sound very restrictive. In practice it was less restrictive than it sounds, because some of the offences which were forbidden by law (for instance, damaging property: see pages 149–53) were very widely interpreted. The vagueness of Athenian laws left much to the discretion of the juries.

PUBLIC PROSECUTORS

There were certain cases in which the prosecutors were men acting in an official capacity. Sometimes a magistrate himself noticed an offence concerning his own sphere of responsibility; for example, a strategos (general) might need to prosecute for desertion from the army, or an agoranomos (market controller) for disorderly conduct in the Agora. If the offence required a penalty greater than the magistrate could impose on his own authority, he had to introduce the case into a court for trial by a jury and act as prosecutor himself (see page 237).

A group of magistrates who had virtually no function except to prosecute was the ten synegoroi (advocates) who presented the case against any ex-magistrate who was being prosecuted on a financial charge at his *euthyna* (see page 170). These synegoroi were ten citizens selected by lot, and were paid one drachma a day.[88]

Another kind of synegoros (alternatively called kategoros) was a man appointed by the Ekklesia or the Boule to speak for the prosecution in a particular case. When the Ekklesia or the Boule passed a decree ordering that someone should be tried, either when accused by *eisan-gelia* (see pages 170 and 183) or when the Areopagos had made a report (see page 190), the decree would state who was to prosecute at the trial. In practice this would often be the man who had originally raised the matter; but it was quite possible for the Ekklesia or the Boule to appoint other speakers for the prosecution, either instead or in addition. Ten such prosecutors were appointed for the trial of Demosthenes and others in 324/3.[89]

Thus it would not be true to say that publicly appointed prosecutors did not exist in Athens. Nevertheless, most public cases were brought by volunteers.

SYCOPHANTS

The device of encouraging volunteers to prosecute was an ingenious one for getting offenders brought to justice in a community which had virtually no police force. The kinds of case for which volunteers came forward most readily must have been those in which the prosecutor received a financial reward if he won the case. One of these was *phasis*, used particularly for offences concerning trade; half the fine paid by the offender was given to the successful prosecutor (see pages 158–9). Another was *apographe*, used to recover property which was being withheld from the state; the successful prosecutor received three-quarters of the amount which the state recovered (see page 166). Another was a *graphe* in which an alien man was accused of cohabiting with a female citizen, or in which a man was accused of giving an alien woman in marriage to a male citizen; the offender's property was confiscated and one-third of it was given to the successful prosecutor.[90] But there must also have been some men willing to undertake prosecutions even for cases of the kind in which successful prosecutors received no payment. They may simply have had an altruistic wish to see justice done, or they may have hoped to gain a reputation as patriotic public figures. Or again, they may have found this a convenient way to do some harm to political or personal antagonists; to do harm to one's enemies was considered by most Greeks to be a perfectly proper aim.

But by the latter part of the fifth century the system had given rise to a notorious nuisance. This was the man who made a practice of prosecuting without justification, either because he hoped to get an innocent defendant convicted and so obtain a payment due to a success-ful prosecutor, or because he hoped to blackmail the defendant into bribing him to drop the case. Such a man was called a 'sycophant', a word that has acquired a different meaning in modern English; the Greek *sykophantes* is a vague disparaging word for an unjustified accuser. Its origin is unknown, though many guesses have been made.[91]

To modern readers, sycophants are familiar mainly from Aristophanes's satire of them. There is a well-known scene in *Akharnians*, in which a Megarian comes to the market to sell his daughters, disguised as pigs, and a sycophant attempts to accuse him by *phasis* of selling goods imported from an enemy state. 'What an evil this is in Athens!' comments the Megarian after the sycophant has been chased away. Soon afterwards a Boiotian would like to have a characteristic Athenian product which he cannot get at home in Boiotia; so a sycophant is parcelled up for him to take away. Another sycophant appears in *Birds*, and one of the lost plays apparently had an attack on sycophants as its main theme.[92] By the time of his last surviving play, *Wealth*, Aristophanes's view of sycophants seems to have mellowed a little, since he allows a sycophant to defend his activities in the following dialogue.

Sycophant: O Zeus and gods! Must I put up with being treated ignominiously by these men? How distressing that I, a worthy, patriotic man, should suffer this!
Good man: You, patriotic and worthy?
Sycophant: Yes, more than any man.
Good man: Tell me something, will you?
Sycophant: What?
Good man: Are you a farmer?
Sycophant: Do you think I'm crazy?
Good man: A merchant, then?
Sycophant: Oh yes; at least I give that excuse sometimes.
Good man: Well then, have you learned a craft?
Sycophant: Certainly not.
Good man: How do you get your living then, if you don't do anything?
Sycophant: I supervise all public and private affairs.
Good man: What makes you do that?
Sycophant: I volunteer.
Good man: How can you be a worthy man, you villain, if you make enemies over matters that are not your business?
Sycophant: Isn't it my business to serve my own city as far as I can, you idiot?

Good man: To serve it? Do you mean to meddle with it?
Sycophant: No; to support the laws that have been made, and not to
allow anyone to do wrong.
Good man: Doesn't the city appoint jurors for that purpose?
Sycophant: But who prosecutes?
Good man: The man who volunteers.
Sycophant: Well, that's who I am. So the city's affairs depend on me.
(Aristophanes *Wealth* 898–919)

The laws of Athens did indeed depend to a considerable extent on
the volunteer prosecutor for their enforcement, but it was necessary to
discourage him from pestering the innocent. So a penalty was introduced for a prosecutor in a public case who obtained less than one-fifth
of the jury's votes. The same penalty was imposed if he abandoned a
case after starting it, which was what a blackmailer would do if he
succeeded in getting a bribe from his victim. The penalty was a fine of
1000 drachmas. Some surviving texts mention only the fine, but others
mention disfranchisement too. It is possible that the rule was changed
in the course of the fourth century. But on the whole the best interpretation of the texts seems to be that the penalty was, in addition to the
fine, the loss of the right to bring in future cases of the type (*graphe* or
phasis or whatever it was) that he had brought on that occasion. This
ban on future prosecutions of the same type was a kind of partial
disfranchisement. But if he failed to pay the fine, he would automatically
suffer total disfranchisement as a debtor to the state (see page 165).[93]
However, some exceptions must be noticed. In one kind of public
case, *eisangelia*, until about 330, a prosecutor suffered no penalty if
he obtained less than one-fifth of the votes; after that date he was
liable to a fine of 1000 drachmas, but not to restriction of his right to
bring cases in future. Presumably the kinds of offence for which
eisangelia was used were considered to be so serious that nothing should
be allowed to deter prosecutors from bringing the offenders to justice,
but unjustified cases of this type later became so common that some
deterrent was found to be necessary after all (see page 186).[94] In another
kind of public case, *probole*, in which there was a preliminary hearing
by the Ekklesia, it was permitted for the prosecutor to abandon the case
after that hearing, without proceeding to the trial by jury (see page
195). In cases tried by the Areopagos, it seems likely that a prosecutor
who abandoned a case did not suffer a penalty automatically but the
Areopagos could impose a fine if it thought fit.[95]

Even in the commonest kind of public case, *graphe*, we know of several prosecutors who abandoned cases without apparently suffering any penalty. Two texts seem to imply that, if slaves under torture gave evidence favourable to the defendant, the prosecutor was allowed to abandon the case.[96] In several other instances we read that a prosecutor withdrew his charge from the magistrate or got the magistrate to delete it, but it is not clear why this was permitted.[97] On the other hand, when a prosecutor and defendant agreed privately that the prosecutor would apply for a postponement of the trial on the ground that he was ill, and then never apply for a new date to be fixed, that was undoubtedly a devious means of abandoning a case in fact without formally doing so, in order to avoid the penalty. And even when a prosecutor who abandoned a case did suffer disfranchisement, he may sometimes have been able to ignore it, since in practice he would be able to go on exercising the rights which he had in theory lost, until someone else took the trouble to prosecute him for doing so. Altogether, it is likely that clever sycophants were often able to evade punishment when they accepted a bribe to abandon a case.[98]

But another possibility was that a man could be prosecuted for the offence of being a sycophant. This was done by *probole*: once a year in the Ekklesia (at the principal meeting in the sixth prytany) any Athenian could bring forward a charge that a man was a sycophant. The number of men that could be denounced on this ground on one occasion was limited to three citizens and three metics. (The fact that metics could be sycophants is an indication that prosecutors did not have to be citizens in every kind of case.) The procedure for a *probole* was that the hearing in the Ekklesia was followed by a trial by jury. The penalty was fixed by the jury; in the only recorded instance it was a fine of 10,000 drachmas.[99]

It was also possible to prosecute a sycophant by *graphe*. At one time *eisangelia* was another possibility, but that was probably excluded when the law about *eisangelia* restricted the offences for which that procedure could be used (see page 184). Yet another possibility was opened up when the mercantile laws in the middle of the fourth century authorized the use of *endeixis* and *apagoge* against a sycophant on the ground that he had prosecuted a ship-master or merchant without justification.[100]

It is not known whether any law contained a definition of a sycophant to help the jurors to decide their verdict. It may well be that there was no such definition, and the jurors had to make up their own minds in each case whether the defendant's activities amounted to sycophancy. The most relevant evidence would probably be either that he had been paid to prosecute someone, or that he had threatened that he would prosecute someone if he were not paid, or that he had somehow revealed that he himself did not believe in the truth of a charge which he had made. It must often have been difficult to prove any of these things; and this, combined with the fact that so many different types of prosecution were permitted for this offence, suggests that the Athenians had great difficulty in suppressing sycophancy.

Part Two: The Scope of the Law

v PERSONAL STATUS

The rights of anyone in Athens, including his right to prosecute at law, depended on his status, on whether he was a citizen (*polites* or *astos*) or an alien (*xenos*) or a slave (*doulos* or *oiketes*).

Until the middle of the fifth century a person was a citizen if his father was a citizen. It was not necessary for his mother to be a citizen also, and some well-known Athenians did in fact have foreign mothers. For example, in the first half of the sixth century Megakles, a leading member of the Alkmeonid family, married Agariste, daughter of Kleisthenes, who was the ruler of Sikyon; their children included Kleisthenes, the politician who reformed the Athenian constitution. And towards the end of the sixth century Miltiades married a Thracian princess; their son Kimon was the leading Athenian general in the 470s and 460s.

This was changed by a law proposed by Perikles in 451/0: henceforth a person was to be a citizen only if both his parents were citizens. (The restriction probably applied only to persons born after the law was passed, and did not disfranchise existing citizens.) During the latter part of the Peloponnesian War this law seems not to have been enforced, but it was reaffirmed in 403/2 on the proposal of either Aristophon or Nikomenes (with the proviso that it should not be enforced against persons born before 403/2; thus Timotheos, son of Konon and a Thracian woman, was able to hold office as a strategos in the first half of the fourth century). The motive for the restriction is not clear. *AP* says that it was 'because of the large number of citizens'. Modern scholars have speculated that Athenian citizens wished to share their privileges with as few others as possible, or that they wished to preserve their racial purity, or that they were afraid that, if many Athenian men married foreign women, Athenian women might be left without husbands. These suggestions seem to spring from the interests and moral beliefs of those who make them, rather than from any firm evidence; but the first, at least, accords with *AP*'s comment.[101] (On the other provision of Perikles's law, invalidating marriage between a citizen and an alien, see page 87).

Some scholars have thought that a person could not be a citizen if
he was not of legitimate birth (that is, if his parents had not been married
with *engye* or *epidikasia*, as explained in chapter VI). But in my opinion
that is a mistake, resulting from confusion between citizenship and the
right to belong to a phratry (a hereditary religious organization) or to
inherit property. To establish his right to be a citizen, a man had to
show only that his parents were citizens, not that they were married.
This is indicated by three pieces of evidence: *AP* defines the legal
requirement for citizenship as birth from citizen parents on both
sides, without mentioning marriage; a decree of 411 disfranchises
descendants of Arkheptolemos and Antiphon 'both bastard and
legitimate', implying that bastard descendants might otherwise have
been citizens; and a speaker in the fourth century, at a time when
marriage between a citizen and a non-citizen was forbidden, refers to
the marriage of an illegitimate daughter of Pyrrhos to a citizen named
Xenokles.[102]

In early Athens the citizens were organized in four tribes (*phylai*),
of which membership was hereditary. But in 508/7 these four tribes
were replaced, for all political and legal purposes, by a new organization
on the proposal of Kleisthenes. Its basis was local. Each citizen was
a member of the 'parish' in which he lived. The Greek word is *demos*,
usually anglicized as 'deme'; a deme might be a village with the surrounding rural area, or it might be a district of the city of Athens.
There were about 150 demes. They were listed in ten groups, so arranged that each group included demes from different parts of Attika
(the city of Athens, the coastal area, and the inland plain) and had
approximately one-tenth of the total number of citizens. These ten
groups were called tribes (*phylai*); but they had no connection with the
old four tribes, and indeed one of the main motives of the reorganiza-
tion must have been to end the significance of the old tribes. But the
precise motives and details of the local divisions raise difficult and much
discussed problems, which need not be considered here.[103]

In 508/7 each citizen was a member of the deme in which he lived
(as in a modern parliamentary constituency). But from that date
onwards he always remained a member of the same deme, even if he
changed his place of residence (unlike a modern parliamentary con-
stituent). And a son belonged to the same deme as his father; thus,
though the initial organization was local, its continuation was hereditary. Ancient Athenians changed their place of residence less often than
people in modern times, and many a family probably lived on the same

farm for centuries. But Athenians did move sometimes, and so the membership of a deme tended gradually to become scattered. A speaker in 346/5, when the new organization had been in force for 160 years, remarks that most members of the deme Halimous live in the deme; this implies that there were some demes of which that could no longer be said.[104]

The most important purpose for which this organization by tribes and demes was used was the appointment of officials, either by lot or by vote. For some offices each tribe provided one holder each year, making ten in all. For the Boule (the council of five hundred) each deme provided a number of councillors which was fixed in proportion to its population. So each deme kept an 'office-lot register' (*lexiarkhikon grammateion*) listing all the adult male members of the deme, to show who was eligible for appointment to office. Every adult male citizen was on the register of a deme, and the deme registers were the only lists of citizens. There were no complete lists of women and children of citizen status.

Each deme appointed each year by lot one of its members to be the chief or chairman, the demarch.[105] He presided at meetings of the members of the deme, and had custody of the register between meetings. Additions to the register were made at a meeting held at the beginning of the year, in midsummer.[106] When the son of a member had reached (or, less probably, had completed) his eighteenth year,[107] he presented himself at this meeting, and the deme-members voted under oath to decide whether he should be registered. First they had to decide whether he had reached his eighteenth year, which (since Athenians had no birth certificates) they had to judge from his physical development or from the evidence of witnesses; if they thought he had not, he had to 'go back to the boys'. Secondly they had to decide whether he was qualified by birth to be a member of the deme; if they thought he was not, he had the right to appeal to a court, but if the jury's verdict there went against him he was punished by enslavement. Only when they were satisfied on both counts did they register him. To ensure that no one was registered before his eighteenth year, newly registered youths were reviewed by the Boule. If the councillors thought that any of them was under eighteen, they imposed a fine on the members of the deme which had registered him; the deme-members could appeal to a court against the fine, so that a jury had then to judge his age.[108] This process of review and registration was called *dokimasia*.

All this may seem to suggest that the registers were kept meticulously, but in fact some demes were probably careless. On one occasion, we are told, the demarch of Halimous lost the register, so that the members of the deme had to reconstruct it from their personal knowledge of one another.[109] In 346/5, on the proposal of Demophilos, the Athenians decreed that the members of every deme should review their register, deciding under oath whether each name was to be retained or excluded. This shows that suspicion had arisen that some men not properly qualified had got on to the registers. Any man excluded in this review could appeal to a court; and in fact our information about the affairs of Halimous comes from a speech (Demosthenes 57, *Against Euboulides*) composed for delivery in court by a man appealing against his exclusion from that deme on this occasion, in which he takes pains to prove by the evidence of witnesses that his father and his mother both belonged to Athenian citizen families.[110]

No other occasion is known on which all the deme registers were reviewed systematically. But at any time a person alleged to be masquerading as a citizen (by exercising any of the rights which only citizens possessed) could be prosecuted by *graphe* for 'being an alien' (*xenia*). He was imprisoned until trial, and if found guilty he became a slave and was sold by the state to anyone who would buy him.[111]

Apart from the demes and tribes, many Athenian citizens belonged also to a phratry (*phratria*, 'brotherhood'), and some prided themselves on belonging to a particular genos ('clan'), just as some Scotsmen are proud of belonging to a particular clan; but membership of a genos or of a phratry had almost no juristic significance, and so such bodies need not be discussed in detail here. (The only known legal function of a phratry was in pardoning a person found guilty of unintentional homicide, if no close relatives of the killed person survived; see page 120.) But although membership of a genos or of a phratry did not itself affect a man's legal status, it could be useful as evidence if his legitimacy or citizen status was questioned, since a genos or a phratry would not accept a new member unless satisfied that he was of legitimate Athenian birth (or an alien on whom citizenship had been conferred by decree); this is why we find speakers in several cases taking trouble to show that somebody was, or was not, accepted by a genos or by a phratry.[112]

CITIZENSHIP CONFERRED ON ALIENS

A person who was not entitled by birth to be a citizen could not normally become one. There was no regular procedure of naturalization. However, there were certain exceptional cases in which citizenship was conferred on aliens.

Solon is said by Plutarch to have introduced a law allowing Athenian citizenship to be acquired by an alien if he was permanently exiled from his own state, or if he brought his entire household to live in Athens to practise a trade or profession.[113] But there is no other information about this law, and Plutarch's statement may not be reliable. Certainly in the fifth and fourth centuries such aliens did not normally become Athenian citizens. Perhaps the law was soon repealed or fell into disuse; or perhaps Plutarch has misreported a law which really only allowed such aliens to become metics, not citizens.

When Kleisthenes in 508/7 introduced his new system of demes and tribes, he is said by Aristotle to have included in them 'many' foreigners and slaves who were resident in Athens.[114] We are not told how many, or by what criterion they were selected. Kleisthenes may have thought that the government would be more democratic, and therefore better, if as many as possible of the adult male population were entitled to participate. He may also have thought that he himself was likely to receive political support from citizens who owed their citizenship to him.

The small city of Plataia made an alliance with Athens in 519 (some scholars emend the text of Thucydides to give the date 509); and either at the same time or afterwards (Thucydides does not make the date clear, but it was before 429) the Plataians were declared citizens of Athens.[115] As long as they lived in Plataia, this honorary citizenship probably had not much practical significance. But in 427, when Plataia was captured by the Spartans and Thebans, the Athenians allowed the Plataians to take refuge in Athens and passed a further decree enabling them to be registered in demes and so exercise the rights of citizenship. No Plataian was allowed to hold office in Athens as a priest or as one of the nine arkhons (who had charge of some religious ceremonies), but their descendants were not subject to this restriction, and otherwise Plataians had all the same political and legal rights as native Athenians.[116] The speech *Against Pankleon* (Lysias 23), which will be discussed in chapter XIV, concerns the case of a man who claimed that he was a Plataian and consequently had the status of an Athenian citizen. In 421 some Plataians moved from Athens to Skione, and after the King's Peace was made in 387/6 some gave up their Athenian citizenship and returned to Plataia, but others may have stayed in Athens as citizens permanently. [117]

In 406 the Athenians became so desperate for men to man their ships for the war against Sparta that they offered citizenship (on the same terms as to the Plataians) to any man who would serve in the navy; and a number of men, including some slaves, did thus obtain citizenship by taking part in the battle of Arginousai.[118]

In gratitude to the people of Samos for their loyalty to Athens in the closing stages of the Peloponnesian War, the Athenians decreed in 405 (and confirmed by another decree in 403/2) that the Samians should be Athenian citizens, and that those Samians who were present in Athens at the time should be allotted to demes forthwith.[119] But a man could not exercise the rights of citizenship until he was registered in a deme, and it may well be that not many Samians actually came to Athens to be registered.

In 403, when democracy was restored after the oligarchic regime of the Thirty, the democratic leader Thrasyboulos proposed a decree granting citizenship to all who had participated in the democrats' occupation of Peiraieus, some of whom were slaves (and one of the others was the orator Lysias); however, Arkhinos attacked this decree by *graphe paranomon* (for this procedure see page 50) on the ground that it had not been passed by the Boule, and so got it annulled.[120] But in 401/0 another decree was passed: the inscription is fragmentary and the restoration doubtful, but this decree seems to have granted citizenship to some men who had taken part in the democrats' advance from Phyle to Peiraieus, as a reward for their service to democracy.[121]

The small Peloponnesian city of Troizen was, like Plataia, an old ally of Athens; and the Athenians gave citizenship to the Troizenians who were expelled from their city in the 320s by a pro-Macedonian ruler.[122]

Besides these grants to whole groups or categories, the Athenians sometimes gave citizenship to an individual alien. This could be a political gesture to cement an alliance with a foreign state, as when Sadokos, son of the king of Thrace, was made an Athenian in 431;[123] or it could be a reward for services to Athens, as when in 409 Thrasyboulos of Kalydon and Apollodoros of Megara were granted Athenian citizenship as a reward for killing Phrynikhos, a leading member of the oligarchic regime of the Four Hundred, in 411.[124]

In the fourth century, around the year 370, a settled procedure for granting citizenship to individual aliens was established by law. The ground for conferring it was supposed to be 'manly virtue' (*andragathia*). A decree granting citizenship to the alien in question was proposed in the Ekklesia. If passed, it did not take immediate effect; at the next meeting of the Ekklesia there was a secret ballot, for which a quorum of 6000 citizens was required, and the decree became effective only if it obtained a majority in this ballot. Even after that it could still be attacked by *graphe paranomon* (see page 50), in which the new citizen lost his citizenship if the jury voted against it. There was also a law forbidding anyone who was a citizen by decree, not by birth, to hold an Athenian priesthood or be one of the nine arkhons.[125]

From this period we have inscriptions of a number of decrees granting citizenship to various individual aliens. Some of them were rulers of foreign states, such as Dionysios, tyrant of Syracuse, to whom the grant of Athenian citizenship cannot have been much more than a compliment.[126] Others were men who had come to live in Athens because their friendship to the Athenians had caused them to be exiled from their own states, such as Phormion and Karphinas, two Akarnanians who fought with the Athenians at the battle of Khaironeia.[127] The fact that a special decree was drafted, passed, voted on by ballot, and inscribed on stone for each case shows that the conferment of citizenship on an alien never became a routine matter. And the fact that the official wording in every decree was not 'citizenship is to be given to X' but 'X is to be Athenian' (even in the case of Dionysios) shows that it was thought of not just as an honour, but as a real assumption of a new nationality.

OUTLAWRY AND DISFRANCHISEMENT ('ATIMIA')

A citizen's status could be affected by *atimia*, which was imposed as a penalty for various offences. This meant that he forfeited rights and privileges, but it is not easy to define exactly what that meant in practice. Modern discussions of the subject have not been entirely satisfactory. A recent account by M. H. Hansen is the best given so far, but some problems are still unsolved.[128]

In the sixth and early fifth centuries *atimia* was outlawry: if a man was *atimos*, anyone could kill or otherwise maltreat him or plunder his property without becoming liable to prosecution or penalty. This would make it virtually impossible for him to remain in Athenian territory. Such *atimia* was roughly equivalent to expulsion from Attika, and it could be imposed on aliens as well as Athenians. We have part of the text of a decree, probably proposed by Kimon at some time between 477 and 450, imposing *atimia* on a foreigner (from Zeleia in

Asia Minor) named Arthmios, because he had bribed people in the Peloponnese to support the Persians; this was in effect a measure prohibiting him from entering Attika.[129]

By the late fifth century a different form of words ('Let him die with impunity') was used for outlawry, and *atimia* had come to mean less than this. Roughly, it meant exclusion from the privileges of Athenian public life, and it was a penalty imposed only on citizens, not applicable to aliens. It is convenient to translate it 'disfranchisement'. However, it involved loss of more than just the right to vote. A disfranchised citizen was not allowed to enter temples or the Agora. He could not hold any public office, nor be a member of the Boule or a juror. He could not speak in the Ekklesia or in a law-court (though he could be present in a court without speaking). But it is not clear that he lost any of the other rights and duties of a citizen; probably he could still marry an Athenian wife and own land in Attika, and was still liable to pay taxes and perform military service. A disfranchised citizen was not equivalent to an alien. In some respects he was better off than an alien, but in others worse; for example, an alien could not marry an Athenian woman, but he could trade in the Agora and speak in a law-court. The ban on speaking in court may well have been in practice the most irksome part of disfranchisement: a disfranchised citizen may have had to endure many personal injuries and insults because he was not able to prosecute. But if he was the victim of some kind of maltreatment for which a public case could be brought by anyone who wished (for example, a *graphe* for *hybris*: see page 129), he might be able to get a friend to bring one; and if he was killed, there was nothing to prevent his relatives from bringing a case for homicide. Thus *atimia* in its fourth-century sense of disfranchisement, though a serious handicap, was much less serious than *atimia* in its sixth-century sense of outlawry.

Disfranchisement was normally for life. It could be made hereditary, applying also to the offender's descendants; more often it was imposed only on the offender himself. But state debtors were in a rather different position: a man who owed money to the state (for example, a man sentenced to pay a fine, or a tax-farmer who failed to pay the price fixed for his tax-collecting privilege on the date when it fell due) was regarded as disfranchised from the moment when he incurred the debt until the moment when he paid it, and if he died before paying it his heir inherited not only the debt but also the disfranchisement; but as soon as the debt was paid the disfranchisement automatically ended.

Partial disfranchisement was also possible: a citizen could be deprived of one or two specific rights. Thus citizens who performed military service for the oligarchic regime of the Four Hundred in 411 were (when democracy was restored) forbidden to speak in the Ekklesia or be members of the Boule; those who served in the cavalry for the Thirty in 404/3 were likewise forbidden to be members of the Boule. Other examples are given by Andokides in his account of *atimia*, and probably any of the rights which were forfeited collectively in total disfranchisement could also be forfeited individually.[130]

If a disfranchised man was seen to be in any of the places, or to be performing any of the functions, which were forbidden to him, anyone who wished could use the procedure of *endeixis* against him. *Endeixis* literally means 'pointing out', and in origin no doubt it meant drawing attention to a culprit who could be seen. But by the fourth century the first step, as in other kinds of public case, was simply to give a charge in writing to the appropriate magistrates, who for *endeixis* were generally the thesmothetai; and the most important distinguishing feature of *endeixis* was that after delivering the charge to the magistrates the prosecutor could, if he wished, arrest the defendant and take him to the public prison to be kept in custody until the trial.[131] However, some variations in the procedure occurred: sometimes the defendant was not imprisoned nor even required to produce sureties; sometimes he was arrested without having first been denounced to a magistrate (this was the procedure called *apagoge*); sometimes the magistrates who received the charge and took the case into court for trial were not the thesmothetai but the Eleven (the officials who controlled the prison) or even the basileus (in a case in which the defendant, Andokides, was being prosecuted for attending a religious festival when banned from doing so).[132] The penalty also varied: for some offenders (for example, a man who held a public office while owing money to the state) the death penalty was required by law, while for others the penalty was left to the jury to decide.[133] The rules governing these variations in the procedure and the penalty have not yet been clearly explained; *atimia* remains one of the most difficult topics in the study of Athenian law.

ALIENS

It goes without saying that an alien could not hold any public office in Athens, nor be a juror or a member of the Boule or Ekklesia (though a foreigner such as an ambassador could be invited to attend and address the Boule or Ekklesia on a particular occasion). He was also not allowed to own land or houses in Attika, nor (after 451/0: see page 87) to marry an Athenian woman. If he wished to trade in the Agora, he had to pay a special aliens' tax (*xenika*).[134]

An alien was allowed to speak in an Athenian law-court, whether as the prosecutor or as the defendant or as a witness (and in this respect was better off than a disfranchised citizen). There were, however, three ways in which his rights in legal cases were less than the rights of a citizen. First, there were some types of public case which an alien could not bring, because the laws specifying the procedure for those cases laid down that the prosecutor must be an Athenian.[135] Yet there were also some types of public case which could be brought by an alien: there is one clear instance in which an Andrian named Epainetos prosecuted Stephanos, a citizen, by *graphe* before the thesmothetai for wrongfully confining him.[136] It is not known why aliens were allowed to bring some public cases and not others.

Secondly, when an alien was prosecuted (certainly in some types of case, and very likely in all), the prosecutor could demand sureties (*engyetai*) for his appearance in court. Naturally there was a greater risk that an alien might evade trial by leaving Attika than that an Athenian might do so. The procedure was that the prosecutor, taking the defendant alien with him if possible, applied to the polemarch, and the defendant had to produce some friends who undertook to pay up if he himself failed to appear for trial. Presumably the amount which they undertook to pay was the value of the matter in dispute. If the defendant failed to produce such sureties, he was imprisoned until the trial.[137]

Thirdly, in many types of case the magistrate responsible for bringing a case to court was not the same one when it involved an alien as when it involved citizens only. The arrangement did not remain the same throughout the classical period, and it was affected by the existence of treaties governing legal proceedings between Athenians and foreigners, and also by the mercantile laws introduced in the fourth century; and so it is discussed along with those topics in chapter XV.

RESIDENT ALIENS (METICS)

Some aliens settled in Attika with the status of 'resident alien'; the Greek term is *xenos metoikos* or just *metoikos*, usually anglicized as 'metic'. A metic was not a citizen, and had no more political rights than any other alien, but he was accepted as a member of the community. He was liable to taxation, including a special metics' tax (*metoikion*) of 12 drachmas a year for a man, 6 for a woman, and was liable to enslavement if he did not pay it; this in fact happened to the philosopher Xenokrates, but Demetrios of Phaleron purchased him and set him free.[138] A metic had also to serve when required in the Athenian army or navy. If he tried to avoid service by going to live elsewhere when war broke out, he was not allowed ever to return to Athens.[139]

Whether the status of metic was held by all aliens (other than slaves) who resided in Attika, or only by some of them, has been a disputed question. Many scholars have thought that there were aliens who lived in Attika but were not metics. But there is no clear evidence for that, since references in various texts to aliens in Attika can all be explained as meaning either metics (who were one kind of aliens) or aliens who were not residents. The counter-argument is stronger: if aliens had been allowed to live permanently in Athens without becoming metics, none of them would have been likely to choose metic status. Paying taxes and performing military service were liabilities, not privileges. All resident aliens must have been subject to them; why should the Athenians let a foreigner enjoy the advantage of living in their city without contributing to their revenues and defence? So we may take it that every free alien residing permanently in Attika was a metic; the question is how a permanent resident was distinguished from a visitor. There must have been a legal definition, but unfortunately no preserved Athenian text gives it. One possibility is that an alien staying with an Athenian or at an inn counted as a visitor, while an alien who set up his own household was a metic. Another possibility is that there was a time-limit: an alien ceased to be reckoned a visitor and became a metic when he had been in Attika for some specified length of time. Aristophanes of Byzantion in the second century BC defined a metic like this: 'A metic is when a man comes from abroad and resides in the state, paying tax for some fixed requirements of the state; up to a certain number of days he is called a visitor and is free from taxation, but if he exceeds the limited period he then becomes a metic and subject to taxation.' But it is not certain that he was referring to classical Athens.[140]

An alien wishing to take up permanent residence had to apply for registration as a metic in a particular deme, if that is a fair inference from the fact that official documents usually designate a metic as resident in a particular deme.[141] He had to have an Athenian citizen as his sponsor or patron (*prostates*), and probably he had at the same time to make his first payment of the metics' tax, but there is no evidence that any other qualification or action was required; as long as he paid the tax and produced a sponsor, registration was presumably automatic.

The exact function of a metic's sponsor is not explained for us by any ancient author. It seems safe to guess that he certified in some way that the alien was a suitable person to be accepted as a permanent resident in Athens. Once the alien was registered as a metic, there is no clear evidence that the sponsor had any further responsibility. Some scholars have thought that when a metic was involved in a legal case his sponsor had to speak for him, but this is a mistake (based on a false analogy with the Roman *patronus*); for we know of several cases in which aliens spoke for themselves but none in which a metic remained silent while his sponsor spoke for him. Prosecution for not having a sponsor (*graphe aprostasiou*) was possible, with enslavement as the penalty, but scholars have had difficulty in imagining what circumstances might give rise to it. Probably this form of words simply means prosecution for residing in Attika without having been registered as a metic.[142]

Otherwise, all that has been said about aliens on pages 75–6 applies equally to metics (though for some legal cases metics had a different magistrate from other aliens for bringing the case to court: see pages 221–4).

PRIVILEGED ALIENS

Apart from metic status, other privileges were sometimes given to an alien as a favour or a reward for services to Athens. Some were given only to metics, others could be given to any alien.

(1) *Enktesis*, which could be 'of land and a house' or just 'of a house', was the right to acquire ownership of land and buildings in Attika.[143]

(2) A metic could be given *isoteleia*, which was the privilege of paying the same taxes as a citizen, instead of the higher taxes paid by metics; or he could be given exemption from the metics' tax (*metoikion*) only. An alien could even be given complete exemption from all Athenian taxation (*ateleia*), but it was probably very rare for this to be given to an alien permanently resident in Athens.

(3) A metic, who had to serve in the Athenian army or navy when required, could be given the privilege of serving alongside citizens, instead of in the separate metics' division.

(4) *Asylia* was immunity from attack or plunder by Athenians abroad.

An alien could be placed under the protection of the Athenian strategoi.
(5) An alien in Athens could be placed under the protection of the
Athenian Boule. He could also be given the right to present complaints
or petitions to the Boule or Ekklesia at the beginning of a meeting.
(6) An alien who was not a metic could be given the same right of
trial before the polemarch as a metic had (see pages 221–4).
(7) An alien could be granted the privilege that, if anyone killed him,
the killer was to suffer the same penalty as a killer of an Athenian
citizen, or was to be exiled from Athens and all other cities in the
Athenian alliance.[144]

The titles *proxenos* and *euergetes* ('benefactor of Athens') seem to have
been honours which did not by themselves give the recipient any
specific right or privilege (except probably no. 6), but a man who was
given these titles was generally given privileges at the same time. We
possess many fragmentary inscriptions of fourth-century decrees
conferring one or other of these privileges, and often several of them
together, as in this example.

'. . . is to be *proxenos* and *euergetes* of the people of Athens, both
himself and his descendants, and *isoteleia* is to be given to them while
living in Athens, and they are to contribute *eisphorai* and pay taxes
like the Athenians, and to serve on campaigns with the Athenians.
They are to have *enktesis* of land and a house. The Boule in office
at any time and the strategoi are to see that no offence is committed
against them by anyone. The secretary of the Boule is to inscribe
this decree on a block of stone and set it up on the Akropolis . . .'

(*IG* ii² 287)

SLAVES

Many books have been written about slavery in ancient Greece,
especially about its moral and its economic significance. Here the
purpose is only to define the legal status of a slave in classical Athens.

Most slaves were foreign captives or their descendants. It was the
accepted practice in Greece for a person captured by an enemy in war
to be the slave of his captors, unless his relatives or friends paid a ransom
to get him freed. There were also some other ways in which a free
person might become a slave in Athens: enslavement could be imposed
as a penalty for an offence (see page 256); a man who had been captured
in war and then ransomed was required to repay the amount of the
ransom to his ransomer, and if he did not he became the ransomer's

slave.[145] In some Greek states a debtor who could not repay his debt became the slave of his creditor, but in Athens enslavement for debt was abolished by Solon in the sixth century. Plutarch says in his *Life of Solon* (13.5) that previously some Athenians had sold their children as slaves, and (23.2) that Solon made a law forbidding this, except for girls who had committed fornication before marriage. But it seems unlikely that Athenian fathers still sold even their naughtiest daughters in the fifth and fourth centuries.

A person whose parents were both slaves was himself a slave from birth. No ancient author tells us explicitly what happened in classical Athens if one parent was a slave and the other not, but it seems possible that a person was a slave if his mother was a slave, and free if his mother was free.[146]

Anyone who tried to enslave a free person was liable to arrest (*apagoge*: see page 148) as an enslaver.[147] Alternatively the person being wrongly enslaved might get a friend formally to 'remove him to freedom'.[148] If the man who claimed to own him as a slave still wished to maintain his claim, he could then prosecute the friend, who had to provide sureties before the polemarch to guarantee the appearance of the alleged slave for the trial. The jury's verdict decided whether the alleged slave was really the slave of the man who claimed him; if so, the friend had not only to hand over the slave or the slave's value in money (or perhaps both) but also to pay an equal amount as a fine to the state.[149]

Like other items of property, a slave could be bought, sold, hired, bequeathed, or given away. A law required a person selling a slave to declare any physical defect in him; if the buyer discovered a defect which had not been declared, he could return the slave and demand his money back.[150] A slave could not himself own anything: the owner, besides providing food and clothes, might give his slave pocket money and other things, or allow him to keep part of any money which he earned by his labours,[151] but these items would remain legally the owner's property, like the slave himself.

It seems (though the evidence is not quite conclusive) that an owner was not allowed to kill a slave,[152] but otherwise he could beat or maltreat him as he liked. Slaves afraid of getting a beating from their owner are common in Greek comedy, and it is a joke that a young man who has recently come into property does not restrain himself from beating his slaves, because he has not yet learned to treat his possessions carefully.[153] But a slave did have one protection against maltreatment by his owner: he could take asylum in the Theseion and ask to be sold to someone else. It was illegal to punish a slave for doing this, but it is not clear what happened next if no purchaser came forward offering a price which the owner was willing to accept.[154]

In Athens (unlike some other Greek cities) persons other than the slave's owner were not allowed to strike him, though an exception to this was that a farmer was allowed to beat a slave whom he caught stealing his produce.[155] But a slave could not himself take legal action against an offender; any case had to be brought by his owner, and if his owner took no action, there was nothing that the slave could do about it. (If the offence was one, such as *hybris*, for which a public case was appropriate, of course any citizen was entitled to prosecute, but probably few or none would take the trouble to bring a case for the benefit of someone else's slave.) Likewise if a slave was killed, it was for his owner to take action against the killer.[156]

If a slave committed an offence against another person, the legal procedure depended on whether he was acting on his owner's orders. If he was, the correct procedure was simply to prosecute the owner. If he was not, the accusation was made against the slave, but any damages or fine imposed had to be paid by the owner.[157] Presumably, though no ancient author actually tells us this, the procedure and the magistrate introducing the case were the same as if the owner were himself being prosecuted, whether he was a citizen or a metic or other alien; and the owner, not the slave, spoke for the defence.

Evidently this arrangement was based on the assumption that a slave was normally under his owner's supervision and control. By the fourth century the assumption had become unrealistic in some cases. Of course there remained many slaves who lived and worked under their owner's eye in his house or farm or workshop; but it was also common for trusted slaves to live and work on their own, carrying on some trade or business and seldom seeing their owner except to deliver a payment (*apophora*), which might be a proportion of the profits of the trade or just a fixed amount, payable once a month or even less often. In Menander's *Arbitration* there is a simple example: one of the characters is Syriskos, a slave of Khairestratos; Syriskos lives with his wife in the country and works as a charcoal-burner, and on the day on which the action of the play takes place he comes to Khairestratos's house to pay his *apophora*.[158] In real life, Timarkhos is said to have owned nine or ten leather-workers; the one in charge paid him *apophora* of three obols a day and the others two obols each, keeping the rest of their proceeds for themselves.[159] Then there was Midas, a slave of Athenogenes. Athenogenes owned three perfume-shops. Midas was in charge of one of them, and got the business into debt; and Athenogenes would have been liable to pay the debts, if he had not sold the shop and Midas to a purchaser who unsuspectingly agreed to take responsibility for any debts without realizing how large the debts were.[160] This case shows that even as late as the 320s it remained the law that the owner was responsible for debts incurred by his slave. The only exception to this seems to have been that the mercantile laws introduced in the middle of the fourth century (see pages 231–4) treated all merchants and ship-masters equally, as independent persons, regardless of their civic status, and we do know of one ship-master who was a slave. Apart from mercantile cases, there is no satisfactory evidence that a slave belonging to an individual owner could take independent legal action. In this matter Athenian law was conservative.[161]

FREEDMEN

The owner could, if he wished, liberate a slave; this made the slave a freedman (*apeleutheros*). No formal procedure was legally required for doing this. A slave of foreign origin might well return to his homeland when freed. If he stayed in Athens, he was registered as a metic, with his former owner as his sponsor (*prostates*). The law forbade a freedman to have anyone else as his sponsor; thus the owner could, if he wished, prevent his freedman from becoming a metic. The law also imposed on a freedman other duties towards his former owner. It is not known what these were, but they probably included the duty to fulfil conditions which the former owner imposed as the price of freedom; he might, for example, demand to be paid a sum of money, which the freedman, since he could not have owned anything legally while a slave, would probably have to borrow from friends until he earned enough to repay it. If the freedman failed to fulfil his obligations to his former owner, or got himself registered as a metic with someone else as his sponsor, his former owner could bring a case for 'departure' (*dike apostasiou*); if the freedman was found guilty, he became a slave again.[162] Since the case was a private one, he surely became once again the property of his former owner; when we read in Demosthenes 25.65 that the state sold a woman convicted *apostasiou*, we should take that as a mistake for *aprostasiou*.[163]

The liberation of a slave could be included in the owner's will, taking effect only on his death. It is not known whether, in this case, the freedman had to perform any duties towards his former owner's heir, nor whether he had to have the heir as his sponsor for registration as a metic. When an owner who was himself a metic liberated a slave, he cannot have been his freedman's sponsor for registration as a metic, since a sponsor had to be a citizen.

In certain circumstances the state liberated a slave without his owner's consent. A slave who gave information that his owner had committed sacrilege, if the information was found to be true, was liberated; it is possible, but not certain, that the same reward was given for information about some other offences.[164] In 406 slaves who fought for Athens at Arginousai were given not only freedom but citizenship too (see page 72).

PUBLIC SLAVES

Some slaves belonged not to individual masters but to the state; for example, caretakers of public buildings, the public coin-tester (see page 158), and the archers who carried out police duties under the orders of the Eleven or other officials.

The only public slave about whom we have much information is Pittalakos, of whom Aiskhines speaks in his speech *Against Timarkhos*. He is described as 'well off for money'. At one stage in his quarrel with Hegesandros and Timarkhos he began legal proceedings against them; then Hegesandros claimed that Pittalakos belonged to him, and tried to take him into slavery, but Glaukon 'removed him to freedom' in the way described on page 80. From all this it is clear that the legal position of a public slave was quite different from that of a slave belonging to an individual owner; it could even be called 'freedom'. It may have been something like the status of a metic.[165]

VI THE FAMILY

The last chapter was about the status of the individual person in relation to the state. But equally important was the relationship of the individual to other individuals, by birth or by marriage. There were two ways in which the law took account of such relationships.

First, it was realized that children and women could not be expected to act independently, but were generally protected and controlled by men; and so the law recognized the position of a man who was *kyrios* ('lord', 'controller') of another person. The *kyrios* of a child or woman had authority over, and responsibility for, the dependant. He was expected to see that his dependant was housed and fed, and the dependant was expected to obey him. He had charge of any property which belonged to the dependant; and if the dependant was involved in legal proceedings, he had to speak for the dependant in court. A child's *kyrios* was normally his father; when the father was dead, the *kyrios* could be an adult brother or paternal grandfather, but if neither of these existed a guardian had to be appointed. A woman's *kyrios* was normally her father until she was married, her husband thereafter. If her father died before she was married, his heir became her *kyrios*. If her husband died, she might either remain in her husband's family with his heir as *kyrios* (especially when the heir was her own son), or she might return to her father's family and have her father or his heir as *kyrios*. If a woman's *kyrios* was going to travel abroad and expected to be away a long time, he could appoint someone else (probably his nearest adult male relative) to act as her *kyrios* during his absence.[166] An Athenian woman seems never to have been independent, with no *kyrios*. But a metic woman might have no male relatives in Athens and so be '*kyrios* of herself' (Demosthenes 59. 46), though, as a metic, she would have a sponsor (*prostates*) who might speak for her in legal affairs.

Secondly, the law recognized that Athenian society consisted not just of individuals but of *oikoi*. *Oikos* literally means 'house', and is the term used for members of a family living together in one house. The *oikos* was particularly significant in two ways: the family property (which in many cases would include the farmland which supported the family, as well as the house itself) was in the hands of the man who was *kyrios* of the *oikos*, so that the other members of it relied more or less on him for their subsistence; and the *oikos* had its hearth and religious ceremonies, including observances in honour of its dead members. Consequently an Athenian (or indeed any other ancient Greek) attached great importance to the preservation of his *oikos*, and to its continuation after the death of its present *kyrios*.

Servants, concubines, and illegitimate children, though they might live in the house and take part in its religious observances, were not members of the *oikos*, which was confined to the legitimate relatives of the man who was its *kyrios*. Besides his own wife and children it might include his widowed mother, his unmarried sisters, and other dependants. If his daughters or sisters were married, they left the *oikos* and passed into the *oikoi* of their husbands; conversely, if his sons married, they could bring their wives into the *oikos*, which in due course might include his grandchildren and even great-grandchildren. When he died, his son became *kyrios* of the *oikos*. If he left more than one son, each son might be *kyrios* of an *oikos*, so that two or more *oikoi* replaced the previous one. (In Demosthenes 43. 19, for example, the speaker relates that Bouselos had five sons, who divided the property among them, and each had a wife and children, so that five *oikoi* came into being out of one.) If he left no son, a problem of succession arose. It was thought deplorable for an *oikos* to become extinct; though the property and the surviving female dependants could be taken over by another *oikos*, the religious observances of the *oikos* would be neglected if it had no heir.

Care must be taken to distinguish control of an *oikos* (which means primarily the ownership of the family property and the responsibility for the family's religious ceremonies) from control of a woman or child, even though the same word *kyrios* is used for a controller of either sort. Of course it often happened that one man was at the same time *kyrios* of an *oikos* and *kyrios* of all the other persons in that *oikos*. But it was not necessarily so: for example, when an *oikos* contained a father and his adult son, the father was *kyrios* of the *oikos*, but he was not *kyrios* of his son; and if the son married, the son, not the father, was *kyrios* of the son's wife.

The nature of the *oikos* and other aspects of family life are fully and well described by W. K. Lacey in another book in this series, *The Family in Classical Greece*. The purpose of the present chapter is not to go over all the same ground again, but only to explain how Athenian law regulated the ways in which a person became *kyrios* of another, or became a member or the *kyrios* of an *oikos*, and the legal rights which that person obtained.

MARRIAGE

In some ancient states financial or other penalties were imposed on a man who did not marry and have children, but it is not certain that this was ever so in Athens. A few texts say or imply that a man who did not marry could be prosecuted by *graphe*, and the orator Deinarkhos declares that a man without legitimate children was forbidden by law to be an orator or a strategos.[167] But these rules, if they ever existed, seem not to have been enforced in the fourth century, when it was certainly possible for a man to choose not to marry.[168]

If he wished to marry, he had to come to an agreement with the father or other *kyrios* of a suitable woman, because a marriage was legally valid only if it was preceded by the act called *engye*. (The only exception was that, when a woman's father had died, *epidikasia* could be a substitute for *engye*: see page 103). *Engye* was the giving of a woman to the prospective husband by her *kyrios*, and it simply consisted in the *kyrios*'s saying formally 'I grant (*engyo*) my daughter (or sister, etc.) to you'. It was not legally necessary for the woman to be present or to consent or even to know that she was to be married.[169] The actual marriage (*gamos*), when the woman moved into her husband's house, took place later, whenever it was mutually convenient. The legal difference between *engye* and *gamos* was, roughly, that *engye* was making a contract and *gamos* was carrying it out.[170]

In some scenes of New Comedy we find a son asking his father to consent to his marriage, or even a father arranging a marriage for his son. Presumably this means that, as long as his father was *kyrios* of the *oikos*, it was difficult in practice for a son to go against his father's wishes. But this was rather a question of domestic practicality than of law; there is no evidence that a marriage made by a son without his father's consent was invalid legally.[171]

A woman could not be legally married to a direct ascendant or descendant (grandfather, father, son, grandson), nor to her brother or half-brother by the same mother. But she could be married to her half-brother by the same father, to her brother by adoption, or to her uncle, cousin, or more distant relative, or of course to a man who was not a relative at all.[172]

In early times an Athenian citizen could marry an alien woman; thus for example Kleisthenes, tyrant of Sikyon, could say 'I grant (*engyo*) my daughter Agariste to Megakles, son of Alkmeon, in accordance with Athenian law' (Herodotos 6. 130.2). After the middle of the fifth century this was no longer legal: Aristophanes in *Birds* 1650-2 (in the year 414) comically makes Peisthetairos apply Athenian law to the gods and tell Herakles that he is a bastard, not a legitimate son of Zeus, because his mother was an alien. The law that a citizen could not marry an alien was part of the same enactment as the law that a child of a citizen and an alien was not to be a citizen, proposed by Perikles in 451/0 (see page 67).[173] It is not known whether the fifth-century law merely declared marriages between a citizen and an alien invalid or also imposed penalties, but by the middle of the fourth century there were certainly penalties. At that time an alien who joined the *oikos* of a citizen as husband or wife (the word *synoikein* implies a purported marriage, not mere concubinage) could be prosecuted by *graphe* and, if found guilty, was sold as a slave; the citizen man who thus received an alien woman into his *oikos* as his wife was fined 1000 drachmas. A man who, acting as her *kyrios*, gave an alien woman to a citizen for marriage could also be prosecuted by *graphe*, and if he was found guilty he was disfranchised and his property was confiscated.[174]

A bride's father (or whoever was her *kyrios* before the marriage) was not legally required to give a dowry with her, but it was usual to do so. A dowry was a contribution towards the expense of maintaining the wife and her prospective children. It was regarded as capital, rather than income; the husband was expected to make use of it and devote the proceeds to supporting them, but not to spend the capital amount, which might have to be returned to its original donor if the marriage came to an end. The amount of the dowry, which must sometimes have been the subject of bargaining between a prospective husband who wanted a large dowry and a father who offered a small one, was usually agreed and stated by the bride's *kyrios* at the *engye*: 'I grant my daughter to you, and I give three talents as a dowry for her', for example.[175] It might consist of money only, or it might be, or include, some land or other property (which was valued, in case dissolution of the marriage later made it necessary for its value to be repaid). It might be handed over at the time of the *engye*, or later. It might be paid by instalments. If it was not all handed over at once, the bride's *kyrios* might make a formal agreement specifying what was to be paid later; he might agree to pay interest in the meantime; he might

provide security for the amount promised.[176] If he failed to carry out
the agreement, the husband could prosecute him (or his heir) for
infringement of the agreement. But, since a dowry was not a legal
requirement, a bride's *kyrios* could not be prosecuted for failing to
provide one if he had not formally agreed to do so.[177]

A husband was not required to be sexually faithful to his wife, but a
wife was required to be so to her husband. A husband who detected
his wife in adultery was required by law to divorce her,[178] and the
seducer could be severely punished (see page 124). Divorce was simple,
at least for the husband: if he wished, he could just send his wife away,
and that terminated the marriage without further formality. Likewise
the wife's father had the right to take her away from her husband
(though it has been suggested that this right lapsed when there was a
child of the marriage).[179] For a wife wishing to divorce her husband the
procedure may have been more difficult. It was not enough just to
leave him; the divorce was valid only when she went to the arkhon's
office and gave in written notice of it.[180] It is not clear how much of an
obstacle this was. Some scholars dismiss it as a mere formality, and
conclude that divorce was as easy for a wife to obtain as for a husband.
But it seems more likely that the proceedings before the arkhon gave
the husband some opportunity to intervene, if he wished. Plutarch at
any rate believed that the purpose of the rule was to give the husband a
chance to get hold of his wife and take her home again.[181] Possibly the
arkhon would not accept notice of divorce from a wife if her husband
entered an objection to it; if so, a wife could not obtain a divorce
without her husband's acquiescence.

If a marriage was terminated by divorce, for whatever reason, the
dowry had to be returned with the woman to her original *kyrios* (or his
heir). In some cases the prospect of having to return the dowry must
have been the chief thing which deterred a husband from divorcing his
wife, and this was one strong incentive for a bride's *kyrios* to provide
a dowry in the first place: it was a safeguard for the woman and her
relatives against divorce.[182]

If a wife died leaving no children, her dowry had likewise to be
returned to her original *kyrios* (or his heir); but if she left children, they
inherited it.[183] If a husband died leaving a widow without children, she
had to return to her original *oikos*; in this case her husband's heir had to
return the dowry.[184] But if she had children (or was pregnant), she
could remain with them in her husband's *oikos*; then they (or their
guardian) kept her dowry.[185] The situation of a widow with children

had this striking exceptional feature: it was perhaps the only situation in which an Athenian woman could choose for herself between alternative *oikoi* and *kyrioi*.[186]

In every case the rule was maintained that whoever had control of a woman's dowry was responsible for her maintenance. A man who kept a woman's dowry when no longer entitled to keep it was liable to prosecution for it (*dike proikos*) by the person who claimed it. If he was unable or unwilling to pay the whole amount at once, he could meanwhile pay interest on it at the rather high rate of 1½ per cent per month for the maintenance of the woman or (if she was dead) of her children; if he failed to pay this, he was liable to prosecution for maintenance (*dike sitou*).[187] To guard against this possibility, a husband sometimes, at the time of his marriage, provided security for the repayment of the dowry if that should eventually be required (*apotimema*: see pages 144–5).

A woman who was either widowed or divorced could be married again. If she had returned to her original *oikos*, her *kyrios* could give her to a new husband by *engye* in the ordinary way, with the dowry recovered from her first husband.[188] Alternatively her first husband on his deathbed or in his will could give his widow, with dowry, to a new husband.[189]

CONCUBINAGE

A man could not legally be married to more than one wife at a time (nor a woman to more than one husband). But there was no legal objection to his having a concubine in addition, or instead. I use 'concubine' to translate the Greek word *pallake*; it means a woman who resides in a man's house and has sexual relations with him but is not formally married to him. (Two other words should be distinguished from *pallake*: *hetaira* is a more general word, not necessarily implying that the woman lives with the man on a long-term basis; and *porne* means a prostitute, whose sexual services are available for purchase by any man.)

The law distinguished concubines kept 'with a view to free children' from other concubines.[190] A concubine who was not kept 'with a view to free children' must normally, perhaps always, have been a slave of the man who kept her. Her children will then have been his slaves also, and her legal position the same as any other slave's.

A concubine who was kept 'with a view to free children' might be an alien woman, of free but not citizen birth. One well-known example was Aspasia, a talented woman from Miletos who lived with Perikles for many years. As a special concession to Perikles a decree was passed conferring legitimacy and citizenship on their son, also named Perikles, who otherwise would have been excluded by the law, which Perikles himself had proposed, laying down that there could be no valid marriage between a citizen and an alien and that a person was to be a citizen only if both his parents were citizens (see pages 67 and 87).[191]

Alternatively a concubine kept 'with a view to free children' could be the daughter of an Athenian citizen. Isaios 3. 39 refers specifically to citizens who give 'their own' women for concubinage, with gifts of an agreed amount, like a dowry. And a seducer of a concubine of this kind was liable to the same penalties as the seducer of a wife.[192] Thus this kind of concubinage may have been much like marriage, except that there was no *engye*. One may guess that a father would prefer to give his legitimate daughters for marriage, and would give only bastard daughters for concubinage; but there is no evidence that it was actually illegal to give a legitimate daughter for concubinage.

Several late authorities mention in connection with Sokrates or Euripides that because of a shortage of population the Athenians passed a decree allowing any citizen 'to marry one citizen woman and procreate children also from another'.[193] Although some modern scholars have doubted the truth of this statement, there is no strong reason for rejecting it. During the Peloponnesian War the Athenians may well have become worried at the number of citizens who were killed in battle or died from the plague, and there may have been many Athenian girls for whom no unmarried men were available as husbands; so the motives of the decree would have been to encourage citizens to have more children and to reduce the number of Athenian women who were left to become old maids. If its existence is accepted, what the decree must have said is not just that a citizen could have a concubine as well as a wife (since that was permitted already) but that his children by the concubine, provided that she was a citizen, would be regarded as legitimate, like those by the wife. The marital circumstances of Sokrates may then have been that Myrto was his wife and Xanthippe his concubine, but his son by Xanthippe (named Lamprokles) was, nevertheless, legitimate; however, the evidence about Sokrates's marriage is so confused that we cannot be certain about this.[194] The decree making a concubine's children legitimate, if it did exist, must have been annulled at the end of the fifth century; in fourth-century speeches it is clear that only the children of a duly married wife were legitimate.

CHILDREN

When an Athenian woman bore a child, it was normal for the father to make a formal acknowledgement that the child was his. This was usually done at the *dekate*, a family gathering on the tenth day after the birth, when the child was named.[195] The *dekate* was a religious celebration rather than a legal requirement, but legally it was important to the child that his paternity should be acknowledged, for on it depended both his membership of the *oikos* and his citizen status. A father who failed to acknowledge paternity of a child who was in fact his could be compelled to do so by legal proceedings: there is the notorious case of Boiotos, who prosecuted Mantias for failing to acknowledge paternity of Boiotos and so depriving him of citizenship.[196] It was also possible for a father who had acknowledged paternity to withdraw this acknowledgement later by a formal rejection (*apokeryxis*) if he found reasons to believe that the child was not his after all.[197] (Some scholars have taken *apokeryxis* to mean 'disinherison'; but the Athenian evidence is against the view that it was legally permitted for a father to disinherit one who was in fact his son, except by having him adopted by someone else. So it is preferable to take *apokeryxis* as denial of the fact of paternity.)

A child was legitimate if his parents were married with *engye* (see page 86) or *epidikasia* (see page 103). Otherwise, apart from the temporary change which may have been made during the Peloponnesian War (see page 90), the child was a bastard (*nothos*).

Parents were under no legal obligation to rear a child, as we see from the plays of New Comedy, in which the exposure of an infant is often an essential part of the plot. Although an Athenian father (unlike a Roman father) did not have the right to put his child to death, simply leaving a living child did not count as homicide.

A father remained *kyrios* of his daughter until he gave her away in marriage. He was *kyrios* of his son only until the son became adult; this was in his eighteenth year, when, provided that he was of citizen birth, he was registered in his deme (see page 69). After that the son was legally independent of his father; but he remained a member of the *oikos* of which his father was *kyrios*.

If a father was getting old and had an adult son, he could retire, handing over control of the *oikos* to his son; so in Aristophanes's *Wasps*, for example, Bdelykleon has taken over control of the household from his father Philokleon. If he had more than one son, they could take over control jointly, or they could divide the property between them.

There is an example in the speech *Against Euergos and Mnesiboulos*. The speaker, wanting to find Theophemos, questioned his brother, Euergos: 'I asked him whether he had made a division with his brother or they held their property jointly. Euergos answered me that he had made a division, and Theophemos lived separately, while he himself lived with their father' (Demosthenes 47. 34–5). Evidently the father had retired and handed over his property to his two sons, who had chosen to divide it. Normally a father's retirement will have been voluntary; but if he had not retired and senility or insanity made him incapable of managing the *oikos*, his son could prosecute him for insanity (*paranoia*) and so, if he won the case, get legal control.[198]

Under a law attributed to Solon a son was liable to prosecution for maltreatment of parents (*kakosis goneon*) if he failed to provide his parents or grandparents with food and housing, used physical violence against them, or failed to provide proper funeral rites when they died. (The requirement to provide food and housing presumably did not apply until the parents became elderly or incapacitated.) The penalty was disfranchisement. The procedure for such a prosecution was probably *eisangelia*, as for maltreatment of orphans (see page 94), though the evidence for it is not entirely clear.[199] But Solon's law excused a son from the duty of supporting his father if his father had failed to teach him a trade or craft, or had prostituted him, or if his birth was not legitimate; for in these cases his father was at fault.[200]

SUCCESSION BY LEGITIMATE SONS

If a man died leaving one legitimate son, that son inherited all his property (including any debts owed to him, and also liability for any debts owed by him): and if the dead man had been *kyrios* of an *oikos*, his son became *kyrios* of it.

If a man died leaving more than one legitimate son, those sons inherited all his property equally; the eldest son had no advantage over the others. They could agree to hold the property or some part of it (such as the house in which they lived) jointly; but the usual practice was to divide it into shares of equal value, and if the dead man had been *kyrios* of an *oikos*, several *oikoi* replaced the previous one (see page 85). If a legitimate son had predeceased his father leaving legitimate sons of his own, those sons were entitled to their father's share of their grandfather's estate; and so on. When property was to be divided, the normal practice seems to have been first of all to agree what the shares were to be, and only then to decide who was to have which share. This decision could be made by drawing lots; an alternative method, when there were two heirs only, was for one to define the shares and let the other choose between them.[201]

As long as there were living legitimate sons or their direct descendants, no other relative had any right to any part of the property. The sons just took possession of it without legal formality, and any attempt by any other person to claim it could be blocked by testimony (*diamartyria*) that legitimate sons existed (see pages 102 and 217-18).

But a problem arose if a son was not yet adult when his father died: one or more guardians had to be appointed to assume responsibility both for the child and for his property while he was a minor. The law required the arkhon to 'look after' orphans;[202] this must mean that he had to see that an orphan had a guardian. (I use 'orphan' to translate *orphanos*; the Greek word here means 'fatherless', not necessarily implying that the child had lost his mother too.) Presumably there were some occasions when no one came forward for appointment as guardian and the arkhon imposed the duty compulsorily on someone, and other occasions when there was competition for the appointment (for example, if the orphan had extensive property) and the arkhon chose between the competitors. On what principles the arkhon made his choice, we do not know. But in each of the cases about which we have clear information the father before dying named one or more guardians for his children, and when this happened probably the arkhon just formally ratified the appointment of the father's nominees. The best-known case is that of Demosthenes, described later by himself in his speeches *Against Aphobos* and *Against Onetor*. He was seven and his sister was five when their father, also named Demosthenes, died. On his deathbed the elder Demosthenes gave his wife (by *engye*: see page 86) with a dowry to be married to his nephew Aphobos; he gave his daughter with a dowry to be married to his nephew Demophon (when she was old enough: this must have meant a remarkably long interval between *engye* and marriage); and he appointed Aphobos, Demophon, and a friend named Therippides, who was not a relative, to be jointly guardians of the young Demosthenes and his property. Thus we see that an orphan could have several guardians, and that a guardian did not have to be a member of the family.

A guardian provided his ward with housing, food, clothing, and education, and represented him (as his *kyrios*) in any official or legal business in which the ward or his property became involved. He also had to see that the ward's property was properly kept and employed; for example, if the property included some agricultural land, the guardian would have either to farm it or to let it to a farmer. The income from the property was available for paying the expenses of maintaining the ward. When the ward came of age in his eighteenth year, the guardian had not only to hand over the property but also to provide accounts, showing that the property now being handed over was equal to the property left by the ward's father, plus the accumulated income from it, minus the expenses incurred in maintaining the ward. A common practice was for the guardian to take the ward to live with him in his own house and let the whole of the ward's property to a tenant; this made it easy not only for the guardian to keep a fatherly eye on the ward, but also to calculate the income received from the ward's property, which was simply the total amount of rent paid by the tenant.

Lease of estate (*misthosis oikou*) for an orphan had to follow a special procedure, to prevent an unscrupulous guardian from exploiting it: the guardian applied to the arkhon, and the arkhon held an auction in the presence of a jury in a law-court, awarding the lease to the highest bidder, who had also to offer property of his own as security (see page 144).[203] If a guardian did not let his ward's property, anyone who wished could prosecute him by the procedure called *phasis*, but he could defend himself by showing that it was a satisfactory arrangement for him to occupy and manage the estate himself.[204]

Maltreatment (*kakosis*) of an orphan was another offence for which a public prosecution could be brought, though it is not known what kinds of act or neglect counted as maltreatment. The procedure for this was called *eisangelia*; but it must not be confused with the other kinds of *eisangelia* (see pages 170, 183, 210). It is likely that originally *eisangelia* for maltreating an orphan simply consisted of reporting the offence to the arkhon, and it was then the arkhon's duty, not the informer's, to take further action. By the fourth century this was no longer true; a normal trial was held, at which the informer was the prosecutor, just as for an ordinary *graphe*, and sometimes the case was even referred to loosely as a *graphe*. But one important difference remained: the prosecutor in an *eisangelia* for maltreatment of an orphan paid no fee or penalty, even if he failed to obtain one-fifth of the votes.[205]

The fact that such offences were made subject not merely to prosecution by any volunteer but to *eisangelia* (in which the prosecutor ran no risk) or *phasis* (in which he stood to gain a reward) marks the Athenians' keenness to protect orphans against bad guardians. An orphan child was *par excellence* the kind of person who needed the community's protection.

When an orphan came of age, he could at any time within the next five years bring a private 'guardianship case' (*dike epitropes*) against his guardian if he claimed that the guardian had not handed over the right amount of property – as Demosthenes did against Aphobos.[206]

HEIRESSES

If a man died leaving no legitimate son (or grandson or great-grandson), he might nevertheless leave a daughter (or granddaughter or great-granddaughter). In this case there was the prospect that she might eventually produce a son to inherit the property and continue the *oikos*; all that was required, therefore, was a man to be her husband and look after the property until her son came of age. By the latter part of the fifth century it became common for a father to arrange this before his death by means of adoption during his lifetime or by will. That procedure is discussed later in this chapter; in the present section I refer only to cases in which the father had died without making any such arrangement.

A woman or girl left in this position was called *epikleros*. The only possible English translation of this word is 'heiress', but if this translation is used it is important to be clear that she did not really own the property herself in the sense of being able to dispose of it as she wished; it just remained with her until her son was ready to inherit.[207]

Still less did the husband of an *epikleros* own the property. Nevertheless he had the control and use of it until her son came of age. If it was at all substantial, this might be an attractive proposition, and consequently there might be a number of competitors for the hand of an *epikleros*. The rule was then that the nearest surviving male relative of her deceased father was entitled to claim her in marriage. If he did not wish to, the next nearest relative could claim her, and so on. (What relationship counted as the nearest, in other words the order of succession, is explained on pages 98–9.) If there were several men of equally close relationship (several paternal uncles, say), the eldest had preference.[208] If there were two or more daughters who were all jointly *epikleroi* (that is, each was 'heiress' of an equal share of the estate), the two or more nearest relatives could claim one each. If an *epikleros* happened to be married already, that was no obstacle; her father's nearest relative could still claim her in marriage, so that she was divorced from her previous husband.[209] (But this could only happen if she had no son; if she had a son, he was the heir, being the deceased man's grandson, and she was not an *epikleros*.) If the nearest relative was himself married already, he had to divorce his wife, or else forgo his claim. He could not obtain control of the *epikleros* and the property that went with her unless he married her; for the chief aim was to get a male heir in direct descent from her father.

But if the deceased man left little or no property, there might be no claimant for the *epikleros*. To obviate the possibility that she might be left without a husband, so that the *oikos* would become extinct, the law laid down that, if an *epikleros* belonged to the lowest property-class (*thetes*), the arkhon was to compel her father's nearest male relative either to marry her himself or to give her in marriage to someone else; if he chose to give her in marriage to someone else, he had to provide a dowry for her out of his own property unless he himself belonged to the lowest property-class too.[210] It was considered creditable to marry a poor *epikleros*, as Andokides indicates in the following passage.[211]

'Epilykos, son of Teisandros, was my uncle, my mother's brother. He died in Sicily without male offspring, but leaving two daughters, who were to pass to Leagros and me. The family's affairs were in a bad way: the visible property which he left amounted to less than two talents, but the debts were over five talents. Still, I invited Leagros to meet me in the presence of members of the family, and said to him that to behave like relatives in such a situation was the thing for good men to do. "It's not right for us to prefer another estate or a successful man, and look down on Epilykos's daughters. After all, if Epilykos were alive, or had left a large amount of money when he died, we should expect to have the girls, because we're the nearest relatives. So, whereas in that case we should have done so because of Epilykos or because of his money, as things are we'll do it because of our good character. So you put in a claim for one, and I will for the other." ' (Andokides 1. 117–19)

The fact that the chief aim was to enable the *epikleros* to produce a male heir is illustrated by the law, attributed to Solon, requiring the husband of an *epikleros* to have sexual intercourse with her three times a month; if he was unable to do so, he had to allow her to be claimed (probably in marriage rather than, as Plutarch thought, for sexual intercourse without marriage) by the next nearest relative.[212] What is astonishing, to modern eyes, is that the law gave the woman herself no choice in the matter. The object was the welfare of the family as a whole and the transmission of its property to the next generation, not the gratification of a woman's personal preference. Andokides, in the passage just quoted (written at the beginning of the fourth century), gives various reasons for marrying the *epikleroi* or not marrying them, but there is no indication that it ever occurred to him to ask the girls whether they wanted to be married to himself and Leagros. Love is not mentioned in this context; nor is it considered whether the prospective husband and wife are suitably matched in age or in temperament.

But at the end of the fourth century there is evidence of a different attitude to this matter. One of the most recent finds of Greek literature is part of Menander's comedy *Aspis* (meaning *The Shield*), first published in 1969. At the beginning of the play Kleostratos is believed to have died in battle, leaving his sister as *epikleros* of their father's estate. Previously she was to have been married to Khaireas, stepson of her uncle Khairestratos; but now her elder uncle Smikrines, a miserly old man, proposes to exercise his right to claim her in marriage, since she is an *epikleros* and he is the nearest relative.

Khairestratos: Are you intending to marry a girl, at your age?
Smikrines: What age?
Khairestratos: You seem to me quite old.
Smikrines: Am I the only old man who has ever got married?
Khairestratos: Please, Smikrines, do be humane about it. Khaireas here, who's intending to marry her, has been brought up with her. What can I say? You needn't lose. This property, such as it is, have it all, take charge of it, we give it to you; but let the girl, on her own, have a husband suitable to her age. I'll provide a dowry of two talents from my own money.
Smikrines: Good heavens, do you think you're talking to Melitides! What's this! Am I to take the property and let him have the girl, so that, if a child is born, I may be prosecuted for having his property?
(Menander *Aspis* 258–73)

A few lines later (288) Khaireas speaks of his love for the girl. Afterwards Smikrines is tricked into believing that Khairestratos too has died, leaving his daughter as a much richer *epikleros* for Smikrines to claim if he abandons his claim to the sister of Kleostratos; but eventually (we can assume, though the end of the play is lost) he gets neither *epikleros*, because it turns out that both Kleostratos and Khairestratos are really still alive. Throughout the play Smikrines is only trying to exercise his legal rights; yet he is presented as the villain of the piece, because he prevents the marriage of two young lovers. Menander tells the story in such a way as to imply that the law about claiming heiresses is unsatisfactory, and it is right to go against it. To attach so much importance to love in arranging a marriage was probably a novelty in Menander's time; the law made no allowance for it.

The arkhon was required by law to 'look after' *epikleroi*, just as he was required to 'look after' male orphans (see page 93); this meant primarily that he had to award them to husbands (by the procedure described on pages 102–3). A public prosecution for maltreatment of an *epikleros*, as for maltreatment of male orphans (see page 94), could be brought by *eisangelia*.[213]

What happened if an *epikleros* was still a child when her father died is not clear. It seems possible that a guardian was appointed for her and 'her' property in the same way as for a male orphan, and then the award to a husband was made in her fourteenth year (the age of puberty); this is suggested by the fact that *AP* 56. 7 mentions the lease of estates of *epikleroi* until their fourteenth year.

If a man died leaving his wife pregnant, the arkhon had to see that she was looked after, presumably by appointing some kind of temporary guardian.[214] Although no instance is known, we may infer that the child born posthumously became an heir (if male) or *epikleros* (if female and without brothers) on birth.

INTESTATE SUCCESSION BY OTHER RELATIVES

If a person left no legitimate descendants, the nearest relative could claim the property. For the purpose of deciding who was the nearest relative, the following was the order of precedence:[215] brother (or half-brother by the same father), and his descendants; sister (or half-sister by the same father), and her descendants; other relatives on the father's side 'as far as children of cousins'; half-brother (by the same mother), and his descendants; half-sister (by the same mother), and her descendants; other relatives on the mother's side 'as far as children of cousins'. The precise limit denoted by the expression 'as far as children of cousins' is not quite clear, and is discussed later (pages 106-7). These were the 'close relatives' (*ankhisteis*). If there were no relatives within these limits, more distant relatives on the father's side could claim. Males took precedence over females in the same degree of relationship, but otherwise, if there were two or more claimants in the same degree of relationship, they shared the property equally.

The deceased man's wife had no right of inheritance and could not become *epikleros* of his property. It seems probable that his ascendants (father, mother, grandfather, grandmother) were also excluded, though this point has been disputed.[216] If the nearest relative was a sister (there being no brother nor descendant of a brother), the death of her brother might have the effect of making her *epikleros* to their father's estate, so that she could then be claimed in marriage by the nearest male relative.[217] But otherwise a female relative did not become *epikleros* but became the owner of inherited property in her own right.

Whether bastards had any right to inherit property from their father (when he left no legitimate children and no will) is not clear. A law of the year 403/2 excluded bastards from the 'close relatives';[218] that may mean that they had first claim if no close relatives existed, but such cases were probably rare. For the position before 403/2 we have no evidence except the comic scene in Aristophanes's *Birds* in which Peisthetairos tells Herakles that he is a bastard and cannot inherit Zeus's property, because his mother was an alien. The wording of the 'law of Solon' which Peisthetairos quotes may mean that, when there were no legitimate sons or daughters, bastards could share the property with the next nearest relatives. But we cannot be certain that this is an accurate reproduction of the wording of the real law.[219]

ADOPTION AND WILLS

In prehistoric times probably the order of succession described in the preceding paragraphs was invariable, and a man could not choose who would inherit his property. But evidently the normal order of succession came to be felt not entirely satisfactory in cases where a man had no direct descendants. If his heir was only an uncle or nephew or cousin, and his property thus became absorbed into the property of another branch of the family, that meant that his *oikos* was extinct; religious observances in his honour would probably be neglected, since the heir would be more concerned with religious observances for his own *oikos* and ancestors.

To avoid this misfortune, it became possible (at some period too early for us to identify it) for a man without sons to adopt a son during his lifetime. The adoptee would usually be a young man with at least one brother, so that his departure from his own family would not lead to the extinction of that *oikos*. By his adoption he entirely lost his membership and right of succession in his own family and became in all legal respects the son of his adopter. When his adoptive father died, he could take possession of the property without any legal formality, just like an ordinary son.

Solon, in the first half of the sixth century, was responsible for the next stage of development. He introduced a law permitting a man without sons to adopt a son by will, so that the adoption took effect only after his death. The most significant feature of this innovation was that it gave the wishes of the deceased individual, as expressed in a written document, precedence over the rights of other members of the family.[220]

So adoption was the means by which an individual could choose his own heir. But it was open only to a man who had no son; a son could not be disinherited. Nor could a daughter be deprived of her position as *epikleros*: a man who had a daughter could adopt a son, but in this case the adopted son had either to marry the daughter himself or give her in marriage to another man with half her father's property as dowry, and when she eventually had children they could claim the whole of her deceased father's property.[221] There were also other rules limiting the possibilities of adoption; but some of the details are disputed, and they need not be discussed here.[222] And in practice the adopted son was usually a relative; sometimes he was actually the nearest relative, who would have inherited the property anyway. 'It has happened', says one fourth-century speaker, 'that men who were not on good terms with their families have preferred [sc. as heirs] unrelated friends to close relatives' (Isaios 4. 18); but he clearly means to imply that this was exceptional, not usual.

We generally think of adoption as being primarily intended for the benefit of the adopted child, to provide parental care for a child who would otherwise lack it. That was not how the Athenians saw it. To them, adoption was a means of obtaining an heir, to support one in one's old age and continue one's *oikos* after one's death. Consequently there was no need for the adoptee to be a child; adults were often adopted. On the other hand, it was not so common (though it was possible) to adopt a girl or a woman, who would become *epikleros* when her adoptive father died;[223] to obtain a male heir, it was obviously more efficient to adopt a male at once than to adopt a female and hope that she would produce a son eventually.

Because a man would not usually adopt a son while he still had hopes of begetting one, an adopter was often old and might be weak in body or in mind. So, to protect the interests of other members of the family, a law laid down that an adoption was not valid if the adopter made it 'when out of his mind because of madness or old age or drugs or sickness, or under the influence of a woman, or compelled by force or restriction of liberty'. This applied both to an adoption taking effect during the adopter's lifetime and to one made by will.[224]

A further development was posthumous adoption. If a man died leaving no son, his heir, or one of his heirs, could become his adoptive son even though he had left no will to that effect. This device must have been useful chiefly when two (or more) brothers would otherwise have been joint heirs. For example, suppose that two brothers were the heirs of their father and also of their maternal grandfather, and that their father's property was a farm on one side of Attika and their maternal grandfather's a farm on the other side of Attika. It would have been highly inconvenient for each brother to own half of each farm; much better for one brother to become the adopted son of their grandfather, so that he would have the whole of their grandfather's farm, leaving his brother as sole heir of their father's farm. And from the religious point of view this meant that their grandfather's *oikos* continued, and was not merged in their father's. It must have been to achieve this kind of convenient arrangement that the members of a family sometimes carried out a posthumous adoption; but details of the procedure are obscure.[225]

Apart from adoption, there was not much scope for a will. A man could not use a will to bequeath his property as a whole to anyone except by adopting him as a son. There was a law permitting a man to make a bequest to a bastard son, provided that it did not exceed a fairly small amount (it is uncertain whether it was five mnai or ten mnai);[226] and in the fourth century we know of a few cases in which a man who had sons made a will to give instructions about the sharing of his property between the sons, or to make small bequests to his widow or other close relatives or for a dedication to a god;[227] but that is all. It was not until after the end of the classical period that it became possible for an Athenian to use a will freely to bequeath all his property to anyone he wished.

CLAIMING AN INHERITANCE

Legitimate sons or grandsons of a deceased man (including a son adopted during his lifetime) could just take possession of his property without formality, but anyone else wishing to claim an inheritance had to follow a legal procedure before the arkhon. (If the deceased was a metic, the polemarch acted instead of the arkhon.) He had to maintain either that the deceased had left a will adopting him as a son, or that he was the nearest relative of the deceased; or he might maintain that, the deceased's nearest relative being a daughter and therefore *epikleros*, he himself was the nearest male relative and so was entitled to marry her and assume control of the property.

If he claimed as the nearest relative, he might find that other claimants disputed his legitimacy, or disputed the relationship which he claimed to the deceased; since Athenians had no birth certificates or marriage certificates, he might find it hard to prove that he was (for example) the son, by a second husband, of a daughter of the deceased's mother's sister, all of these intermediate relatives now being dead. If on the other hand he produced a document which he claimed was the deceased's will adopting him as a son, other claimants might say that it was a forgery (ancient seals were less reliable than modern signatures for guaranteeing the genuineness of a document) or that it was legally invalid because the deceased made it 'when out of his mind because of madness or old age or drugs or sickness, or under the influence of a woman, or compelled by force or restriction of liberty' (see page 101).

To make his claim, the claimant had to make a written application to the arkhon. The claim was read out at a meeting of the Ekklesia, to alert any other citizens who might wish to dispute it.[228] After that, there were three possibilities:

(*a*) If no one disputed the claim, the arkhon formally awarded the inheritance to the claimant.

(*b*) Someone might come forward and declare that the inheritance was 'not awardable', because one or more living legitimate sons of the deceased existed (or a son adopted by the deceased during his lifetime). If testimony (*diamartyria*) to this effect was produced, no other claim could then be admitted unless someone challenged the truth of the testimony (maintaining, for example, that the sons were not legitimate) by bringing a prosecution for false witness (see pages 217–18).

(*c*) One or more other persons might make claims to the inheritance.

Then the arkhon had to arrange for a trial by jury, in which each claimant presented his claim and the jury's verdict decided the case.

The procedure of claim and award was called *epidikasia*. If the claim was disputed, the term *diadikasia* was generally used instead. Whereas an ordinary trial had two disputants (prosecutor and defendant), the peculiarity of a *diadikasia* was that there could be any number of claimants, all on an equal footing; apart from this, it was an ordinary private case. When the claim was for an *epikleros*, the procedure was exactly the same as when it was simply a claim for an inheritance; and the award (*epidikasia*) of an *epikleros* to a man was equivalent to *engye* for the purpose of making the marriage valid and the children of it legitimate.

Even after the arkhon awarded an inheritance to a claimant, it was still possible for a new claimant to come forward at any time during the life of the first heir or not more than five years after the first heir's death. The new claimant issued a summons to the first heir to appear before the arkhon, and another *diadikasia* was held.[229]

 A number of surviving speeches were composed for inheritance cases. The orator Isaios, in the first half of the fourth century, seems to have specialized in the intricacies of Athenian inheritance law, and all his complete surviving speeches were composed for delivery by various speakers in cases connected with inheritances. Some of them are very complicated. One of the best-known and most interesting concerns the property left by Hagnias. This is the subject not only of Isaios 11 (*On the estate of Hagnias*) but also of Demosthenes 43 (*Against Makartatos*), and these two speeches well illustrate the complexity of Athenian inheritance procedure.[230]

Hagnias, son of Polemon, was killed by the Spartans in 396, leaving substantial property. He is shown in capital letters in the family tree on page 104. † marks a relative whom we may presume to have died before him. M or F denotes a male or female relative whose name is not known. The dotted line marks a disputed relationship. For simplicity some relatives not involved in the events to be described have been omitted from the diagram.

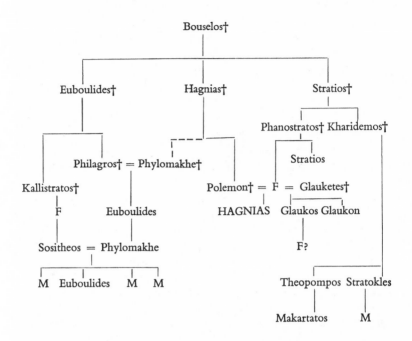

Hagnias had no sons or daughters, but he left a will adopting his niece
(perhaps, though not certainly, a daughter of his half-brother Glaukos).
So on his death she became *epikleros*: when she was married, her
husband would take possession of Hagnias's property, and eventually
her son would inherit it. Whether she ever was married is not known,
but anyway she died childless some years later. Who was to inherit
Hagnias's property now?

Hagnias's half-brothers Glaukos and Glaukon (sons of his mother by
her second husband Glauketes) produced a document which they said
was Hagnias's will. This document specified that, if Hagnias's adopted
daughter died childless, his property was to go to Glaukon (who would
thus become Hagnias's posthumously adopted son). Glaukon put in a
claim to the arkhon. But this claim was disputed by Phylomakhe,
daughter of Euboulides. (Euboulides himself, son of Philagros, had
died by now.) Phylomakhe's case will have been conducted on her
behalf by her husband, Sositheos (who, being her second cousin, had
claimed her when she became *epikleros* of her father's estate). They
claimed that the alleged will was a forgery, that Hagnias had left no

will, and that his property should pass to Phylomakhe as his nearest surviving relative; for she claimed to be Hagnias's first cousin once removed on his father's side, whereas Glaukon was Hagnias's brother only on his mother's side, and relatives on the father's side took precedence over relatives on the mother's side. The case came to trial (*diadikasia*), and the jury voted for Phylomakhe. A document preserved in Demosthenes 43. 31 records this verdict and dates it to 361/0; if the date is right, thirty-five years had already passed since Hagnias's death.

But Phylomakhe and Sositheos did not keep the property long. Once the will had been rejected as a forgery, other relatives began to take an interest. Hagnias's second cousins Stratios (son of Phanostratos), Theopompos, and Stratokles all considered putting in claims. Stratios and Stratokles both died before taking any action, but Theopompos submitted a claim to the arkhon. Since his claim had not been considered at the previous *diadikasia*, a fresh *diadikasia* had to be held. This time there were the following claimants:

(*a*) Theopompos, who was Hagnias's second cousin.

(*b*) Phylomakhe, who claimed to be Hagnias's first cousin once removed.

(*c*) Glaukos and Glaukon. It is not clear whether they based their claim this time on the assertion that the 'will' was genuine, or merely on their relationship to Hagnias, which was close through his mother but only distant through his father.

(*d*) Hagnias's mother. She, we are told, did not base her claim on the fact that she was her own son's second cousin, since Theopompos was also a second cousin and it was the rule that males took precedence over females in the same degree of relationship; she simply pointed out that she was Hagnias's mother. To a modern reader maternity seems a close relationship, but actually Athenian law gave priority to relatives on the father's side 'as far as children of cousins', and seems not to have given the mother any place at all in the order of succession. A man named Eupolemos, who is mentioned in connection with this *diadikasia*, was probably not a separate claimant but a relative who conducted Hagnias's mother's case for her, possibly her third husband.

Phylomakhe claimed to be the granddaughter of an elder Phylomakhe, who was Hagnias's aunt. Theopompos undermined her case by declaring that the elder Phylomakhe was not in fact a legitimate sister of Polemon, so that the younger Phylomakhe's only relationship to Hagnias was as second cousin once removed (through her great-grandfather Euboulides). The jury accepted this argument and awarded Hagnias's estate to Theopompos.

But the dispute still had a long future before it. The next thing that happened was that Theopompos was prosecuted for not giving half of the estate to his nephew, the son of Stratokles. This boy, after the death of Stratokles, was under the joint guardianship of Theopompos and some other relative (possibly a brother of Stratokles's wife). The other guardian declared that, since Theopompos and Stratokles were brothers, equally related to Hagnias, Stratokles's heir had the right to share the estate with Theopompos; when Theopompos refused to hand over half, the other guardian, acting on the boy's behalf, brought against Theopompos a prosecution by *eisangelia* for maltreatment of an orphan (see page 94). Theopompos's speech in his own defence in this case is the speech *On the estate of Hagnias* which we have (Isaios 11). The most important point which he makes in it concerns the definition of 'close relatives' (*ankhisteis*). According to the law close relatives were relatives 'as far as children of cousins', so that the order of precedence for inheritance was: first, relatives on the father's side 'as far as children of cousins'; secondly, relatives on the mother's side 'as far as children of cousins'; thirdly, more distant relatives on the father's side. In the Greek phrase 'cousin' should probably (though this has been disputed) be taken to mean 'first cousin', and 'as far as' means 'down to and including, but not beyond'. Theopompos explains that Polemon (father of Hagnias) and Kharidemos (father of Theopompos and Stratokles) were cousins; therefore Hagnias and Theopompos were within the category 'as far as children of cousins', but the son of Stratokles belonged to the next generation and thus was outside that category. The jury presumably accepted this argument, for Theopompos kept the estate until his death.

When Theopompos died, the estate passed to his son Makartatos. Sositheos and Phylomakhe now decided to make a further attempt to recover it, by an ingenious use of the Athenian practice of posthumous adoption. Phylomakhe had been the only child of her father Euboulides; thus on his death she was *epikleros*, and her son would be his eventual heir. By now she had four sons, and she and her husband proceeded to make one of them, also named Euboulides, Euboulides's adopted son and heir. When this formality was completed, the boy Euboulides was legally the son, not the grandson, of Phylomakhe's father Euboulides. On the assumption that the latter was the son of Polemon's sister (as Sositheos and Phylomakhe had maintained all along), the boy Euboulides was now legally a first cousin once removed of Hagnias. On his behalf a claim for Hagnias's estate was submitted to the arkhon. Makartatos opposed it, and another *diadikasia* was held. Sositheos's speech presenting the claim of the young Euboulides is the speech *Against Markartatos* which we have (Demosthenes 43). In meticulous detail he describes the genealogy of the descendants of Bouselos, and he calls witnesses to confirm relationships which he alleges. Apart from his insistence that the elder Phylomakhe was Polemon's sister, his most significant point is his interpretation of the legal phrase 'as far as children of cousins'. Euboulides (son of the elder Phylomakhe) was Hagnias's cousin; therefore the young Euboulides, posthumously adopted, is the child of Hagnias's cousin and comes into the category of 'close relatives'. But Kharidemos (father of Theopompos) was the cousin not of Hagnias, but of Polemon; therefore Theopompos was not the child of Hagnias's cousin, and was outside that category. In effect, Sositheos maintains that 'as far as children of cousins' means that the limit of 'close relatives' is first cousin once removed, whereas Theopompos in the earlier speech (Isaios 11) maintains that it is second cousin.

We do not know what verdict was given in this *diadikasia*, and we do not know whether the jury accepted Sositheos's interpretation of the law or not. On the face of it, it seems a more reasonable interpretation of the Greek words than Theopompos's, which the earlier jury accepted. Modern scholars have expressed contrary opinions: on the one side, that Sositheos's interpretation was right and Theopompos hoodwinked the jury into giving a wrong verdict;[231] on the other side, that Theopompos could not have hoodwinked a jury on such a point, and so his interpretation should be accepted.[232] Neither of these alternatives seems quite correct. The truth is that 'as far as children of cousins' is an ambiguous phrase. The fact that Theopompos and Sositheos could propound different interpretations, each with some hope of convincing a jury that his interpretation was right, indicates that its meaning was obscure to the Athenians, as to us, and both interpretations had some plausibility. The original drafters of the law must have known what they meant, but they failed to express their meaning clearly.

The date of this last *diadikasia* is not known, but it appears to have been some years after the one in which the estate was awarded to Phylomakhe; if that one was correctly dated to 361/0, this one was about half a century after Hagnias's death. Probably none of the participants in it had known Hagnias. Yet there is no suggestion that there was any particular difficulty in identifying the property of which the ownership was in dispute. How could Hagnias's estate remain clearly defined for so long? The explanation is that in ancient Greece an inheritance was primarily real, rather than financial. A modern inheritance is usually thought of in terms of money, which can easily be spent or dispersed. But the most significant part of Hagnias's estate will have been a piece of land with a house; long after his death the other members of his family would still know which piece of land was Hagnias's.

This long and involved dispute has been worth recounting in full because it illustrates six most important features of Athenian inheritance: the real (rather than financial) character of an estate; the role of an *epikleros* in securing succession to a man who left no son; the use of adoption to provide an heir when a man had no children; the comparative uselessness of a written will, because documents could be forged easily; the difficulty of proving relationships, in the absence of official birth certificates; and the ambiguity of the law, due to incompetent drafting.

VII DEATH

THE FUNERAL

Death was an event which concerned primarily the other members of the dead person's family. It was customary for the women of the family to wash, dress, and lay out the body in the house, where lamentation took place. Then it was carried out in a family funeral procession for burial. There was, however, a law regulating these matters: the funeral had to be on the next day after the laying out (not later than the sunrise of the third day); the men had to walk first in the procession, and the women behind; no women who were not members of the family (the *ankhisteis*: see pages 98–9) might participate, except for women over sixty years old; if the funeral was at night, women had to travel in a waggon with a lamp; sacrifice of an ox was forbidden; there were limits to the amount of clothing, food, and drink which might be taken for burial with the dead; and disorderly lamentation was not allowed. The main purpose of these rules appears to have been to ensure that a funeral was a discreet family event, not an occasion for extravagant displays of feminine grief to disturb the general public.[233]

Another law provided for a person who died away from home, when no members of his family were there to take up the body. In these circumstances the demarch of the deme (district) in which the death occurred was required to notify the dead person's family (or the owner of a dead slave) and tell them to take up the body for burial. If they failed to do so, the demarch was to hire persons to bury it as cheaply as possible, and exact twice the cost from the family or pay it himself; the purpose of this rule was evidently to get the family to do their duty. In any case, the law insisted that the body must be removed on the day of death, whether by the family or by the demarch, and the deme must be 'cleansed'; this word's implications are religious rather than hygienic.[234]

HOMICIDE AND THE FAMILY

Further duties fell upon the family if there were grounds for believing that a person had not died from natural causes or from suicide, but had been killed, whether deliberately or accidentally, by another person or by external circumstances. The steps which had then to be taken appear to have had three distinct purposes. One was, of course, to deter people from homicide, but there were also two others: vengeance and purification.[235]

Vengeance was required by the deceased himself. He had suffered unjustly by being made to die before the due time, and the only way in which he could be compensated was by punishment of the killer. If with his dying breath he forgave his killer, that gave the killer legal immunity from prosecution and punishment; but no one else had authority to forgive a killer on the victim's behalf.[236] Here we see a difference between classical Athens and some other communities. In the Homeric society depicted on the shield of Achilles, for example, a killer atones for his act by paying compensation to the victim's family (see page 19); but in Athens there was no payment of 'blood-money' because it was the victim himself, rather than his family, who required compensation.

Purification was required because killing was believed to cause pollution (*miasma*). Pollution was a kind of supernatural infection, which was liable to spread from the killer to others who consorted with him, and to the whole community, unless they took steps to bring him to justice. A polluted person was considered likely to suffer disease, shipwreck, or other disasters sent by the gods. The Athenians' belief in pollution is reflected in one of the best-known situations in their drama: at the beginning of Sophokles's *Oidipous Tyrannos* a plague afflicts the citizens because a killer is living among them unpunished. So it was considered very important, for practical religious reasons, that legal action should be taken against anyone believed to be guilty of homicide. Yet even for this most serious offence there were no public officials to prosecute; the duty of prosecution was laid upon the victim's family.

The law laying down the procedure for cases of homicide was probably the oldest law still in force in Athens in the fourth century. It was believed to be the only law made by Drakon which had not been superseded by the laws of Solon, and part of the reinscription made in 409/8 survives (see page 42); but much of it is lost or damaged, and we still have to use surviving speeches, especially those of Antiphon and the Demosthenic corpus, to reconstruct the law. Two sentences partly preserved in the inscription, supplemented from oratorical evidence, specify which relatives were to take action.

'Relatives as far as cousinhood [this may mean "children of cousins";
cf. pages 106–7] and cousin are to make proclamation to the killer in
the Agora. The prosecution is to be shared by cousins, children of
cousins, sons-in-law, fathers-in-law, and members of the phratry.'

(*IG* i² 115. 20–3)

Thus a very wide circle of the victim's relatives had responsibility for
taking steps against a killer, though in practice probably the closest
adult male relative would take the initiative and the others would just
give support if it was needed. If the victim was a slave, it fell to the
owner to take action. It is less clear what happened if the victim was
free but had no relatives in Athens, as could be the situation of a former
slave who had been freed. One such case is described in the speech
Against Euergos and Mnesiboulos and another in Plato's *Euthyphron*. I
have elsewhere argued from those texts that the law did not forbid,
though it did not require, non-relatives to bring a case of homicide. My
interpretation has been both disputed and supported, and this remains
one of the most controversial questions in the study of Athenian law.[237]

The first thing which the relatives were legally required to do was
to make a proclamation in the Agora. (Another proclamation made at
the funeral was a religious act rather than a legal one.) The proclamation instructed the killer 'to keep away from the things laid down by
law'. They then went to the basileus (the arkhon particularly concerned with religious matters) and presented to him their charge
against the killer. The basileus too is said in *AP* 57. 2 to have made a
proclamation ordering the accused person 'to keep away from the
things laid down by law'; it is not clear whether this was additional to
the family's proclamation or replaced it at some date in the fourth
century. Although no complete list is preserved of 'the things laid down
by law', they certainly included all temples and public religious
ceremonies, the Agora, and law-courts (except of course for his own
trial), and presumably public meetings of all kinds. In effect, the
accused man suffered temporary disfranchisement (what was called
atimia in the fourth century, though not in Drakon's time: see page
74). The purpose may have been to protect other people from being
polluted by contact with a killer, or it may have been just that the
prospect of exclusion from public life was thought likely to deter
prospective killers.[238]

These proceedings are exemplified in Antiphon's speech *On the
Chorister*. The case concerns a boy named Diodotos, a member of a

chorus rehearsing for the festival of the Thargelia, who died after being given a drink which was presumably intended to improve his voice. The surviving speech is composed for delivery by the khoregos (manager of the chorus), who is accused of being responsible for causing the boy's death. The leading prosecutor is Philokrates, elder brother of Diodotos. In his defence the khoregos impugns the sincerity of Philokrates. At the time of Diodotos's death, he says, he himself had begun taking steps to prosecute certain other men, including two named Aristion and Philinos, for embezzlement; and these men bribed Philokrates to bring a homicide charge against him because the proclamation made against a killer would prevent him from entering a court to prosecute in the embezzlement case. Subsequently, the homicide charge was dropped, but some months later Philokrates brought it forward again for the same purpose, the khoregos alleges, at the request of another group of men whom the khoregos was to prosecute; Philokrates and the other members of Diodotos's family are alleged to have proceeded with the homicide charge or abandoned it whenever they received or did not receive bribes from men who wanted the khoregos kept away from law-courts.

'On the first day, when the boy died, and on the next day, when he was laid out, even they did not see fit to accuse me or do me any injustice in this matter, but they met me and conversed with me. But on the third day, when the boy's funeral was held, they were corrupted by my enemies, and took steps to accuse me and to proclaim to me to keep away from the things laid down by law. . . . When they [Aristion and others] persuaded these men to charge me and make a proclamation to me to keep away from the things laid down by law, they thought that this would be their salvation and escape from all their troubles. For the law goes like this: "Whenever anyone is charged with homicide, he is to keep away from the things laid down by law." I should not be able to proceed against them while keeping away from the things laid down by law.'
(Antiphon 6. 34–6)

It was thought improper for the dead person's family to associate in any friendly manner with the person whom they accused of being the killer. Philokrates and the other members of Diodotos's family revealed their insincerity by their social behaviour towards the khoregos.

'They met me and conversed with me in the temples, in the Agora, in my house, in theirs, and everywhere else. Why, Zeus and all gods! this man Philokrates himself stood with me on the platform in the Bouleuterion, with the Boule looking on; he touched me and talked with me, he addressing me by name and I him. So the Boule thought it extraordinary when they heard that a proclamation had been made to me to keep away from the things laid down by law, by people whom they saw meeting me and conversing with me on the previous day.' (Antiphon 6. 39–40)

If, after the proclamation had been made, the accused man was found in the Agora or any of the other places from which he was ordered to keep away, anyone could arrest him and deliver him to the Eleven, who kept him in prison until he was tried (the procedure called *apagoge*). This trial for infringement of the proclamation was quite distinct from the trial for homicide; it was held in an ordinary court, and the penalty was fixed at the discretion of the jury.[239] But as long as the accused man kept away from the forbidden places, he was not imprisoned and presumably could go about his ordinary private business until his trial was due. There was no anxiety that he might evade trial and punishment: as long as he stayed in Attika it would not be too difficult to find him; and if he left Attika, that would mean that he voluntarily underwent exile (which Athenians regarded as a severe penalty) and thus freed Attika from the pollution caused by the homicide. But it was a different matter if an Athenian was killed by a foreigner, since a foreigner who stayed in his own city and refused to come to Athens for trial would not be suffering the penalty of exile. In such a case Athenian law permitted the victim's relatives to make a seizure (*androlepsia*) of any three citizens of the city where the alleged killer was, and hold them until that city either extradited the killer to Athens or proved that they were not harbouring him.[240]

KINDS OF HOMICIDE

Some kinds of killing were lawful and incurred no penalty. In an athletic contest, such as boxing or wrestling, a man who accidentally killed his opponent was not liable to punishment; neither was a man who, in war, killed another by mistake for an enemy. If a patient died while under the care of a doctor, the doctor was not liable to punishment. A man who was attacked by another and in the course of defending himself killed his assailant incurred no penalty, but to prove his innocence he had to show that the other had struck the first blow. It was permitted to kill a highwayman who waylaid one on a road, a brigand who was using force to seize one's property, or anyone caught stealing anything at night. A man was allowed to kill a man whom he caught in sexual intercourse with his wife, mother, sister, daughter, or concubine kept 'with a view to free children' (see page 89). If a man who had been sentenced to exile for homicide was found within Athenian territory, he could be killed with impunity; so could anyone attempting to set up a tyranny or overthrow the democracy.[241]

This range of situations in which homicide was lawful is wide, by modern standards. Under modern legal codes the killing of a nocturnal thief or an adulterer, for example, would not be condoned. But in Athens in the fifth and fourth centuries there was a much more recent tradition of self-help. It seemed natural that a man who stole one's property or one's wife should be resisted by an immediate use of force, instead of being calmly referred to some higher authority for trial, and there had probably never been a period when killing in such circumstances was not permitted. The usual direction of development for a society is from habits of self-help towards the use of legal trials; so the fact that an Athenian was still permitted in the fourth century to kill a nocturnal thief or an adulterer for himself instead of taking him to court shows that Athenian society in this respect remained primitive, while the existence of laws restricting such 'private executions', and of a court to examine claims that they were justified (at the Delphinion: see page 117), was a sign of progress.

Among killings which were not lawful, the most important distinction was between intentional and unintentional homicide. Aristotle discusses this distinction, and gives an example of unintentional homicide.

'Whenever a person hits another or kills him or does anything of that sort with no previous deliberation, we say that he did it unintentionally, on the ground that intention lies in deliberation. For instance, it is said that on one occasion a woman gave a man a philtre to drink, and afterwards he died from the philtre, but she was acquitted on the Areopagos, where they let off the accused woman for no other reason than that she did not do it deliberately. For she gave it to him for love, but she failed to achieve this aim; so they decided it was not

intentional, because she did not give him the philtre with the thought
of killing him. So here the intentional is classed with the deliberate.'
(Aristotle *Ethika Megala* 1188b 29–38)

In other areas of law (and of religion too) it often strikes a modern
reader that the Athenians seem to take notice only of actions, dis-
regarding the intentions which gave rise to them. This makes it all the
more interesting that intention plays such a crucial part in their law on
homicide, one of the oldest parts of their legal code. But their distinction between intentional and unintentional homicide remained crude,
by our standards. We should distinguish between an act planned in advance and an act committed in a moment of anger without premeditation; and so indeed did Aristotle.[242] But in their law the Athenians,
though they had a phrase which we may translate 'deliberate' or 'with
premeditation' (*ek pronoias*), did not employ it to make a distinction
but treated it as a mere synonym of 'intentional' (*hekon* or *hekousios*).[243]

There is also some evidence that an act was counted as intentional
homicide if the offender intended to harm his victim and death in fact
resulted, even if he did not intend to kill. In the speech *Against Konon*
Ariston claims that Konon assaulted and injured him. He recovered,
but he says that if he had died from the injuries Konon would have
been liable to be prosecuted for homicide on the Areopagos. Since
cases of unintentional homicide were not tried on the Areopagos (see
page 117), this means that the charge would have been one of intentional homicide. Yet, though Ariston (or Demosthenes) does not mince
his words about Konon, nowhere in the speech does he allege that
Konon actually intended to kill him. So it seems that the Athenians
classed as intentional homicide any act which, at the moment of committing it, was intended by the doer to harm the victim and which in
fact caused the victim's death.[244]

A distinction was also made between 'planning' (*bouleusis*) and killing
with one's own hand. A person was guilty of *bouleusis* of homicide if
he had planned or was responsible for an act of killing performed by
someone else. Good examples are provided by two speeches of
Antiphon, both concerned with cases of poisoning.

In Antiphon 1 (*Against the Stepmother*) the speaker is the dead man's
illegitimate son. He is prosecuting the dead man's wife, his own stepmother, who is defended by her sons, the prosecutor's half-brothers.
His father had a friend named Philoneos, and Philoneos had a concubine, of whom he was tiring. His father's wife (alleges the prosecutor)

told the girl that she possessed a love-potion which would increase the two men's affection for the girl and herself, and they made a plan by which the speaker's stepmother was to provide the philtre and the girl was to put it in the wine when the two men were drinking together. An opportunity was found when Philoneos was entertaining the speaker's father at his house in Peiraieus. The girl put the potion in the wine, inserting a rather larger share in Philoneos's cup. Philoneos died at once. The speaker's father fell ill, and died some twenty days later. The girl was executed. Now, some years afterwards, the speaker prosecutes his father's wife for killing his father. He claims that she caused his death deliberately; the charge is one of *bouleusis* of intentional homicide.

Antiphon 6 (*On the Chorister*, already mentioned on pages 111–13) is a speech for the defence. The speaker was the khoregos for a boys' chorus at the festival of the Thargelia. In the course of the rehearsals one of the boys took some kind of drink, and soon afterwards died; and the speaker is accused of causing his death by poison. His defence is that he did not attend the rehearsals himself, owing to pressure of other business, but appointed four men, including his own son-in-law, to act as his deputies and manage the chorus; so far from giving the boy the drink or ordering him to take it, he was not even present at the time. The prosecutors themselves agreed that he was not present and that the boy's death was not caused deliberately. So the offence alleged was responsibility for an act which resulted in death although no harm was intended; the charge was one of *bouleusis* of unintentional homicide.

Yet another distinction depended on the status of the victim: killing an Athenian citizen was more serious than killing an alien or a slave.

It was these distinctions which decided which court was to try a particular case. In the fifth and fourth centuries homicide cases were still tried by the Areopagos or the ephetai (see page 27 for their earlier history). The Areopagos now consisted entirely of ex-arkhons. Each year the nine men who had held the arkhonships automatically became members of the Areopagos for the rest of their lives. This will have made a body of between a hundred and two hundred men at any one time. It had lost almost all its political functions, so that its main function now was its judicial one: it tried cases on the three days preceding the last day of each month. Every member had some legal experience, because he had presided over trials as an arkhon, and this was enhanced by the continuity of membership of the Areopagos. Consequently the Areopagos was a good jury, and widely respected.[245]

'This court alone neither tyrant nor oligarchy nor democracy has dared to deprive of homicide trials, but all believe that their own verdicts in these cases would be inferior to the verdicts of these men. That is remarkable enough; but in addition this is the only court where no defendant who was condemned or prosecutor who lost his case ever proved that the verdict was unjust.' (Demosthenes 23. 66)

The ephetai were fifty-one men over fifty years of age, chosen by lot (perhaps from the members of the Areopagos, though there is no clear evidence for this).[246] Their trials were held in different places, according to the nature of the case.

The rules for allocating homicide cases to courts were as follows. If a person accused of killing put forward as his defence that the killing was lawful, the case was tried by the ephetai at the Delphinion (a temple of Apollon Delphinios and Artemis Delphinia, situated in south-east Athens, near the Olympieion). Otherwise, any person accused of killing an Athenian citizen intentionally with his own hand was tried by the Areopagos. A person accused of unintentional homicide, or of *bouleusis* of homicide, or of homicide of an alien or a slave, was tried by the ephetai at the Palladion (a temple of Pallas Athena just outside Athens). If someone already exiled for unintentional homicide was accused of committing another homicide intentionally, he could not enter Attika for trial, but he was allowed to make his defence from a boat offshore at a place called Phreatto (perhaps at Zea, on the east side of Peiraieus), while the ephetai sat on the beach.[247]

Finally, there was a separate court for homicide alleged to have been committed by an unknown person, or by an animal or inanimate object. Such cases were heard at the Prytaneion, a building on the northern side of the Akropolis. Here the basileus, who presided over all homicide cases, sat with the four phylobasileis (the heads of the four ancient Athenian tribes, who by the fifth century had otherwise only religious functions), probably without the ephetai. If they decided that homicide had been committed by an unknown person, they proclaimed that he ('the person who killed so-and-so') was to go into exile from Attika. An animal found guilty of homicide was presumably put to death or driven out of Attika. An inanimate object, such as a stone or a tree which had fallen on a person and killed him, was cast beyond the frontiers of Attika by the phylobasileis. At first sight this may seem to a modern reader to have been a pointless ritual, but it was not. If someone was killed by an object, an animal, or an unknown person, it was desirable that the state should take note of the manner of his death, and take any steps that were practicable to see that no one else died in the same way in future. This court served some of the purposes of a modern coroner's court.[248]

PROCEDURE IN HOMICIDE CASES

The trial procedure for homicide was more elaborate than for other offences, either because it was considered more serious or just because of religious tradition. When the basileus received a charge of homicide from the victim's family and a proclamation against the alleged killer had been made, his next duty was to hold three pre-trials (*prodikasiai*). These had to be held in three separate months, and the trial itself in a fourth month. Since all these had to be conducted by the same basileus, one effect was that no homicide prosecution could be begun in the last three months of the year, when the basileus no longer had time to complete all the proceedings before he demitted office. We learn this from the case of the chorister, already mentioned, in which the khoregos maintains that the basileus of the preceding year acted quite properly in refusing to accept the homicide charge.

> 'After accepting the charge, the basileus had to hold three *prodikasiai* in three months and bring the case to trial in a fourth month (as has now been done). But only two months of his term of office remained, Thargelion and Skirophorion. So you see he could not have brought it to trial in his own term of office; and it is not permitted to pass on a case of homicide to a successor, nor has any basileus in this country ever done so. Since therefore he was permitted neither to bring it to trial nor to pass it on, he decided not to accept the charge at all in contravention of the laws of Athens.' (Antiphon 6. 42)

We know nothing of what happened at these pre-trials, except that speeches were made on both sides of the case. One purpose must have been to enable the basileus to decide which court was to try the case, in accordance with the rules already mentioned. But that could surely have been done after a single pre-trial; why were there three? Perhaps ust to compel the parties to take plenty of time to calm down and reflect whether they really needed to proceed to a full trial for homicide.

All homicide trials were held in the open air; if other people shared a roof with a killer, that would be a mark of friendship and might pollute them. So a trial at the Palladion, for instance, must have been outside the temple, not in it.[249]

Oaths were particularly elaborate at homicide trials. At the beginning the prosecutor swore that the defendant had committed the homicide, the defendant (except of course at the Delphinion) that he had not; at the end the winner swore again that he had told the truth and that the jurors' decision was the right one. Witnesses too had to swear, not just that their evidence was true, but that the defendant committed the homicide, or that he did not commit it. There are some grounds for thinking that in homicide cases witnesses gave their evidence orally, even when this had ceased to be the practice in other cases (see pages 242–3), and also that women, children, and slaves were allowed to appear as witnesses; even though the information which we have does not allow certainty on these points, it does seem that in these cases it was thought appropriate to take extra trouble to check the allegations.[250]

Each side made two speeches (in the order: prosecutor, defendant, prosecutor, defendant). At the end of his first speech the defendant was permitted to leave the court and go into exile if he wished.[251] In this way a man who expected to be condemned to death for intentional homicide could avoid execution by condemning himself to banishment for the rest of his life. This may appear a humane rule, especially to modern opponents of capital punishment. But in practice the choice must often have been agonizing, because it had to be made before the court gave its verdict. To be sure of avoiding death, a man had to go into exile without waiting to see whether the jury would acquit him. If he waited for the verdict at the end of the trial and then was convicted, it was too late to go into exile. But if he went into exile before the end of the trial, the jurors would probably take his flight as a sign that he had a guilty conscience and expected to be convicted, and so they would be more inclined to convict him than if he had stayed. Thus a gamble was involved. This suggests that the rule originated not from a humane belief that a guilty man should be allowed to choose exile instead of death, but from the fact that it was not practicable in early times to pursue a man beyond the boundaries of the state, perhaps combined with a belief that the state was not polluted by a man who had left it.

At the end of the speeches the jury (the Areopagos or the ephetai) voted and the basileus formally pronounced the verdict. The penalty for a person found guilty of intentional homicide was death, and his property was confiscated. For unintentional homicide the penalty was exile: the offender had to keep out of Attika and also to avoid the great religious festivals and games attended by people from all parts of Greece, but he could retain his property and live a free life abroad. If he was found in Attika, whoever found him could either kill him at once or arrest him and take him to the thesmothetai, or simply point him out to the thesmothetai, for execution without any further trial; and anyone harbouring him was liable to the same penalty. His exile lasted for life, unless he obtained pardon (*aidesis*) from the family of the person whom he had killed. Pardon for unintentional homicide could be granted by the victim's father, brothers, and sons, if they were unanimous; if none of these survived, it could be granted by the other relatives; if not even these existed, the ephetai could select ten members of the victim's phratry to decide whether the unintentional killer should be pardoned. Pardon, once granted, could not be revoked.[252]

The penalty for *bouleusis* of intentional or unintentional homicide was the same as for committing it with one's own hand. The penalty for killing an alien or a slave appears not to have been fixed by law but to have been assessed by the jury in each case, and it must usually have been less severe than for killing an Athenian citizen.[253]

THE USE OF 'APAGOGE' FOR HOMICIDE

The homicide law attributed to Drakon and the courts of the Areopagos and the ephetai, as described so far in this chapter, apparently had by the fourth century existed with little change for more than two hundred years, and represented one of the most antique and conservative parts of the Athenian legal system. But by that time another way existed of bringing a killer to justice, which did not involve those courts at all. This was by using *apagoge*, which meant that the prosecutor himself arrested the defendant and took him to the Eleven, who had charge of the prison, and a trial was held before an ordinary jury. I have already mentioned that this procedure could be used against a person who was found in a sacred or public place after a proclamation had been made against him as a person to be tried for homicide, and that a person sentenced to exile for homicide was subject to *apagoge* if he was found in Attika. But those were persons against whom other steps had already been taken. What we have now to consider is the possibility of walking up to a person and seizing him as an alleged killer without any previous legal proceedings at all. Demosthenes, after describing the courts of the Areopagos and the ephetai, mentions this alternative possibility.

'If one is ignorant of all these methods, or the various times for employing them are past, or for any other reason one does not wish to proceed in these ways, and one sees the killer going around in sacred places and in the Agora, one is permitted to arrest him and take him to the prison ... When arrested, he will suffer no penalty at all until he is tried, but if he is convicted, he will be punished by death.' (Demosthenes 23. 80)

The mention of sacred places and the Agora is significant. The offence which justified this procedure was not just killing, but mixing with the general public afterwards, because this might pollute other people. We can conjecture how this procedure came to be introduced. There must have been some occasions when a person, generally believed to have killed somebody, was not immediately prosecuted, either because the killing was done in the last three months of the year when homicide proceedings could not be started (see page 118) or because the killed man had no relatives or the relatives failed to act. Other people thought it objectionable, and indeed dangerous because of the risk of pollution, if the killer rubbed shoulders with them in the Agora. So the new procedure by *apagoge* was instituted, which could be used by any citizen at any time to get rid of a killer from a sacred or public place.

The case of Agoratos was one in which this procedure was used. We have a speech *Against Agoratos* (Lysias 13), written to be delivered for the prosecution in this case. Agoratos was alleged to have caused the death of Dionysodoros in 404/3 by denouncing him to the oligarchic regime of the Thirty, who executed him. Several years later, when democracy was restored, Dionysodoros's brother Dionysios wanted to avenge his brother by bringing Agoratos to justice. But in 403 an amnesty had been declared, exempting from prosecution all offences committed before the restoration of democracy in that year (with certain exceptions, not relevant to Agoratos). This meant that Dionysios could not accuse Agoratos of *bouleusis* of intentional homicide before the ephetai at the Palladion. So instead he arrested him; the ground for the arrest, though not clearly stated in the speech which we have, can only have been that Agoratos had since 403 (in the period not covered by the amnesty) frequented sacred and public places although guilty of homicide. Thus, in this case, for the purpose of circumventing the amnesty, the *apagoge* procedure was used by the victim's family simply as a substitute for a homicide prosecution of the traditional kind.[254]

VIII ASSAULT AND ABUSE

BATTERY AND DELIBERATE WOUNDING

It was an offence to strike a blow at another person, and an ordinary private case of battery (*dike aikeias*) could be brought for it. If two men had a fight in which each hit the other, only the one who struck the first blow was guilty. Probably it often happened that each alleged that the other had struck first, and we know of one instance in which two men each prosecuted the other as a result of the same fight. The penalty seems normally to have been payment to the victim of a sum of money assessed by the jury.[255]

If the person struck was the offender's parent or grandparent, a prosecution for maltreatment of parents could be brought (see page 92). The penalty for this was disfranchisement.

A more serious charge was deliberate wounding (*trauma ek pronoias*). The distinction between this and battery appears not to have been defined by law. One speaker accused of deliberate wounding argues that condemnation on this charge should be limited to attempted homicide, to persons who intended to kill but failed; but he is trying to avoid condemnation himself, and his words are not an impartial interpretation of the law.[256] A better guide is a passage of the speech *Against Konon* which ranges several offences in an order of escalation.

'For instance, there are cases of slander; these, they say, were instituted in order that men who are abused should not be induced to hit one another. Next there are cases of battery; these, I am told, exist in order that no one, when losing, should defend himself with a stone or anything of that sort, but he should await the legal case. Next there are *graphai* for wounding, to prevent homicide being committed when people are wounded. The most trivial offence, I suppose, that of abuse, has been provided for to guard against the last and most serious, so that homicide should not be committed, and one should not be gradually led on from abuse to blows, and from blows to wounds, and from wounds to death, but there should be a legal case for each of these, and they should not be decided by the individual's anger or whim.' (Demosthenes 54. 17–19)

This passage, besides showing how the possibility of legal proceedings could deter the victim of one offence from committing a worse offence in retaliation, indicates that, as a fight got worse, the stage at which the men were liable to *graphe* for wounding came before the stage at which they tried to kill one another. So deliberate wounding was not necessarily attempted homicide. Instead, this passage and one other (Lysias 4. 6) suggests that in practice a blow with a stone or other weapon was generally regarded as deliberate wounding, whereas a blow without a weapon was just battery.

Several features of the procedure show how much more seriously the Athenians took a case of deliberate wounding than mere battery. First, it was tried by the Areopagos, like a case of intentional homicide.[257] Secondly, it was a *graphe*,[258] which meant that it need not be brought by the victim himself; if the victim was too seriously hurt to take legal proceedings, the offender could still be brought to justice by someone else. Thirdly, the penalty was exile and confiscation of property.[259]

SEXUAL OFFENCES

It seems strange to us that the Athenians thought that sexual intercourse outside marriage was a more serious offence if the woman consented than if she did not. Seduction was worse than rape, because it implied corruption not only of the woman's body but also of her mind; a raped wife had not ceased to be loyal to her husband.[260]

The penalty for rape of a free woman was only financial. Solon's law fixed it at 100 drachmas. By the beginning of the fourth century the amount was assessed by the jury for each case; the offender had to pay this amount to the woman's husband or other *kyrios*, and the same amount again to the state. The prosecution was called 'a case for violence' (*dike biaion*), just as for violent theft of property; since it was a *dike*, not a *graphe*, it could be brought only by the woman and her *kyrios*.[261]

A seducer was liable to much more severe treatment. A man who caught a seducer in the sexual act with his wife, mother, sister, daughter, or concubine kept 'with a view to free children' (see page 89), could kill him immediately, and if accused of murder could defend himself by pleading that the homicide was lawful.[262] Or he could maltreat him; favourite kinds of treatment for a seducer were to push radishes up his anus and to pull out his pubic hair.[263] Or he could demand a sum of money in compensation, and keep the seducer imprisoned until he paid or provided sureties to guarantee payment. If the alleged seducer protested his innocence, he or a friend could counter this by bringing a *graphe* for wrongful confinement as a seducer. If he won this case, he and his sureties were released from the obligation to pay the money; but if the jury decided that he was indeed a seducer, his opponent could, besides exacting the money, subject him in the presence of the court to any treatment he wished, short of bloodshed.[264] Yet another possibility, perhaps the only procedure permitted if the seducer was not caught in the act, was that anyone could bring a prosecution for seduction (*graphe moikheias*); it is not known whether the penalty for this was fixed by law or assessed by the jury.[265]

The seduced woman was also punished, though less severely. If she was married, her husband had to divorce her. She was forbidden to attend public religious ceremonies and to wear any kind of ornament, presumably to reduce the chances of her attracting other men. Anyone who saw her infringing this rule could pull off her clothes and ornaments and slap her.[266] In Solon's time an unmarried daughter who committed fornication could be sold as a slave, but probably that was no longer done in later times (see page 80).

Procuring a free woman for seduction (accepting payment for bringing a man and a woman together) was also an offence for which a prosecution (*graphe proagogeias*) could be brought against either a man or a woman. The penalty for this in Solon's law was a fine of 20 drachmas, but in the fourth century it was death.[267] It is not known when or why the Athenians thought it necessary to change the penalty so drastically. But prostitution of women was not illegal: if a woman was an inmate of a brothel or an open street-walker, intercourse with her did not count as seduction.[268] Thus the proprietor of a brothel would not be guilty of procuring.

These laws about rape and seduction applied to free women, whether they were of citizen birth or not. There was no law against a man's having sexual intercourse with a slave. However, slaves were mentioned in the law about *hybris* (see page 129).

Homosexual conduct as such was not illegal. But rape and procuring of free males were subject to the same laws as rape and procuring of free females, with the possibility of a *dike biaion* or a *graphe proagogeias*.[269] And the organization of boys' schools and boys' choruses at festivals was controlled by legislation to discourage homosexual affairs: a school could only be open during daylight hours, the khoregos of a boys' chorus must be over forty years old, and so on.[270]

Male prostitution was not forbidden, but in law it was incompatible with the status of an Athenian citizen. Thus an Athenian man who was or had ever been a prostitute was required to observe the restrictions of disfranchisement (see page 74); if he infringed them, but only then, he was liable to a prosecution for prostitution (*graphe hetaireseos*), for which the penalty was death. The same kind of *graphe* and penalty were incurred by a man who caused a citizen man or boy to become a prostitute and so to disfranchise himself: that is, a man who hired him, or one (a boy's father or other *kyrios*) who let him out for hire.[271] The penalty seems remarkably heavy, but perhaps cases were rare. No instances are recorded; and the existence of a law that, if a man let out his son for hire as a prostitute, the son was not required to support him in his old age (see page 92), and of a law that a prostitute who spoke in the Ekklesia could be accused by *dokimasia*, leading to disfranchisement only (see page 174), implies that a *graphe* for prostitution was not always brought when it could have been.

RESTRICTION OF LIBERTY

In certain circumstances one man could arrest another. A seducer caught in the act could be held (see page 124), and some kinds of offender could be arrested and taken to the Eleven for imprisonment (*apagoge*: see page 148). The Ekklesia or the Boule could authorize someone's imprisonment, or it could be imposed by a court as a penalty. But otherwise, as a fourth-century inscription indicates, it was against the law to confine an Athenian citizen. A case for confinement (*dike heirgmou*), mentioned by two late lexicographers, would presumably have been brought for this offence, but nothing else is known about that kind of prosecution.[272]

If a man, whether citizen or alien, was confined because he was accused of being a seducer caught in the act and he denied it, a *graphe* for wrongful confinement as a seducer could be brought.[273] The penalty for wrongful confinement was presumably assessed by the jury in each case, but no instance is known.

SLANDER

Personal attacks can be made verbally as well as physically, and the Athenians had several laws prohibiting slander and abusive language. Solon made it illegal to speak ill of the dead at all, or of the living in temples, at legal trials, in public offices, or at festival contests; the penalty for speaking ill of the living was a payment of 3 drachmas to the person slandered and 2 to the public treasury. The first of these laws, about speaking ill of the dead, was still in force in the fourth century; and another law had been added, presumably at the end of the sixth century, specifically forbidding anyone to speak ill of the tyrant-slayers Harmodios and Aristogeiton or to sing disparaging songs about them.[274] Whether Solon's law about speaking ill of the living remained in force is uncertain. Probably it was abolished at the time when another law, forbidding certain specified slanders, was introduced.

This more specific law was in force in 384/3, when the speech *Against Theomnestos* (Lysias 10) was written. The speaker is bringing a case for slander (*dike kakegorias*) against Theomnestos (who was allegedly a coward who had thrown away his shield to flee from a battle) for saying that he had killed his own father in the time of the Thirty, twenty years before. From part of the speech it is clear that the law listed a number of expressions which were forbidden. The speaker argues that its intention is to ban not just those particular words but any statement having the same meaning.

'Perhaps he will say . . . that it is not one of the forbidden words if one says someone has killed his father, because the law does not forbid that, but prohibits calling him a murderer. But surely, men of the jury, you should go not by the words but by their sense, and you all know that those who have killed people are murderers and those who are murderers have killed people. It would have been a long business for the law-maker to write out all the words which have the same meaning; by mentioning one he indicates them all. You would not, I suppose, Theomnestos, demand legal satisfaction from someone who called you a father-beater or a mother-beater and yet, if someone said that you hit your female parent or your male parent, think he should go unpunished because he had not said any of the forbidden words. I should like you to tell me this, since you are an expert on this subject and have made a practical and theoretical study of it: if someone said you had flung away your shield (when the law says "if anyone alleges that he has thrown it away, he is to be liable to penalty"), would you refrain from bringing a case against him and be content to have flung away your shield, saying that it did not matter to you, because flinging is not the same as throwing?' (Lysias 10. 6–9)

We can infer from this that it was illegal to say that a man was a murderer, a father-beater, or a mother-beater, or had thrown away his shield, and that the law did not say explicitly that other expressions having the same meaning were also banned, though no doubt the speaker was right to maintain that this was its intention. Presumably the list of forbidden slanders included others not mentioned here, and one other is in fact mentioned in Demosthenes 57. 30: it was forbidden to disparage the work in the Agora of any male or female citizen. (Perhaps the purpose of this was to prevent remarks like the fifth-century jokes against Euripides's mother for being a greengrocer.) But a person was guilty of slander only if what he had said was false; if he could show that he had merely spoken the truth, that was sufficient defence.[275] The penalty on conviction for any of the slanders specified in the law was a payment of 500 drachmas.[276] Inflation had made it necessary to raise the figure since Solon fixed it at three drachmas paid to the person slandered and two to the state; it is not known whether the payment continued to be divided in the same proportions or now went entirely to the person slandered.

There was also a separate law, or laws, about abuse of magistrates. A law authorized a magistrate to fine anyone who abused him in a public office or meeting. The same or another law specified disfranchisement as the penalty for anyone who assaulted or abused one of the nine arkhons when he was performing his official functions.[277]

There seems to have been no separate law about libel (defamation in published writing), but presumably reading a defamatory statement aloud would have come under the law of slander.

Comedies performed at public festivals appear, at least at some periods, to have been exempt. But a decree which in some way limited or forbade satire of individuals in comedy was passed in 440/39 and annulled in 437/6, and there is also some less clear evidence that a politician named Syrakosios got a decree passed to restrict it again shortly before 414.[278] The surviving plays of Aristophanes composed before 414 are full of rude personal remarks, some of which would surely have fallen foul of the law of slander if it had been applicable to them; for example, the politician Kleonymos is often said in those plays to have thrown away his shield, and this allegation was probably false, or at least exaggerated.[279] But in *Birds* (performed in 414) the two references to Kleonymos and his shield are oblique, and in general the later plays, though they contain many jokes against individuals, seem not to contain statements contravening the law of slander as far as we know it from the speech *Against Theomnestos*. This suggests, though it does not prove, that what the decree of Syrakosios did was to make comedy subject to the law of slander.

'HYBRIS'

Another way of dealing with assault or abuse was available if the offence was an act of *hybris*. *Hybris*, though a fairly common word, is difficult to define or translate. Modern writers often use it to mean 'arrogance', but that does not represent the range of the Greek word adequately. Study of its use by Greek authors indicates that a fundamental element of it is having energy or power and misusing it self-indulgently. Characteristically its driving force is the energy of a young man who has had plenty to eat and drink and behaves like a frisky horse, and it is often found in men who have wealth and political power; but it is not necessarily confined to the young or the wealthy. Its characteristic manifestations are further eating and drinking, sexual activity, larking about, hitting and killing, taking other people's property and privileges, jeering at people and disobeying authority both human and divine. A person shows *hybris* by indulging in conduct which is bad, or at best useless, because it is what he wants to do, having no regard for the wishes or rights of other people.[280]

The text of the law about *hybris* is preserved as follows.

'If anyone treats with *hybris* any person, either child or woman or man, free or slave, or does anything illegal against any of these, let anyone who wishes, of those Athenians who are entitled, submit a *graphe* to the thesmothetai. Let the thesmothetai bring the case to the Eliaia within thirty days of the submission of the *graphe*, if no public business prevents it, or otherwise as soon as possible. Whoever the Eliaia finds guilty, let it immediately assess whatever penalty seems right for him to suffer or pay. Of those who submit private *graphai* according to the law, if anyone does not proceed, or when proceeding does not get one-fifth of the votes, let him pay 1000 drachmas to the public treasury. If a money penalty is assessed for the *hybris*, let the person be imprisoned, if the *hybris* is against a free person, until he pays it.' (Law quoted by Demosthenes 21. 47)

Most of this law describes the normal procedure for trial and punishment in a *graphe*. (The odd phrase 'private *graphai*' may mean merely '*graphai* for offences committed against themselves', not referring to a different procedure.) Only the first sentence is concerned with defining the offence, and there is no attempt at all to define *hybris* itself. That shows that the word does not have any special legal meaning but is just being used in its ordinary sense with which all readers of the law are assumed to be familiar. But the law does not refer to all *hybris*, only to acts of *hybris* against any child or woman or man. It is limited to behaviour involving a victim; if a man is full of energy and wastes it on some useless activity, that may be *hybris*, but as long as he does no harm to anyone else it is not contrary to the law. Another limitation is that acts of *hybris* against a god, for instance disobeying a god's command or denying his existence, such as are sometimes mentioned in tragedies, are not forbidden by this law. But slaves are specifically protected. As long as the act of *hybris* is directed against another human being, there is no further limitation on the kind of behaviour that can be punished under this law. The law allows a man to prosecute another for hitting, killing, rape, disobeying authority, jeering at someone, depriving him of a privilege or indeed any kind of misbehaviour whatever towards another person, if he thinks that he can convince a jury that the act was an act of *hybris*.

Clearly there is a considerable overlap between the scope of a *graphe* for *hybris* and the scope of a *dike* for battery, violence, slander, and so on. But the Athenians, with their concern for personal honour and their resentment towards anyone who diminished it, may well have felt that the difference between them was more important. The difference lay in the motive and state of mind of the offender. If, for example, a man hit someone because he lost his temper, or even by accident, that was just battery (*aikeia*). But if he hit him because he considered himself and his own wishes more important than the rights and esteem of his victim, that was *hybris*, a much more serious offence.

'If one hits, one does not in all cases commit *hybris*, but only if it is for a purpose, such as dishonouring the man or enjoying oneself.'
(Aristotle *Rhetoric* 1374a 13–15)

'*Hybris* is doing and saying things at which the victim incurs dishonour, not in order to get for oneself anything which one did not get before, but so as to have pleasure.' (Aristotle *Rhetoric* 1378b 23–5)

So a *graphe* for *hybris* is not to be regarded as duplicating the other legal procedures for assault and abuse, and the suggestion that it was intended to supersede them is not correct.[281] It existed alongside them in the fourth century; being a *graphe*, it was a more serious kind of prosecution, which could be brought if necessary by any Athenian against a man whose behaviour was an offence to the whole community.

'So for *hybris* too the legislator allowed *graphai* to everyone who wishes, and made the penalty entirely payable to the state. He considered that a man who attempts to act with *hybris* wrongs the state, not just the victim; and that vengeance is sufficient compensation for the victim, and he ought not to take money for himself for such offences. And he went so far as to allow a *graphe* even for a slave, if anyone treats one with *hybris*. For he thought that what mattered was not the identity of the victim but the nature of the act; and since he found the act inexpedient, he did not allow it to be permitted either against a slave or at all. Nothing, men of Athens, nothing is more intolerable than *hybris*, or more deserving of your anger.' (Demosthenes 21. 45–6)

But although the surviving speeches often contain complaints about an opponent's *hybris*, actual prosecutions for *hybris* appear to have been rare. One reason for this may have been the difficulty of producing proof of it. In a court it is difficult to establish a state of mind. It may be fairly easy to prove that someone hit you, but much harder to prove that what made him hit you was self-indulgent egotism and not some other motive or accident. Demosthenes points out how one may feel sure that *hybris* was the motive and yet be unable to explain it.

'There are many things which the hitter might do, some of which the victim might not even be able to report to someone else, in his stance, his look, his voice . . .' (Demosthenes 21. 72)

A look or a voice may be hard to describe, and so one would think that Ariston was lucky to have such clear evidence of Konon's *hybris*. In his speech (Demosthenes 54) he describes how he and his friend, Phanostratos, while walking in the Agora one evening, were set upon by Konon and several other men.

'When we came up to them, one of them, whom I did not know, fell upon Phanostratos and held him down, while this man Konon and his son and Andromenes's son fell upon me. First they pulled off my cloak, and then they tripped me up and pushed me into the mud, and they put me in such a state, by jumping on me and treating me with *hybris*, that my lip was cut and my eyes closed. They left me in such a bad condition that I could not stand up or speak. And while I was lying there I heard them saying a lot of dreadful things. Most of them were scurrilous, and some I should not like to repeat in front of you. But the thing which shows Konon's *hybris*, and indicates that he was the ring-leader, I will tell you: he crowed in imitation of cocks that have won fights, and the others suggested he should beat his sides with his elbows like wings.' (Demosthenes 54. 8–9)

To show that Konon committed not just battery but *hybris*, Ariston needed to show what was Konon's motive and state of mind at the time. And since it is characteristic of *hybris* to feel pleased with oneself and to crow over other people, there could hardly be any sound revealing *hybris* more clearly than the one which Ariston describes Konon as uttering. Why then did he not bring a *graphe hybreos* against Konon, but only a *dike aikeias*? One reason may be that it was easy to prove that he received blows, because many people saw him in his injured state, but he may have had no witness able and willing to testify to the crowing. Another may be that he did not think that vengeance alone was sufficient (as Demosthenes maintained in 21. 45, already quoted) but wanted financial compensation, which he could not get by a *graphe*. Athenians thought honour and reputation important, but that does not mean that they ignored opportunities for material profits. *Hybris* was a fine subject for rhetorical denunciation, but for the practical purposes of the courts the other procedures for dealing with assault and abuse were more precise and more profitable.

ix PROPERTY

The Athenian laws concerning property were on the whole simple and primitive by comparison with the elaborate property laws of Roman and later systems. There was, for example, no Greek noun for ownership, as distinct from possession; and other concepts and principles which are precisely defined in modern law were left undefined by the Athenians, who just took their own customs for granted in an unsophisticated manner. Some modern scholars, especially in Germany, have applied their own juristic expertise and subtlety to the analysis of Athenian laws about property, often in terms of Roman law or of modern civil law. No such analysis will be attempted here; my aim is rather to present a summary of the subject as the Athenians themselves saw it. Readers wanting more detail should turn to A. Kränzlein's *Eigentum und Besitz im griechischen Recht* and A. R. W. Harrison's *The Law of Athens* i.

The most obvious and important kind of property, especially before the invention of money, was land. With land went any buildings erected on it and crops growing on it. Another valuable kind of property was slaves. It was also possible to own animals, ships and other vehicles, furniture, clothes, jewellery, and so on. And there were gold, silver, and other metals; and, from about the beginning of the sixth century, there was coined money, which made transfer of property easier.

An alien could not own land or buildings in Attika, unless specifically given the right of *enktesis* (see page 78), and a privately owned slave could not legally own anything (see page 80); but otherwise any individual could own any of these kinds of property. It was also possible for two or more individuals to own property jointly: thus brothers might jointly own land inherited from their father, or commercial partners might jointly own a ship or a workshop. Property could also be owned by a corporate body such as a deme or a phratry or a religious group; or it could be owned by the state of Athens itself.[282]

One common way of acquiring ownership of property was inheritance, which has already been described in chapter VI. Other methods of transfer of ownership were sale and gift; and the state could, through its magistrates and courts, confiscate property as a penalty. By lease or loan the use of property could be transferred without transfer of ownership.

Although in general an owner was entitled to dispose of his property as he wished, there were some exceptions: the right to bequeath property on death was strictly limited (see page 101); a minor could not dispose of his property, which was under the control of a guardian (see page 94); neither could a woman dispose of her property, except for small items (no more than the value of one medimnos of barley).[283] A man who held office was subject to restrictions on the disposal of his property until he had undergone his *euthyna* (see page 170), in case he was found to have misappropriated money belonging to the state.[284] Property owned jointly could not be disposed of unless both or all the owners agreed; but if there was disagreement, one of the owners could demand a division of the property to enable him to do as he liked with his own share, and could bring a legal case against a co-owner for appointment of liquidators.[285]

LAND AND BUILDINGS

In early times it was customary for the same family to remain in possession of a farm for many generations, and it is possible that land was then regarded as belonging to a family rather than an individual, so that no individual had power to dispose of it, and it was practically inalienable, except for changes arising when two families intermarried or a family died out. However, there is no clear evidence that this was ever a rule of law in Athens, and certainly by the fifth century sale of land was permitted.[286]

Though we have no evidence of an explicit law to this effect, probably the Athenians took it for granted that ownership of a piece of land implied ownership of any trees, crops, water, or other natural produce of it, and also of any buildings on it. (When an alien was given *enktesis* 'of a house' but not 'of land and a house', does that mean that he could own a house without owning the land on which it stood, so that he would have to pay rent or feu duty to an Athenian citizen for the site? I think it is more likely that *enktesis* 'of a house' implies the right to own enough land for a house to stand on, but not land for farming; I doubt whether it occurred to the Athenians that ownership of land underneath someone else's house could have any use or meaning.) And it would also be taken for granted that ownership implied the right to do what one liked with one's own, so that on one's own land one could build or demolish a house, cut down trees, and so on, without asking anyone's permission. However, there were several laws which restricted a landowner's rights in certain respects.

One subject of restriction was olive-trees. Olive-trees were one of the commonest kinds of fruit-tree in Attika; they were associated with the goddess Athena, and also olive-oil was a most important product for domestic food and lighting and for export. Certain olive-trees were regarded as sacred ones (*moriai*), belonging to Athena and Athens; these included trees growing in sacred precincts, but also some on privately owned land. The fruit of these trees belonged to the state (the state offered it for sale), and if anyone felled any of them, a law prescribed trial before the Areopagos, with death as the penalty. This law was still in force at the beginning of the fourth century, when we have the text of a speech (Lysias 7) delivered before the Areopagos by a man accused of destroying the old stump of a sacred olive-tree (not even a live tree) on his own land. But by Aristotle's time the law, though not formally repealed, was no longer enforced, and the owner of land on which sacred olive-trees stood was allowed to keep the fruit on payment to the state of 1½ kotylai (less than three-quarters of a pint) of olive-oil per tree per year. (It was distributed to the winners of the gymnastic and horse-racing competitions at the Panathenaia.) Other olive-trees were not sacred and belonged to the landowner. But even with these he could not do just what he liked; a law forbade any one man to fell more than two olive-trees per year for his own use, on pain of a fine of 100 drachmas per tree, though felling for a public religious ceremony or a funeral pyre was permitted without limit.[287]

Another kind of restriction on an owner's use of his land was that which forbade him to plant trees or dig ditches so near the edge of it as to interfere with his neighbour's farming. Laws on this subject, and also on the circumstances in which one must allow a neighbour on to one's land to draw water, are attributed by Plutarch in the following passage to the wisdom of Solon; though other evidence is lacking, they may well have remained unaltered throughout the classical period.

'Since the country is not adequately provided with water either by ever-flowing rivers or by any lakes or by copious springs, but most people used artificial wells, he made a law that, where there was a public well within horse-distance, people must use it. (Horse-distance was four stades [800 yards].) Where it was farther off, they must try to get a private water supply. But if after digging a depth of ten orguiai [60 feet: the figure seems high and may be an error] on their own land they did not find any water, then they were to take it from their neighbour, filling a six-khous jar [4¼ gallons] twice a day; for he thought it right to help those in need, not to provide for the idle. He also laid down limits for planting, in a very expert manner: he ordered those planting any other tree in a field to keep five feet away from their neighbour's, but those planting a fig-tree or an olive-tree, nine feet, because these spread further with their roots and injure some trees if they are next to them, taking away nourishment and emitting an exhalation which is harmful to several. As for pits and ditches, he ordered that anyone wishing to dig them should keep them the same distance away from anyone else's land as their own depth; and beehives were to be set up three hundred feet away from ones already installed by anyone else.' (Plutarch *Solon* 23)

Water is not a plentiful commodity in Attika, especially in summer, and laws existed to control interference with it. A good surviving example is a law of about 420 which laid down that no one was 'to soak skins in the Ilissos above the precinct of Herakles, nor to dress hides, nor to [throw rubbish?] into the river'.[288]

There seems also to have been some restriction on building walls. The speech *Against Kallikles* (Demosthenes 55) is not easy to interpret in detail, but it is clear that the speaker's farm and Kallikles's both lay on a hillside, and in wet weather a stream of water ran down the hill between them. For the rest of the year the watercourse was dry and was used as a track or path. Because the stream tended after heavy rain to run over his land, the speaker maintained a wall, which he says his father had built, to keep the water out. Now, after one severe storm, the water, excluded from the speaker's farm by the wall, has flooded Kallikles's farm and caused some damage. So Kallikles brings a case for damage (*dike blabes*) against the speaker, claiming to have suffered losses due to the speaker's wall. From the speech we gather that the speaker will have to pay 1000 drachmas if found guilty, but also that Kallikles has some hope of getting hold of the speaker's land. The best explanation of this seems to be Wolff's, that there must have been a law penalizing anyone responsible for a man-made obstruction to a natural flow of water, which caused the water to damage someone else's property; he had to pay the injured party 1000 drachmas or else forfeit the land to him (surely not his entire farm, as Wolff supposes, but merely the land on which the obstruction stood).[289]

There may have been other similar laws restricting the right of a landowner to do as he wished with his own land; but those already mentioned are the only ones for which we have Athenian evidence, apart from the special circumstances of the owner of land under which a mine was situated.

MINES

Some of the richest silver mines in Greece were situated in Attika, mainly in the area of Laureion. The exact legal status of the mines has been a matter of much doubt and dispute among scholars, but it now seems to be generally agreed that at least the underground area of a mine was always the property of the state. Anyone wishing to open up or work a mine had to register it with the poletai (the sellers of state property); it was an offence to work an unregistered mine. He had then to buy from them a lease of the mine for a period of years. Besides brief references in literary texts to the purchase of mine leases, fragments have been found of stone inscriptions of the poletai's accounts which record such leases, giving the name of the mine, its location, the name of the purchaser, and the price. Three years is the period of a lease for a mine in current operation, but a longer lease appears to have been given for a new mine or one transferred to a new lessee.[290]

What is not so clear is the legal position of the land surface above a mine. Although some mines may have been under mountainous or rocky ground which was not owned by anybody, there were certainly some which were situated under land owned by private individuals, for the poletai's accounts sometimes identify a mine as being 'in X's estate'. The sinking of a mine would inevitably interfere with agricultural operations on the surface, and one would suppose that some payment was made to the farmer on this account, but no evidence shows whether this was done. Possibly the state bought from the individual owner the land immediately around a mine shaft, so that it became state property like the underground part of the mine; or possibly the farmer retained ownership of the land surface and received from the poletai some part of the rent paid for the mine by the lessee.

References to workshops for ore-crushing and other operations, situated on the surface near a mine, show that they were owned by individuals, like other buildings, and were not state property.

There was a 'mining law' (*nomos metallikos*) which made it an offence 'if anyone excludes anyone from operation'; no doubt this would apply especially to the farmer of surrounding land who obstructed the lessee of a mine from access to the mine. It also forbade 'any other offence concerning the mines', apparently without defining such offences. Cases brought under this law (*dikai metallikai*) came before the thesmothetai, and in the fourth century they were one of the types of case accepted every month (see page 233). The *phasis* procedure (see pages 158–9) could be used by any citizen for at least some kinds of mining case, particularly prosecution for operating an unregistered mine.[291]

SALE

Sale developed out of barter. Before the invention of coinage, we find in the Homeric poems that exchange is a normal way of acquiring property. Indeed the ox is treated almost as a unit of currency: modern readers find striking the passage of the *Iliad* where Achilles provides prizes for the wrestling match, a cauldron worth twelve oxen for the winner and a woman worth four oxen for the loser; and there are many other examples.[292] It is the essence of the exchanges that the ownership of the two items exchanged changes at the time when the exchange occurs. This principle remained unaltered after coinage was invented. Then money was normally one of the items exchanged, and the exchange can be called sale, but it remained a cash sale: legal ownership of the property sold changed when, and only when, the money was paid. Apparent exceptions are the allocations by the state to individuals of the right to work mines or to collect taxes; the verbs 'buy' and 'sell' were used for these, even though the money was not paid when the allocation was made. But these are special cases, not affecting the general rule. That the principle of the cash sale prevailed throughout Greece and in Hellenistic Egypt is one of the main themes of Fritz Pringsheim's exhaustive study *The Greek Law of Sale*, and has been generally accepted.

Thus sale on credit was not recognized in Athenian law; until the buyer paid, the sale had not legally been made and the land or goods remained the property of the seller. If the buyer did not have sufficient cash available, he had to borrow it in order to make the purchase. But we hear of one case in Athens in which the buyer seems to have solved this problem by borrowing the required sum from the man who was selling him the slaves he wanted to buy. If this practice was common, it must have been much the same in effect as a system of sale on credit, even though formally the sale and the financial loan were separate.[293]

A prospective buyer who did not yet have enough cash to make the purchase and wanted to secure an option (to prevent the property from being sold to someone else in the meantime) could offer part of the purchase money in advance, as a deposit (*arrabon*). Although this device is mentioned only once in surviving Athenian texts, it occurs several times in comedies of Plautus which are based on Athenian plays and probably follow Athenian law. In *Mostellaria* Tranio says that Philolaches has arranged to buy a house for 2 talents and has paid a deposit of 40 mnai (one-third of the price). In *Pseudolus* Ballio has agreed to sell a slave-girl to Harpax for 20 mnai; 15 have already been paid and the day when the action of the play takes place is the date fixed for payment of the other 5. In *Rudens* Plesidippus wants to buy a girl from Labrax for 30 mnai, and has paid a deposit; when Labrax fails to produce her on the appointed date, Plesidippus prosecutes him and wins the case. These examples show that a seller who accepted a deposit was legally required to keep the property available for the prospective buyer until a certain date. They do not show whether the law laid down any rules about the amount of the deposit and the length of time allowed for payment of the balance, or left these matters to be mutually agreed by the seller and buyer.[294]

As a safeguard for buyers against sellers who might misrepresent the qualities of their merchandise, there was a law forbidding false statements in the Agora.[295] There were also some special rules about the sale of land or slaves. If land was to be sold, some precaution was needed to check that the seller was entitled to sell it. In Athens there was no land register (though some other Greek states had one). Boundary stones (*horoi*) with or without the owner's name were sometimes set up to mark the boundary of a farm, but they were not documents having legal validity. So there was a law that sixty days' notice of any sale of land had to be given in writing to the appropriate authority (presumably the arkhon). This public notice gave time for objection by anyone who claimed to own the land concerned or to have a loan secured on it.[296] When a slave was sold, the seller was required by law to say if he had any physical defect; if the buyer discovered a defect which had not been declared, he could return the slave and demand his money back.[297]

There is an interesting account of the sale of some slaves in the speech of Hypereides *Against Athenogenes*. Athenogenes, a metic resident in Athens, owned several perfume-shops, one of which was managed by a slave named Midas with two sons. The speaker of the surviving (but incomplete) speech, whose name may be rightly restored as Epikrates, took a fancy to one of the boys and wanted to buy him, but Athenogenes was unwilling to sell the one boy separately and persuaded Epikrates to buy all three slaves with the perfume-shop and its contents for 40 mnai. He drew up a written agreement (*synthekai*) by which Epikrates was to be responsible for any debts owed by the perfume business, saying that the stocks of perfumes in the shop were more than enough to cover all outstanding debts. Epikrates, in haste to get possession of the boy, agreed to this and paid over the money to make the purchase. Later it turned out that the debts incurred by the perfume business amounted to the huge total of five talents. Athenogenes had doubtless known this all along, and had tricked Epikrates into buying the whole perfume business for the very purpose of evading his debtors. The speech which we have is delivered in court by Epikrates in an attempt to persuade the jury to declare Athenogenes responsible for the debts.

Had Epikrates a sound case? It depends on the validity of the written agreement. If there had been no agreement, Athenogenes would certainly have been liable for the debts, because the slaves and shop belonged to him when they were incurred. But there was a law saying that any agreement made voluntarily by one man with another before witnesses was valid, provided that the thing agreed was not unjust.[298] Epikrates could not argue convincingly that he agreed under compulsion or without witnesses; so his only hope was to persuade the jury that the agreement was unjust. We do not know whether he succeeded. But the case shows how sale in Athens, though it did not require a written contract, could be accompanied by one.

LEASE

By lease it was possible to obtain use of property without acquiring ownership of it. The word for lease or rent is *misthosis*, and the connection of that word with *misthos* ('fee', 'wages') suggests the following course of development. A landowner might employ a man to work a piece of his land, giving him a fixed amount of the produce each year (*misthos*) and keeping the rest himself. Then, to encourage the labourer to work hard, the landowner might agree to take only a fixed amount of the produce each year, allowing the labourer to keep the rest; in practical effect, this would mean that the labourer had a lease of the piece of land and paid a fixed rent for it. Since the division of the produce between the landowner and the labourer could not be made until it was harvested, this account of the historical development explains why, unlike a purchaser who had to pay up before taking possession, a lessee normally paid his rent not in advance, but in arrears. But it is quite conjectural.[299]

By the fifth century rent was normally paid in cash, not in produce, and houses as well as agricultural land could be leased. The essential feature of a lease was simply that the owner of the property concerned (the lessor) allowed a tenant (the lessee) to occupy and use the property for a number of years in return for rent. It was possible to add more detailed conditions: for instance, dates might be fixed for the payment of the rent, once or twice in each year; a lessee might be required to grow certain types of crop on land which was leased, or to leave a part of it fallow each year; he might be required to preserve certain features of the estate, such as trees; and so on.[300] If the conditions were at all complicated, it would be convenient to have them in writing. But a written agreement was not legally required in order to make a lease valid.

When the lessor was the state, or a public body such as a deme, the conditions of the lease were sometimes recorded on stone. Surviving remains of such inscriptions are the subject of a recent study by D. Behrend entitled *Attische Pachturkunden*, and they give us more information about leases granted by public bodies than is available about leases granted by private owners. The following example, belonging to the late fourth century, is virtually complete. It records a lease granted by a body of *orgeones* (a religious group) allowing a man named Diognetos to use the shrine of their hero Egretes. (The word 'shrine', *hieron*, is used both for the sacred precinct and for the sanctum inside one of the buildings in the precinct.) It shows how quite complicated conditions could be included in a lease.

'The *orgeones* leased the shrine of Egretes to Diognetos son of Arkesilas of Melite for ten years for 200 drachmas a year, to use the shrine and the houses built there as a shrine. Diognetos shall also whitewash those of the walls which need it, and he shall build and carry out other works also, whenever Diognetos wishes. When his

ten-year period expires, he shall take away with him the woodwork
and tiles and doors but shall not disturb anything else. He shall also
take care of the trees planted in the shrine, and if any dies he shall
replace it and hand on the same number. Diognetos shall pay the
rent to the treasurer of the *orgeones* each year, one half, 100 drachmas,
on Boedromion 1st and the remainder, 100 drachmas, on Elaphebolion 1st. When the *orgeones* sacrifice to the hero in Boedromion, Diognetos is to make available the house where the shrine is,
open, with a roof and the kitchen and couches and tables for two
three-couch rooms. If Diognetos does not pay the rent at the times
stated or does not do the other things stated in the lease, his lease
shall be invalid and he shall lose the woodwork and tiles and doors,
and the *orgeones* shall be allowed to grant a lease to whoever they
wish. If any capital levy (*eisphora*) is made, it is to be deducted from
the payment to the *orgeones*. Diognetos is to inscribe this lease on the
stone which is in the shrine. The date when the lease begins is the
next arkhon after Koroibos.' (*IG* ii^2 2499)

If a lessee of property owned by the state failed to pay the rent,
there were laws specifying a procedure for making him pay; in some
cases at least he was disfranchised until he paid.[301] This sanction was not
available to a private lessor whose lessee defaulted on the rent. But he
could bring a private case against the lessee, a case for house-rent (*dike
enoikiou*) or a case for produce (*dike karpou*; the name indicates that
rent for land was at one time paid in kind), or, if he still failed to get his
rent, a case for recovery of his property, as described later in this
chapter.

LOANS AND SECURITY

A man could lend money to another and, if he thought fit, require
interest to be paid on the loan. A usual rate of interest was one per cent
per month, but the rate of interest and the duration of the loan were
not fixed by law but were matters for mutual agreement between the
lender and the borrower.

In early times, if a man borrowed money (or, before the invention of
money, grain or some other commodity) and failed to repay it, the
creditor might take possession of his property or his person (as a slave)
in payment of the debt. Enslavement for debt was abolished in Athens
by Solon early in the sixth century, but a debtor's property continued
to be subject to forfeiture if his debt was not paid. To avoid the risk of

having all his property seized, or any part picked at random, it was convenient for a borrower to earmark a particular piece of his property which should become the creditor's if he could not pay his debt. To have a specific item pledged in this way was also an encouragement to the creditor to make the loan, since it assured him that if he did not recover his money property of sufficient value was available to compensate him. So it became customary for property to be offered as security for any substantial loan.

The simplest form of security was the pawn: an object at least as valuable as the amount of money lent, which the borrower put into the hands of the lender when he borrowed the money and recovered when he paid the money back. Thus Demos, wishing to borrow the sum of 16 mnai from a man named Aristophanes (not the dramatist), offered to deposit a gold cup with him, which he would redeem later by paying 20 mnai; this meant that Aristophanes would obtain interest of 4 mnai on the loan. The father of Demosthenes lent 40 mnai to Moiriades and received as security twenty slaves, who were carpenters making beds; the work done by these slaves served as his interest on the loan. Difficulties arose in another case, when Polykles borrowed 12 mnai, giving his horse as security, and the horse died before he paid the money back.[302]

Land and houses were more reliable as security, because they were not so subject to death or disappearance. If a borrower offered a piece of land or a house as security for a loan, it was generally (though a few exceptions are known) considered unnecessary for the creditor to take it into his keeping, and the debtor was allowed to remain in possession of it unless he defaulted in the payment of interest or repayment of capital when it was due. But he was not free to sell it or give it away without the creditor's consent, and to warn off any prospective buyers it was customary for the creditor to place on the land a stone inscribed with brief particulars of the loan for which it was security. (The same Greek word, *horos*, is used for a stone marking a financial encumbrance as for a stone marking a boundary.) Many such stones have been found, and they are discussed in detail in two books, J. V. A. Fine's *Horoi* and M. I. Finley's *Studies in Land and Credit in Ancient Athens*. One important feature is that most of the stones describe the land to which they were affixed as 'sold with right of redemption' (*pepramenon epi lysei*). The most obvious interpretation of this expression is that legally the 'loan' was regarded as purchase money and the 'lender' as the buyer of the land; but the 'borrower' remained in occupation of it, making regular payments which may be regarded either as interest or as rent, and retained the right to recover full ownership by paying back the money which he had received. This arrangement would be much the same as a modern mortgage. The stones which do not use the phrase 'sold with right of redemption' might indicate a legally different arrangement, by which the borrower remained the owner of the land unless he defaulted However, this account of 'sale with right of redemption' is almost certainly too simple, and several problems remain unsolved. For instance, there is evidence that a man could use one building to raise money from two different sources by this method; but, if it was a kind of sale, how was it legally possible to sell the same house twice? Was each creditor regarded as owning part of the house; or is it, after all, wrong to regard this transaction as a sale at all? The best evidence for answering this and other questions is the case described in the speech *Against Pantainetos* (Demosthenes 37), but it is too complicated to be adequately discussed here, and readers wishing to investigate the subject further had better turn to the discussions of this and other evidence by Finley, Fine, and Harrison.[303]

The word *apotimema*, meaning 'valuation' or more precisely 'property valued and set apart', was used especially for two particular types of security, in which a monetary value was attached to land and buildings. One of these was connected with the lease of an estate belonging to an orphan. When the arkhon awarded the lease of an orphan's estate (see page 94), the lessee was required to offer property of his own as security for the return of the estate, with the rent payable for it, when the orphan came of age. It is possible that the security had to be land or buildings, and that it was required only for that part of the orphan's property which was not land or buildings, though the evidence is not sufficient to make this clear. The arkhon had both the estate and the security valued, to check that the security was as valuable as the estate, and some stones (*horoi*) have been found which marked the land to which they were affixed as security of this type, calling it 'valuation (*apotimema*) for the child of . . .'. During the lease the lessee would retain possession of the land he had offered as security but he would forfeit it to the orphan if he failed to restore the orphan's estate to him when the orphan came of age and the lease expired.[304]

Security for the return of a dowry was also called *apotimema*. If a father gave a large sum of money as a dowry for his daughter (see pages 87–9), he might feel apprehensive that, if the marriage was ended by divorce or death, the husband might be discovered to have spent the money so that it could not be repaid. So a husband could, at the time of the marriage, offer a piece of his land as security, which would not meanwhile be sold and would be handed over to the wife's family if she was divorced or died or was widowed without children and the dowry could not be repaid otherwise. There is a disputed instance of this in the speeches of Demosthenes *Against Onetor*: Onetor maintained that he had given his sister to Aphobos in marriage with a dowry, that Aphobos had offered a piece of land as *apotimema* for return of the dowry if required, and that Aphobos had subsequently divorced Onetor's sister and not returned the dowry, so that the piece of land now belonged to Onetor; Demosthenes rejects most of these allegations and claims that the piece of land is part of his own inheritance and never belonged to Aphobos. There are also some stones which marked an *apotimema* of this kind. One, for example, reads:

'Mark (*horos*) of land and house, valuation (*apotimema*) of dowry for Timodike daughter of Philippos of Anagyrous, 4500 (drachmas).'
(*IG* ii² 2662)

But it was not a legal requirement to provide security for the return of a dowry; and the detailed working of this kind of *apotimema*, and of other types of security also called *apotimema*, remains doubtful for lack of evidence.[305]

One other important type of loan and security was bottomry, in which a ship-master or merchant borrowed money on the security of a ship and its cargo. This came under the Athenian mercantile laws, described in chapter XV.

PROCEDURES FOR CLAIMING PROPERTY

If a dispute arose about ownership, and one man claimed that another ought to hand over a house, for example, or that he owed him a sum of money, what legal procedures were available for deciding who was the owner or whether the debt was indeed owed?

One procedure for settling disputes about property was *diadikasia*, already mentioned in chapter VI in connection with inheritance. When there was a dispute about the right to inherit an estate, a claimant could apply to the arkhon, and the arkhon arranged a trial by jury. The feature which distinguished *diadikasia* from other trials was that no one was the prosecutor or the defendant; there could be any number of claimants, each of whom stated the grounds of his own claim to the property. Besides inheritance cases, a late lexicographer tells us that *diadikasia* was the procedure used when a man's property was confiscated by the state and others claimed that debts owed to them were payable out of the property now under state control; obviously prosecution would have been inappropriate in this case.[306] But there is no evidence that *diadikasia* was used for other kinds of dispute about ownership. Nearly a century ago Leist put forward a theory that all questions of ownership were decided by *diadikasia*, but in the absence of supporting evidence this view should be rejected.[307]

For there is sufficient evidence that an ordinary *dike* could be brought by a person who claimed that land, money, or other property at present held by someone else belonged to himself. In various texts there is mention of a case for property (*dike ousias*), a case for house-rent (*dike enoikiou*), a case for produce (*dike karpou*), a case for cash (*dike argyriou*), a case for debt (*dike khreos*), and cases for slaves and animals.[308] Hitherto (from Roman times onwards) scholars who have believed that each of these phrases was the name of a different 'action' (see page 59) have found it a problem to distinguish one from another; what, for instance, was the difference between a case for cash and a case for debt? The problem disappears when it is realized that there is no adequate ground for believing that these cases were separately defined in law. The legal position was simply that a *dike* could be brought to claim property of any kind from another person. If it was called 'a case for X', specifying a particular type of property, that was just an informal name, not a legal definition; and the informal names were vague, overlapping, and to some extent interchangeable.

However, there was one legal distinction which was introduced during the fourth century. After monthly cases were instituted (see page 233), certain kinds of claim for money or other property were included among the types of case which were accepted every month. In this category *AP* 52. 2 mentions claims for repayment of money lent at the standard interest rate of one per cent per month or lent as capital for starting a business, and claims for slaves and draught animals. At the ploughing season, for example, it would be a serious handicap to a farmer to be unable to recover his pair of oxen promptly.

If the property claimed was a movable object, the prosecutor could demand that the defendant, who had the disputed item in his possession, should produce it in court for the jury to see (*emphanon katastasis*, 'production of items in the open'). If he did not produce it, it seems (if an obscure passage in Demosthenes 53. 14 is rightly interpreted) that he not only forfeited ownership of the property concerned but also had to pay a fine equal to its value. We hear of one case in which a man by this procedure summoned a banker to produce the will which he himself had deposited with him some time before, but he abandoned the case before it came to trial.[309] In another case, when a man, whose brother had lately died, summoned someone to produce some property which he claimed had belonged to his brother and so was now his by inheritance, the defendant blocked the prosecution (by *paragraphe*, a procedure described in chapter XIV) by saying that he himself was the heir, because the deceased man had left him the property by will; this meant that the correct legal procedure was not a *dike* but a *diadikasia* before the arkhon.[310]

One possible line of defence for a man accused of having property belonging to someone else would be to say that he had bought it from some other person, so that, if the prosecutor was in fact the true owner, it was that other person and not he himself who had misappropriated it. Probably a man wishing to defend himself in this way could compel the seller to come to court to state what right he had to sell it, and to refund the purchase money to him if he lost the case. Two lexicographers mention a 'case of confirmation' (*dike bebaioseos*) for doing this, but there is no Athenian evidence for it.[311]

When the item of property claimed was a human being, alleged to be a slave, there was a further possibility: the alleged slave might be not in anyone else's possession, but living and going around independently, as a free person. If so, the man who claimed ownership of him had no need to bring a *dike* against anyone else; all he had to do was to catch the slave and take him away. But if he seized in this way someone who was not in fact his slave but a free person, he might be arrested as an enslaver, or the alleged slave might be 'removed to freedom' (see page 80).

Such were the procedures for simply claiming ownership of an item of property which another person had in his possession, when the claimant had no object beyond recovering it. We now turn to procedures used when there was some further object, to make the defendant pay damages or a fine or other penalty.

THEFT

A person who deliberately took away someone else's property was a thief, deserving not just to be deprived of the property concerned but also to be punished. So we find that cases of theft, unlike the cases described in the previous section, involved penalties.

A person who suspected another of having stolen something of his might demand admission to his house to search it. A law laid down conditions on which this might be done, but we know no details except that the searcher was required to be 'undressed' (this may mean wearing only a tunic, with no cloak) to ensure that he did not smuggle in under his cloak the allegedly stolen object, plant it in the house, and then accuse the householder of theft.[312] Once he believed he had detected the thief, he could bring a case for theft (*dike klopes*). If the defendant was found guilty, besides returning the stolen object or paying compensation, he had to pay to the prosecutor a sum of money equal to twice the object's value, and the jury could if they thought fit impose an additional penalty of confinement in the stocks in a public place for five days and nights. An accomplice or accessory was liable to the same penalty.[313]

If the owner alleged that his property had been taken away by force, he could bring a case for violence (*dike biaion*). In this case a defendant found guilty, besides paying to the prosecutor an amount assessed by the jury, had to pay the same amount again as a fine to the state.[314]

But certain sorts of theft were felt to need severer treatment than this, either because they were so serious or because they were so easy. The stricter procedure could be used against 'wrongdoers' (*kakourgoi*). Though we do not have the actual text of the law, it seems likely that it specifically mentioned thieves, enslavers (stealers of human beings), and clothes-stealers (who would operate especially at gymnasiums and baths), and was not intended to be used for other kinds of offender (even though attempts to use it against others were sometimes made). Thieves came into this category only if they stole at night, or stole from a gymnasium or other place of athletic exercise (the Lykeion, Akademeia, and Kynosarges are mentioned), or stole more than 10 drachmas from a harbour or more than 50 drachmas from anywhere else. Anyone catching such a thief could arrest him and take him to the officials called the Eleven (this was the procedure called *apagoge*), or alternatively fetch the Eleven and tell them to make the arrest (this was the procedure called *ephegesis*). If the thief was caught red-handed (*ep' autophoroi*: this expression is not clearly defined, but it probably covers not only men seen in the act of stealing but also those found with the stolen goods in their possession) and admitted his guilt, the Eleven had him executed without trial. If he denied his guilt, they kept him in the prison until he was tried, and if found guilty he was executed.[315]

One passage of Demosthenes (22. 26) implies that the procedure of *graphe* could be used against thieves. But elsewhere we hear of *graphe* for theft only in cases of theft or embezzlement of public money by public officials (see page 171) or theft of sacred money or property. If *graphe* could be used for any other kinds of theft, we do not know what kinds.

There are two passages referring to *graphe* for theft or embezzlement of money belonging to a sacred treasury.[316] Distinct from this, though we do not know the exact terms of the distinction, was the more serious offence of temple-robbery (*hierosylia*), for which the penalty was death, with exclusion from burial in Attika and confiscation of property.[317] This may have been the charge brought against Pheidias the sculptor. The evidence about his trial is late and inconsistent. It seems probable that he was accused in 438/7 of stealing some part of the precious materials (gold and ivory) entrusted to him for making the great statue of Athena for the Parthenon, and possibly also of the impiety of including representations of himself and Perikles among the figures on Athena's shield. He fled to Elis, and subsequently made his other great chryselephantine figure, the statue of Zeus at Olympia. But it is not clear whether he fled to avoid execution or because exile was imposed on him as a penalty, nor whether he was prosecuted for impiety or temple-robbery or both, nor which legal procedure was used.[318]

DAMAGE

A case for damage to property (*dike blabes*) was one of the commonest kinds of case, because the Athenians used 'damage' in a very wide sense, covering what we should regard as several distinct kinds of offence.

We have no chronological information about how the legal senses of 'damage' developed, but presumably the earliest was physical damage to a piece of property, such as to destroy it or make it useless or less valuable than before, but without taking it away (which would be theft). Thus Kallikles brought a case for damage when he said that a wall on his neighbour's farm caused his own farm to be damaged by flooding, as described earlier in this chapter (page 136). And when Meidias, as Demosthenes alleges, entered the goldsmith's house at night and partly destroyed the gold crowns and clothing which Demosthenes had ordered for his chorus to wear at the forthcoming festival, Demosthenes could have brought a case for damage against him, though in fact he decided not to.[319] (But one kind of physical damage to property was dealt with differently: cases of arson were tried by the Areopagos. These may have been *graphai*, but we have hardly any information about them. A conjecture that they went to the Areopagos only when a fire caused loss of life is not supported by any evidence, and a conjecture that the penalty was death is based only on a rhetorical question in Euripides.[320])

From this, 'damage' was extended to cover any action which caused someone to lose property, particularly money. When the deme of Aixone granted a lease of a piece of land to Autokles and Auteas for forty years, it was specifically stated that anyone who proposed any deviation from the conditions of the lease before the forty years were up could be prosecuted by the lessees for damage; that is, for causing them loss of produce.[321] When Apollodoros prosecuted Timotheos for debt, he needed Antiphanes, who was present when the money was lent, as a witness; Antiphanes failed to attend and testify, with the result that Apollodoros lost the case before the arbitrator; Apollodoros therefore brought a case for damage against Antiphanes, alleging that Antiphanes had caused him to lose the money which he ought to have recovered from Timotheos.[322] Pantainetos brought a case for damage against Nikoboulos; he said that Nikoboulos had caused Pantainetos's payment to the state for the lease of a mine to be made late, so that he incurred double payment as a penalty for lateness. We have the text of his charge, the first part of which is as follows:

'I was damaged by Nikoboulos scheming against me and my property, ordering his slave Antigenes to take away from my slave the money which he was taking as payment to the state for the mine which I had bought for 90 mnai, and being responsible for my being put down to pay double to the treasury ...' (Quoted by Demosthenes 37. 22)

And finally we find instances in which the alleged 'damage' was simply that the defendant had failed to pay the prosecutor a sum of money. Nausimakhos and Xenopeithes brought a case for damage against the sons of their former guardian, now deceased, for not paying over money of theirs which their guardian had had.[323] The speech (Demosthenes 48) in which Kallistratos accuses Olympiodoros of failing to give him a half-share of the money and other property left by Komon, according to a private agreement which they had made between themselves, is entitled *Against Olympiodoros for damage*. Kallippos brought a case for damage against Pasion the banker, on the ground that Pasion had paid out to Kephisiades instead of to himself some money which Lykon had deposited in Pasion's bank.[324] Cases for damage on the ground of failure to repay a loan were brought by Pamphilos and Dareios against Dionysodoros, and by Apollodoros against several men to whom money had been lent by his late father Pasion.[325]

How do these cases differ from an ordinary *dike* to claim money (see page 146)? The crucial difference is in the penalty to which the defendant was subject if he lost the case. If he lost a *dike* for debt he had only to pay the amount of money which the prosecutor claimed was his. But the laws about damage prescribed payment of double the amount of the damage if it was committed intentionally, or of the simple amount if it was committed unintentionally.[326] Any creditor, then, who thought he could convince a jury that his debtor was withholding payment deliberately, and not from inadvertence or from genuine belief that the money was not due, would be sure to bring a case for damage rather than for debt, because he stood to gain twice as much money if he won. That must be the reason why we seldom hear of a *dike argyriou* and much more often of a *dike blabes*.

The use of a case for damage in the hope of recovering twice the amount lost is exemplified by the charge brought by the aged orator Deinarkhos against Proxenos, at whose house he stayed after his return to Athens from Khalkis. The old man lost some money and silver plate, and alleged that Proxenos was to blame.

'Deinarkhos son of Sostratos of Corinth against Proxenos, with whom I live, for damage; assessed at 2 talents. I was damaged by Proxenos receiving into his house in the country, at the time when, after exile from Athens, I returned from Khalkis, 285 gold staters, which, as Proxenos knew, I conveyed from Khalkis and brought into his house, and silver plate worth not less than 20 mnai, scheming against these.' (Quoted by Dionysios of Halikarnassos *Deinarkhos* 3)

Although we do not know the exact rate of exchange between gold staters and Athenian currency, probably the total value of what Deinarkhos claimed to have lost was a little over 1 talent. The figure of 2 talents, then, is not the amount of the loss but the double amount which he claimed Proxenos should pay for causing the loss intentionally, and the word 'scheming' (*epibouleusas*), which we find in Pantainetos's charge too, may have been regularly used to allege that damage was intentional. Yet Deinarkhos does not appear to have said that Proxenos stole his property, but only that he deliberately took some action which caused its loss.

Some cases for damage were based on the allegation that the defendant had broken a specific law. Wolff's suggestion that there was a specific law about obstruction of a flow of water, which Kallikles accused his neighbour of breaking, has already been mentioned (see page 136). Another law sometimes quoted in cases for damage is the one saying that any agreement made voluntarily before witnesses was valid, already mentioned in connection with Athenogenes and the perfume-shop (see page 140). The case in which Kallistratos prosecuted Olympiodoros for failing to give him a half-share of the property left by Komon, in accordance with a written agreement which the two of them had made, appears to have been based on this law.[327] Without this agreement, Kallistratos could hardly have argued that Olympiodoros, by keeping property awarded to him in a *diadikasia*, was guilty of damaging Kallistratos's interests. The law did not specify that an agreement must be written. If there was a written document, that would of course be useful evidence of what had been agreed if the details were later disputed. But an agreement made orally had no less legal validity than one recorded in writing; it was only in the mercantile laws of the mid fourth century that special authority was given to a written contract (see pages 232–3). When Kallippos brought a case for damage against Pasion the banker, his accusation was that Pasion, after agreeing not to pay out a certain sum of money without Kallippos's consent, had in fact handed it over to Kephisiades; but whatever agreement had been made (unless the account given by Apollodoros is grossly misleading) had not been made in writing but in conversation.[328]

Thus 'damage' covered some acts which in modern law would rather be regarded as breach of contract. The law saying that any agreement made voluntarily before witnesses was valid was (apart from the mercantile laws) the only law of contract which the Athenians had, and the legal proceedings for infringement of it were no different from the proceedings for other kinds of damage to property.[329]

Other cases for damage were not based on the infringement of any specific rule. When Pantainetos accused Nikoboulos of causing delay to his payment for his mine-lease (see page 150), or when Deinarkhos alleged that Proxenos had caused the loss of his gold staters and silver plate (see page 151), there is no suggestion, and no likelihood, that there was some particular law on either of these subjects which Nikoboulos or Proxenos had broken. We should therefore assume (though the point has been disputed) that, in addition to some specific laws, there was also a quite general one saying something like 'If anyone wrongly causes damage to anyone else intentionally, let him pay double the amount of it; if unintentionally, the simple amount.'[330] This would be the law under which Pantainetos and Deinarkhos prosecuted, and the jury in each case must have had the task of deciding whether the conduct of Nikoboulos or of Proxenos could justly be called 'damage'.

ENFORCEMENT OF PROPERTY RIGHTS

What if a court had decided the ownership of some property, whether land or money or anything else, and the man who had it in his possession still refused to hand it over? If this happened, the owner could bring against him a case for ejectment (*dike exoules*). To win this case he had to prove two things: first, that he already had legal authority to take possession; secondly, that the defendant had sent him away (*exagein*) when he attempted to do so. The clearest kind of legal authority to take possession was a previous decision by a jury or arbitrator that he was the owner. A person who, on winning another case, had been awarded damages, but had not received payment of the damages from his opponent within the time allowed for it, could likewise bring a *dike exoules* against him.[331] There were also some other circumstances which counted as legal authority to take possession, even without a decision by a jury or arbitrator. The legitimate or adopted son or grandson of a deceased man could take possession of his father's or grandfather's property without awaiting a decision by a jury or the arkhon (see page 102). If a man had lent money, for which land or other property was offered as security (see page 143) and the money was not repaid by the date when it was due, he could take possession of the security forthwith, and could bring a *dike exoules* against anyone who excluded him from it.[332] If the state treasury sold property to a man, that seems to have been legally as good as a court award, though no actual instance is known of a *dike exoules* brought on this ground.[333]

A defendant who lost a *dike exoules* was required to pay as a fine to the state an amount equal in value to the property concerned.[334] His name was recorded in some public list (perhaps of persons who did not deserve the protection of friends and neighbours against eviction),[335] and the successful prosecutor was entitled to eject (*exeillein*) him; that is, to seize the property due to him, or other property of equal value. Athens had no public officials to execute judgements of this sort. The *dike exoules* was a procedure for authorizing self-help, for permitting a man to use force to recover his property when peaceful methods had failed.[336]

X LIFE IN THE COMMUNITY

WORK

The first duty of an Athenian man was to support himself and his family, whether by producing food on their own farm or by some other means. There was in fact a law against idleness. According to Herodotos, who says that the law was still in force in his own time, Solon got the idea from Egypt, where every year each man had to state the source of his livelihood and anyone failing to show that he had an honest source was condemned to death. According to Lysias, Drakon had made a law on the subject, in which the penalty was death, and Solon lightened the penalty to a fine of 100 drachmas for a first or second offence and outlawry (*atimia*) for a third.[337] In the fourth century there was still a law about idleness, but it is not known whether it was the same as in Solon's time.[338] There is some evidence that offenders against Solon's law were punished by the Areopagos; if so, that at least had been changed by the fourth century.[339]

Normally, of course, an Athenian was free to choose his own method of making a living, provided that it was an honest one. But we do hear of one exception. There was a law about the ferrymen who plied between Salamis and the mainland: any of them who unintentionally overturned his boat in the strait was not allowed to be a ferryman any more.[340] No doubt this law was made after some incident in which passengers were drowned. It is interesting as an instance of a law made to protect the general public against a man practising his profession incompetently. Doctors were treated more favourably than ferrymen: if a patient died, the doctor could not be prosecuted for causing the death by his negligence.[341]

TRADE

Far the commonest way of earning a living in the community was by growing or making some product and offering it for sale. The sale of substantial property has been described in chapter IX, but the present chapter is a suitable place to consider retail and wholesale trade.

Most trade was retail trade: a man who made shoes (or who owned slaves who made shoes) sold them directly to the customers who would wear them. This kind of trading was done in the Agora in the centre of Athens. There was another Agora in Peiraieus, and possibly other towns and villages had small markets too, but we know nothing about them, and it seems clear that the Agora in Athens was the principal market for the whole of Attika. It was also a focal point for the life of the community generally, where people would meet and talk and lounge even if they had no buying or selling to do. A man who was excluded from it (for example, a man accused of homicide: see page 111) was cut off not only from the market but from a substantial part of ordinary social intercourse and public life.

The privilege of trading in the Agora was sometimes denied to aliens, but the extent of the restrictions is not entirely clear. It is stated in Demosthenes 57. 31–2 that a 'law of Solon' forbade an alien to do business in the Agora, and that later this law was re-enacted on the proposal of Aristophon. (Perhaps this was done in 403/2, when Aristophon may have been responsible for the re-enactment of Perikles's law on citizenship: see page 67). But a few sentences later (57. 34) there is mention of an aliens' tax (*xenika*) paid by aliens selling goods in the Agora. The best explanation of this seems to be that the law forbade aliens to trade in the Agora unless they paid a tax for the privilege of doing so, but there was a period in the fifth century when the law lapsed and aliens were able to use the Agora without paying tax. However, at the time of the Peloponnesian War (and the same may well have been true during other wars), when men from neighbouring enemy states were naturally forbidden to enter Attika to sell their goods, there was also a ban on goods imported from enemy states, whoever was selling them.[342] It is worth noticing that laws of this sort favoured Athenian producers, who thereby had less competition to face, rather than Athenian consumers, who might have benefited from having more goods available for purchase.

There was also the decree excluding Megarians from the use of the Athenian Agora (and from harbours in the Athenian empire), which was passed about 433 and came to be regarded as one of the principal causes of the Peloponnesian War.[343] G. E. M. de Ste Croix has recently argued that this decree was not intended to prevent Megarians from trading in Athens, since it excluded them only from 'the civic Agora'.[344] But I think that his attempt to distinguish the market from the civic centre is mistaken. The Athenians used the same word for both; de Ste Croix writes of 'the agora' and 'the Agora', but the Athenians do not appear to have felt any need to use two different expressions. Admittedly, there is some vagueness about the boundaries of the Agora. There were boundary stones, two of which, dating from about 600, have been found *in situ*, but these seem to have become covered over, perhaps by the fourth century, and there is little doubt that by then the area of the market extended beyond them.[345] Possibly new and more extensive boundaries were then drawn; more likely the Athenians just called the whole civic centre and market area 'the Agora' without worrying that its boundaries were not defined exactly.

Activities in the Agora were under the supervision of the agoranomoi (controllers of the market). These officials, five for the Agora in Athens and five for that in Peiraieus, were appointed annually by lot. Accusations were made to them if any trader lied about his goods or sold goods which were adulterated.[346] Fishmongers were not allowed to sprinkle water over their stock to make it look fresher than it was.[347] There may have been some regulation of prices too; one scholiast says that prices of fish, including eels, were fixed by law.[348] The agoranomoi also supervised public order in the Agora. Thus in Aristophanes's *Wasps* a woman bread-seller, whose loaves Philokleon has knocked out of her basket on to the ground, proceeds to summon him to appear before the agoranomoi for damaging her goods.[349]

Grain and flour were sold in a special part of the Agora, which in the fourth century was supervised not by the agoranomoi but by the sitophylakes (guardians of grain). They too for some time numbered five in Athens and five in Peiraieus, but by Aristotle's time the numbers had been increased to twenty and fifteen respectively. They enforced a law which forbade excessive prices for unmilled grain, for meal, and for bread. Another law, a breach of which is the subject of the speech *Against the Grain-dealers* (Lysias 22), forbade dealers to accumulate more than 50 phormoi of grain at one time. The purpose of this law must have been to prevent dealers from hoarding grain in the hope of selling it later at a higher price. In the one case known to us the steps to enforce it were taken not by the sitophylakes but by the Boule, in much the same way as the Boule acted against officials for maladministration (see pages 169–70).[350]

That was the retail trade; separate again was the wholesale trade in grain, by which merchants importing grain to Peiraieus from overseas sold it to the grain-dealers. This trading was not done in the Agora but in the *emporion*, which had its own ten supervisors (*epimeletai tou emporiou*). The *emporion* was an area whose limits were marked by signs of some kind; it is not known how far it extended, but it must have included the whole harbour of Peiraieus.[351] In the second half of the fourth century there were several laws which must have been introduced at some time when there was a scarcity of grain in Athens: one law required merchants to transport to the city of Athens two-thirds of any cargo of grain which they imported to the Athenian *emporion*; other laws forbade Athenian citizens and metics to import grain to any market except Athens, or to lend money to finance the importation of grain to any market except Athens. Prosecutions for infringement of any of these laws were brought before the supervisors of the *emporion*. The penalty, at least in some cases, was an 'extreme' one; that may mean death with confiscation of property.[352]

Yet another board of officials was the metronomoi (controllers of measures), five for Athens and five for Peiraieus, who inspected the measures and weights used by traders.[353] It is possible that they had judicial competence like the agoranomoi, sitophylakes, and supervisors of the *emporion*, and thus would receive accusations of use of false measures or weights and take cases into court for trial, though no such case is actually recorded.

False coins were another hazard of Athenian trading. A law prescribed death as the penalty for producing counterfeit coins.[354] There was an official coin-tester, a state-owned slave who sat in the Agora and tested for genuineness any coin brought to him for that purpose. A law proposed by Nikophon in 375/4, which has recently been discovered in the Agora excavations, provided for the appointment of another coin-tester for Peiraieus and laid down that any seller who refused to accept a coin passed by the tester was liable to prosecution before the officials called 'collectors of the people' (*syllogeis tou demou*), or before the sito-phylakes or the supervisors of the *emporion* if the offence was committed in their areas. The penalty was confiscation of all the goods which the offender was offering for sale in the market on that day, and if he was a slave he was beaten fifty lashes with the whip.[355]

For some offences concerning trade the legal procedure called *phasis* was available; it is attested in cases of selling goods imported from an enemy state, of importation of grain to a market other than Athens, and of refusal to accept a coin passed as genuine by the coin-tester;[356] and it may well have been used in other trading cases. A *phasis*, like a *graphe*, could be brought by anyone who wished to prosecute, whether or not he personally was affected by the offence. It is not known what formal differences there were between the two procedures, but the significant practical difference was that the prosecutor in a *phasis*, if he won the case, received half of the fine which was imposed on the offender.[357] That was a strong incentive; presumably the Athenians had found that without it offenders of this kind tended to escape unprosecuted.

The special arrangements made under the mercantile laws in the middle of the fourth century for prompt trial of cases concerning contracts made in the *emporion* are discussed in chapter XV.

TOWN REGULATIONS

Besides the various market officials, *AP* tells us of ten *astynomoi* (controllers of the town), five for Athens and five for Peiraieus, who enforced a number of miscellaneous regulations in the urban area.

'They check that flute-girls, harp-girls, and lyre-girls are not hired for more than two drachmas, and if several men want the same one they draw lots and let her to the winner. They also see to it that no dung-collector deposits dung within ten stades of the city wall; and they stop anyone building over a street, extending railings [balconies?] over a street, making gutters which discharge water into the street from above, and opening windows [constructing shutters so as to open?] into the street.' Assisted by public slaves, they remove those who die in the streets.' (*AP* 50. 2)

There is no reason to suppose this list exhaustive; there were probably other town regulations of which we have no knowledge. Presumably the astynomoi, like other magistrates, could fine or take into court for trial anyone accused of infringing them.

MILITARY SERVICE

Every man between his eighteenth and his sixtieth year, if he was an Athenian citizen or metic resident in Attika, had to turn out for military or naval service when required. He might serve in the cavalry (providing his own horse and equipment) or as a hoplite (a fully armed infantryman, providing his own armour) or as a soldier without full armour (*psilos*) or as a sailor. Some men preferred to serve in the cavalry, whether because it was less dangerous than the infantry or because it was more spectacular; some preferred not to serve in the cavalry, because it was more expensive. Any dispute about whether a man should be enrolled in the cavalry or not was decided by the Boule, which held a review (*dokimasia*) to check whether a man was sufficiently rich and physically fit; anyone who joined the cavalry without first undergoing this review was liable to disfranchisement (the same penalty as for desertion from the army).[358] We do not hear of any legal rule or procedure for deciding whether a man could be enrolled as a hoplite. The modern suggestion that those in the property-class of *zeugitai* became hoplites automatically is unsupported by evidence. Possibly each individual was allowed to choose for himself whether to serve as a hoplite or as a *psilos* or sailor, weighing the greater prestige of hoplite status against the greater expense.

Calling up men for service when they were needed was done by the ten strategoi (generals) assisted by the ten taxiarchs and other staff; for the cavalry, it was done by the two hipparchs, assisted by the ten phylarchs. Presumably illness or tenure of public office was legally acceptable as an excuse for not serving. So was membership of a chorus for a festival or responsibility for collecting a tax, and so also was absence from Attika. A man named Polyainos complained when he was called up only two months after returning to Athens from abroad, but it is not clear whether this complaint had legal justification.[359]

A man who evaded military service was guilty of cowardice (*deilia*). The law about cowardice seems to have mentioned three offences: not performing military service (*astrateia*), leaving one's post (*lipotaxion*), and throwing away one's shield (sc. to run away). But the orators' references show that distinctions between these were not drawn precisely, and did not need to be, since the legal procedure and penalty were the same for them all. The procedure was *graphe*, so that the charge could be brought by any citizen, not only by the military officers. The military officers were the magistrates who brought the case into court; the jury consisted of soldiers who had served on the campaign. The penalty was disfranchisement.[360]

For other offences on active service the strategoi (or the hipparchs in the case of the cavalry) had authority to punish summarily. In the fifth century they seem to have been able to put to death a man caught communicating with the enemy.[361] But they must have lost this power by Aristotle's time, when they had authority to place a man under arrest, or to dismiss him with ignominy, or to impose a fine.[362] If they thought an offender deserved a more serious penalty than they had authority to impose, they would have to bring him to trial in a court in the ordinary way on their return to Athens. It is nowhere stated what constituted an offence on active service, and we must assume that no distinct code of military law existed. Presumably the strategoi could decide for themselves what acts deserved punishment. But anyone who considered that they had misused their authority would be free to make an accusation against them at their *euthyna* at the end of the year. Since they were democratically elected for a year at a time, they would think twice before imposing a penalty likely to be unpopular.

LITURGIES

A liturgy (*leitourgia*) was a kind of public service required of the richest men in Athens, both citizens and (for certain types of liturgy) metics. It involved payment of money in support of some public activity; usually it involved other duties too. Some liturgies were concerned with public religious festivals, such as the Dionysia or the Panathenaia: a man might be appointed a khoregos, to pay the expenses of one of the choruses (tragic or comic or dithyrambic) and provide facilities for it, or a gymnasiarch, to support a team of relay-runners for a torch-race, or an arkhitheoros, to support the Athenian team of entrants for one of the international festivals, such as the Olympic or the Pythian games. The number of men needed to perform these festival liturgies was around a hundred in each year.[363] Another kind of liturgy was the trierarchy. A trierarch had to pay and arrange for the maintenance of a ship in the Athenian navy; he also was its captain if it was sent out to sea, unless he preferred to pay someone else to perform that task for him. From about 411 onwards a trierarchy was normally shared by two men, and later by a larger number: there was a panel of 1200 trierarchs during the years 357–40, and a panel of 300 thereafter.[364] Yet another kind of liturgy introduced in the fourth century was the *proeisphora*: a man was appointed to pay to the state treasury the whole amount of tax (*eisphora*) due from a number of taxpayers, and then proceeded to recover as much of it as he could from those who were liable to pay it. The number of men required to pay *proeisphora* was 300 on each occasion (not every year) when the tax was levied.[365]

Each year men were appointed to all these liturgies by the appropriate magistrates; the arkhon appointed khoregoi for the tragic choruses at the Dionysia, the strategoi appointed trierarchs, and so on. Sometimes a man keen to serve Athens or display his wealth would volunteer for a liturgy. Otherwise the richest men available were appointed, but the law specified certain exemptions. Minors were exempt from all liturgies until one year after coming of age. The nine arkhons were certainly exempt from the trierarchy, and very likely from all liturgies. The preserved clause of the law says 'No one is to be exempt from the trierarchy except the nine arkhons', but in practice it seems clear that disabled men and cleruchs (residents in Athenian settlements overseas) were not appointed. No one could be required to perform two liturgies in the same or successive years, though after 357 membership of the trierarchic panels did not count for this purpose. A law saying that one man need not perform the same liturgy twice must have applied only to festival liturgies, not to the trierarchy or *proeisphora*. There was also a rule that the khoregos of a boys' chorus must be over forty years old. A man who was appointed to a liturgy and claimed exemption on any of these grounds made his excuse (*skepsis*) to the appointing magistrate, who, if not disposed to accept it, brought the case into court for decision by a jury.[366]

If a man appointed to a liturgy could not claim exemption on any of these grounds, he might nevertheless seek to avoid service by claiming that there was some richer man, not exempt, who should have been appointed in preference to him. This was the occasion for the procedure called *antidosis* ('exchange'). The procedure could be initiated only on a day fixed each year for this purpose by the magistrate responsible for each kind of liturgy. On that day any man appointed to a liturgy could challenge another to choose between two alternatives: either (if he admitted being richer) to take over the liturgy from the challenger, or (if he claimed to be poorer) to hand over the whole of his property in exchange for that of the challenger, who would then perform the liturgy himself. If the man challenged chose the second alternative, to exchange property, each of them swore an oath (its wording is not known, but presumably they swore to hand over all their property and keep nothing back) and within three days each had to produce an inventory of his own possessions, showing debts and liabilities as well as assets. Each could also, if he wished, go with witnesses to the other's house or estate to observe what was there and seal the doors of barns or store-rooms, to check that his opponent did not remove anything surreptitiously. A law in force in the 320s allowed property in the silver-mines to be excluded from the exchange, but we are not told when or why this exception was introduced.[367]

The whole procedure is an astonishing example of Athenian logic.

The idea that two men, who each claim that the other's property is superior, should exchange is perfectly rational. Yet it meant that a family who had lived on the same farm for many generations might, at a few days' notice, leaving behind everything they had, move to a farm in another part of Attika, or to a city house with a factory or bank or other means of livelihood. Some modern scholars have found this totally incredible. But their attempts to interpret the evidence differently have not been very successful. Among the phrases which we find in different speeches concerning *antidosis* are these: 'they broke down the doors of the rooms, as if they already belonged to them by the *antidosis*'; 'I am willing to surrender what I have in the mining works too, besides my other property, if he hands over to me just his hill farm without encumbrance'; 'whether I have Phainippos's property or my own'; 'the pair of oxen and the slaves and all that he got from the country by the *antidosis*'.[368] In the face of such expressions we should accept that exchanges of property could actually occur.

Nevertheless, it seems unlikely that they occurred often. Probably the more usual position was that the man challenged, though unwilling to take on the liturgy, did not want to exchange property either. If the challenger submitted to the magistrate a written statement that the man challenged had neither taken on the liturgy nor given his property in exchange, the magistrate arranged for a trial by a jury. The case was a *diadikasia*: neither man was regarded as prosecutor or defendant, but the jury had simply to decide which of them was to perform the liturgy.[369] There is one surviving speech composed for such a case in the 320s, the speech *Against Phainippos* (Demosthenes 42). The speaker (whose name is not known) has been appointed by the strategoi to the liturgy of *proeisphora*. He claims that he has lost much money recently, and that Phainippos, a young farmer who has never performed any liturgies, is much better off; and so he has challenged Phainippos to *antidosis*. At first Phainippos seems to have agreed that he would exchange property. The speaker proceeded to inspect Phainippos's farm and seal the barns, and he also made out an inventory of his own property. But then Phainippos unsealed the barns and neglected to produce his inventory on time; so the speaker reported to the strategoi that Phainippos was not carrying out an exchange of property in the proper manner. Phainippos also made a counter-charge that the speaker had not made out his inventory properly; and it may be that either party, not just the original challenger, could demand a *diadikasia* if he claimed that the exchange was not being correctly carried out. But that does not mean that the jury had to regulate the details of an exchange: when a *diadikasia* took place, the proposal to exchange property lapsed, and the jury simply ordered one man or the other to perform the liturgy. We do not know who was the loser in the Phainippos case.

After it was settled who was to perform a liturgy, one would expect that there were some legal sanctions against a man who failed to perform it properly. For the trierarchy, it is clear that there were indeed procedures for prosecution and punishment, at least in the fourth century. At that time a trierarch, like a magistrate, was subject to *eisangelia* before the Boule, and also to *euthyna* at the end of his year (as described later in this chapter).[370] Some detailed evidence exists for the period after the reform of the trierarchy in 357, when we find references to the apostoleis (dispatchers of ships) and the supervisors of the docks (*epimeletai ton neorion*). These magistrates could imprison a trierarch who failed to perform his duties. If a ship was damaged or destroyed, whether by a storm or by enemy action or by a trierarch's negligence, or if some of its equipment disappeared, they brought into court a *diadikasia*, in which the jury had to decide whether the cost of replacement should be paid by the state treasury or by an individual trierarch or by some other person.[371] For the earlier period there is little evidence, but a sentence of 'the Old Oligarch' and several fragmentary inscriptions show that the supervisors of the docks (for whom *neoroi* seems to have been an alternative name at that time) existed before the end of the fifth century, and that the procedure of *diadikasia* was already in use then for ships' equipment.[372] There is also the speech *Against Polykles* (Demosthenes 50), which shows how a negligent trierarch might have a private case brought against him: Apollodoros was a trierarch in 362/1 and at the end of the year his successor Polykles did not present himself punctually to take over the ship, and so Apollodoros continued as trierarch for several more months and afterwards prosecuted Polykles to recover the extra expenses.

For the *proeisphora*, a man who was appointed to the liturgy and failed to pay was certainly liable to prosecution, but nothing is known about the procedure.[373] There is nothing to show whether procedures existed for enforcing the proper performance of festival liturgies.

DEBT TO THE STATE

The organization of public finance, with the various treasuries, financial officials, and sources of revenue, is too large a subject to be discussed in detail here, but a few words may be said about the legal proceedings to which a man became liable if he failed to pay money which he owed to the state.

Debts could be incurred in various ways. One was lease of public property (including mines: see page 137), for which rent fell due to be paid once a year or at more frequent intervals. Another was taxation. The normal system of securing collection of a tax was that the right to collect it was sold by auction; the highest bidder obtained the right to collect the tax for one year from those who were liable to pay it, and in the course of the year he paid over to the state the amount of his bid, keeping any surplus as his own profit. By this system only the man who had bought the right to collect a tax incurred a debt to the state; the persons who were liable to the tax owed their money not to the state but to the tax-collector as an individual. Another way of incurring a debt to the state was by being condemned to pay a fine for some offence.

The Boule had one meeting in each of the ten prytanies of the year at which payments due at regular intervals, such as rents and taxes, were received by the apodektai ('receivers'), who were also responsible for bringing a case into court for trial if there was a dispute about whether a payment was due. Payments falling due only once a year mostly did so in the ninth prytany (early in the summer). Anyone failing to make a payment when it fell due was reported to the praktores ('exactors'), or to the treasurers of Athena and the other gods if a payment was owed to them, and these officials kept lists of the debtors. A fine was payable from the moment when it was imposed by a magistrate or jury, and was reported to the praktores immediately.[374]

Legal safeguards were apparently found necessary to preserve the accuracy of the lists of debtors, for we hear of prosecutions by *graphe* before the thesmothetai when a name which should have been on a list was not, or when a name which should not have been was. The prosecutions were called *graphe agraphiou* or *graphe pseudengraphes* or *graphe bouleuseos*; these phrases are not well defined in the texts which we have, but probably a *graphe* could be brought both against the official who falsified the record and against the person who induced him to do so.[375]

Any citizen who was recorded as a debtor to the state was regarded as disfranchised until he paid up, and so was liable to prosecution by *endeixis* if he entered any of the places or performed any of the functions from which disfranchised citizens were debarred (see pages 74–5).[376]

Further penalties ensued if the debtor had still not paid up by the ninth prytany. His debt was then doubled; if due to the gods' treasury, it was multiplied by ten.[377] (It is not clear whether payments which only fell due in the ninth prytany, if they were not paid on the dot, were doubled immediately or not until the ninth prytany of the following year.) Moreover his property became liable to confiscation.

The procedure for confiscation was called *apographe*. As in other public cases, any volunteer could prosecute. Anyone who considered that some man had no excuse for failing to pay off a debt to the state, since he possessed some property which could be used for paying it, could propose that his property be confiscated to pay the debt. The method of initiation was the same as for prosecution by *graphe*, except that the written charge submitted by the prosecutor consisted of a list (*apographe*) of the land, houses, slaves, and other property which he proposed should be confiscated. The magistrates in charge of this kind of case were the Eleven. Any such lists that they received were read out at the principal (*kyria*) meeting of the Ekklesia in the next month, to alert anyone else who might wish to claim that some item of property proposed for confiscation belonged in fact to him. At the trial the defendant might maintain that he did not owe any debt to the state, and that his property was therefore not liable to confiscation; it was also possible for anyone else to intervene with a counter-claim (*enepiskep-testhai*) that the property or part of it was his, or that the defendant owed money to him too. When there were several claimants the trial was called a *diadikasia*, though we know little of how it was arranged, except that each man intervening with a counter-claim had to pay a deposit (*parakatabole*) of one-fifth of the value of his claim, which he forfeited to the state if his claim failed. If the jury voted that the property was to be confiscated to the state, it was handed over to the poletai (the officials who sold state property) and they sold it by auction. The amount which it raised was set against the debt owed to the state. If it was enough to pay off the whole debt, the debtor ceased to be disfranchised and any surplus from the sale was returned to him; but if it was not enough, his debt was merely reduced by that amount and he remained disfranchised. The prosecutor was rewarded for his efforts with three-quarters of the amount which the state recovered. It is not clear why this kind of public case was considered to justify such a remarkably high premium.[378]

It was also possible for a debtor to the state to be imprisoned. Andokides tells us that before 403 the Boule had authority to imprison in the stocks any tax-collector who defaulted on his payments to the state. Subsequently this law was modified in some way; it is not quite clear how, but it seems probable that in the fourth century the debtor could avoid imprisonment by paying double the original debt, whereas in the fifth century the Boule could, if it thought fit, keep him imprisoned even after he had paid up, as a penalty for the lateness of his payment.[379] Also, when a person was condemned by a jury to pay a fine for some offence, it was sometimes stipulated that he was to be held in prison until he paid it (see page 257).

Some, perhaps all, of those who contracted to make payments to the state at future dates, such as those who bought the right to collect a tax, were required, when they made the agreement, to provide sureties (*engyetai*), men who promised to pay the sum due if the debtor himself did not. If in the event the debt was not paid either by the debtor himself or by his sureties, the sureties became liable to the same penalties of confiscation and imprisonment as the debtor.[380]

It could, of course, happen that a debtor had too little property to be worth confiscating, and that no one proposed to the Boule that he should be imprisoned. In that case, provided that he observed the restrictions of disfranchisement, he might leave his debt unpaid indefinitely.

PUBLIC OFFICIALS: 'DOKIMASIA'

Any Athenian man of citizen status, if not disfranchised or incapacitated, might be selected to hold some public office. This is not the place for a complete account of the functions of public officials; for that readers must turn to books on the Athenian constitution. Here I discuss only the legal procedures involved.

The first such procedure was *dokimasia*, a review to check that a man appointed to office was entitled to hold it. Public officials were appointed either by lot or by election. In Solon's time certain offices were confined to members of certain property-classes, but by the fourth century such limitations had mostly been annulled, and those which theoretically remained were not enforced in practice.[381] Any citizen then might be selected by lot or election, but before entering upon the office he had to undergo *dokimasia* by a jury in a court under the presidency of the thesmothetai. Those selected by lot to be the nine arkhons for the following year had also first to undergo *dokimasia* by the Boule; at an earlier period rejection by the Boule was final, but by

Aristotle's time the jury always had the final decision, so that the Boule's decision must have been merely prejudicial, suggesting a verdict to the jurors but not binding them. Men picked by lot for membership of the next year's Boule underwent *dokimasia* by the outgoing Boule only, not by a jury (though a man rejected by the Boule may have had the right to appeal to a jury if he wished).[382]

The form of the *dokimasia* was that each candidate was first asked certain standard questions: the names of his father, mother, and both grandfathers, and their demes; the location of his family tombs and shrines of Apollon Patroos and Zeus Herkeios; whether he looked after his parents, paid his taxes, and performed his military service. He had to produce witnesses to confirm his answers. Then anyone who wished was allowed to make an accusation, against which the candidate could speak in his own defence. After that (or immediately, if no accusations were made) the jury (or the Boule) voted to accept or reject him.[383] In strict law presumably the only kind of accusation allowed was that the man was legally disqualified for the office for which he had been selected, either because he was not an Athenian citizen, or because he was disfranchised, or because he was not old enough (for membership of the Boule, and probably for all offices, a man had to be at least thirty), or because he had held the same office before (only military officers could be re-elected without limit; membership of the Boule could be held twice only), or because his appointment infringed some other specific rule, such as the rule in force in the 390s that a man who had served in the cavalry under the Thirty (in 404/3) might not become a member of the Boule.[384] But in practice, as we see from several surviving speeches composed for *dokimasia* proceedings (Lysias 16, 25, 26, 31), the temptation to introduce extraneous questions, and to argue not only whether the candidate was legally qualified but whether he was a good and patriotic citizen, was often not resisted.

The whole procedure of *dokimasia*, whether held in a court or in the Boule, was much like an ordinary trial. There were, however, three important differences. First, most of the candidates selected by lot or election probably had no accusation made against them; nevertheless they still had to appear before the jury or Boule, answer the standard questions, and be voted on. Secondly, an accusation could be made on the spot, without previous notice. Thirdly, if the vote went against a man, he was not subject to punishment; he was merely excluded from the office to which he had been appointed. In that sense it seems not to

have been regarded as an offence for a man to allow his name to go
forward for selection for an office which he was not actually entitled
to hold.

PUBLIC OFFICIALS: 'APOKHEIROTONIA' AND 'EISANGELIA'

Once a man had entered upon a public office, legal procedures were
available for use against him if he misused his authority or neglected his
duties. One was a vote in the Ekklesia. At the principal (*kyria*) meeting
of the Ekklesia in each prytany – that is, once every thirty-six days or
so – there was a vote (*epikheirotonia*) on the question whether the holders
of public offices seemed to be performing their duties well. If the vote
went against anyone, he was deposed from his office; this was called
apokheirotonia. A trial normally followed; and indeed one passage of
AP, referring to the strategoi, says that a deposition led to a trial, and
acquittal in the trial led to reinstatement in the office.[385] But it is not
certain that each of these consequences followed automatically by law.
A vote that an official did not perform his duties well seems too vague
to constitute, in itself, the charge in a trial. It may be better to suppose
that prosecution and trial required a separate initiative, which however
was virtually always taken; and presumably the prosecutor could use
whichever procedure (*graphe* or *eisangelia* or some other) was appropriate to the charge which he wished to make. A decision to re-
instate a deposed official, or alternatively to appoint someone else in his
place, may also have been made separately, by a decree of the Ekklesia.[386] The most notorious deposition was that of Perikles: in 430
he was removed from his position as a strategos and fined. Soon
afterwards he became a strategos again, but it is uncertain whether he
was reinstated in the same year by a decree of the Ekklesia or was
merely elected at the normal election for the following year.[387] Another notorious instance, the deposition of the strategoi who commanded the Athenian fleet at the battle of Arginousai, will be examined
in a later chapter (see pages 186–9).

Another method of checking the misconduct of officials lay in the
hands of the Boule. The Boule's duties included the supervision of
many administrative matters, and ten of its members acted as logistai
(auditors) to inspect officials' accounts every prytany.[388] With this went
the power to punish officials for maladministration. The initiative
would often be taken by the Boule's own members, but any citizen
could make to the Boule an accusation that an official had transgressed

the laws. Examples of both are found in the speech *On the Chorister* (Antiphon 6): on two occasions the speaker of that speech brought prosecutions for embezzlement before the Boule; at the time of the second he was himself a member of the Boule, but the first was in the previous year when he had not yet become a member. This kind of prosecution was called *eisangelia* (at least when brought by a non-member of the Boule; whether cases initiated by the Boule itself were so called is uncertain). It must be distinguished from *eisangelia* for treason (described on pages 183–6), where the Boule could not try the case and decide the verdict unless it was authorized by the Ekklesia to do so. In an *eisangelia* for an official's misconduct the Boule did give a verdict and could impose a fine of up to 500 drachmas, but the case had to be referred to a court if the Boule considered that a heavier penalty was required. There remain a number of uncertainties about the trial of officials by the Boule, and the evidence is too complex to be discussed here. Readers who are interested in it should consult the discussions by P. J. Rhodes, who has shown that the Boule was concerned with a wide variety of administrative cases, and M. H. Hansen, who has made headway in distinguishing the different kinds of *eisangelia*.[389]

PUBLIC OFFICIALS: 'EUTHYNA'

The main investigation of a public official's conduct was the one called *euthyna*. This took place after he demitted office, which for most officials was at the end of the year. A man continuing in office for more than one year probably had to undergo it each year, though if he was abroad on duty (for instance a military officer on a campaign) it would naturally wait until he returned to Athens. It applied not only to the arkhons and other magistrates, but to all who were appointed to perform public duties, including priests, ambassadors, trierarchs, members of the Boule, and members of the Areopagos (but not jurors). Until it was completed, the man under investigation was not allowed to leave Attika, nor to take various other kinds of action which might dispose of any money which he might be found to have misappropriated.[390]

The first part of the investigation was financial. It was conducted by ten logistai (auditors) assisted by ten synegoroi (speakers). These were selected from all the citizens by lot, and thus were distinct from the logistai appointed by the Boule. They called upon each official to submit his accounts of the public money which he had received and spent during his term of office. If he had not received any public money, he still had to submit a written statement saying so, and even that did not exempt him from the rest of the procedure; for it is obvious that even a man whose duties did not involve public money might still be guilty of accepting bribes, which was one of the offences falling within the purview of the logistai. After inspecting the accounts they brought each man into a court with a jury; it appears that the logistai presided in the court and the synegoroi presented the case against any man whose accounts appeared unsatisfactory. Even if no fault was found in the accounts, a herald invited anyone who wished to make an accusation. (Presumably only financial charges were admitted at this stage of the *euthyna*.) The jury might find a man guilty of *klope*, which means theft or embezzlement, deliberately appropriating public money to one's own use; or of *dora*, accepting bribes; or of the vaguer and less serious *adikion*, which probably means causing loss of public money by culpable neglect or inadvertence, as opposed to deliberate deception. For the first two offences, a man found guilty had to repay ten times the amount of money involved, and his descendants as well as himself were disfranchised until he paid up. For *adikion* he only had to repay the simple amount.[391]

When the financial part of the investigation was complete, the investigation of other kinds of misconduct in office followed. This was conducted by ten euthynoi, who were members of the Boule, one selected by lot from each of the ten tribes; each was assisted by two paredroi (assessors), also selected by lot. They sat in the open Agora, where anyone wishing to accuse any man whose investigation by the logistai had recently been completed could hand his charge in writing to the euthynos of the tribe to which the accused man belonged. Presumably the charge might be either of neglect of duty or of positive misuse of power. The euthynos read it, and if he thought it well founded he delivered a formal condemnation. In the fourth century, at least, his condemnation was not final, but was passed on to the appropriate magistrates for trial by their normal procedures: to the tribe judges (see page 206) if the offence was a private one, to the thesmothetai if it was public.[392] This seems to have been the procedure used by Demosthenes and Timarkhos to accuse Aiskhines of misconduct as an ambassador in 346, leading eventually to the trial for which the surviving speeches of Demosthenes and Aiskhines *On the False Embassy* were composed.

In the fifth century the authority of the euthynoi may well have been greater. Inscriptions show that at that period there were thirty logistai, who were concerned with calculating sums payable to the treasuries of Athena and the other gods, including the quota from the tribute paid by the cities of the Athenian Empire; but there is also one passage showing that the euthynoi then held sessions in the rooms called *logisteria*. Perhaps the euthynoi had responsibility for the whole of the *euthyna* of officials, with assistance from the logistai, and it was not until the beginning of the fourth century that the financial part of it was taken over entirely by the logistai, whose other functions had by then been diminished by the ending of the Athenian Empire.[393] There are also several surviving decrees of the fifth century (and only one of the fourth century) in which the amount of a fine to be imposed by a euthynos and his paredroi (either mentioned specifically or implied by the use of the verb *euthyno*) is stated; this suggests, though it does not prove, that in some cases the verdicts of euthynoi may at that time have been final.[394] Certainly it would be in accord with the general trend of development of Athenian legal institutions if powers possessed by individual euthynoi in the fifth century were transferred to juries in the fourth.

CORRUPTION AND IMPROPER PARTICIPATION IN PUBLIC BUSINESS

Bribery seems to have been a serious problem in Athenian public life, if we may judge from the number of references to it in surviving texts. The possibility of conviction for accepting bribes was not limited to officials undergoing *euthyna*. Any person who either offered or accepted a bribe, in connection with either public or private affairs, was liable to prosecution by *graphe*. The penalty was a fine of ten times the amount of the bribe, and the culprit and his descendants were disfranchised until he paid it; Deinarkhos says in one passage that alternatively the death penalty could be imposed.[395]

However, the penalty differed from this in the most notorious of all Athenian trials for bribery, the trial of Demosthenes in 324/3. Harpalos, treasurer of Alexander the Great, fled to Athens bringing with him 700 talents. He was imprisoned, and his money was deposited on the Akropolis; but when he later escaped, only 350 talents were found there, and Demosthenes and others were suspected of receiving the rest as bribes. Demosthenes himself proposed a decree that the council of the Areopagos should be instructed to investigate, and that death should be the penalty for anyone found guilty of taking a bribe from

Harpalos. The Areopagos made a report (*apophasis*: see page 190) against Demosthenes and several others. They were tried in a court by 1500 jurors, but in the end Demosthenes, accused of accepting a bribe of 20 talents, was only fined 50 talents. It seems clear that this case was exceptional: the Ekklesia's decree referring the case to a court must have authorized the jury to decide the penalty on this occasion.[396]

One particularly serious kind of corruption was bribery of members of the Ekklesia or the Boule or a jury to get them to vote for or against something, especially bribery by a defendant to get jurors to acquit him. It is difficult to bribe a large number of voters, but Anytos, when on trial after his failure to prevent the loss of Pylos to the Spartans in 409, is said to have discovered a method of doing so, which was given a special name, *dekazein*. The details of the method are obscure, but it was made the subject of a separate law, with death as the penalty.[397] We have the text of the law as it stood in the mid fourth century.

'If anyone conspires or helps to *dekazein* the Eliaia or any of the law-courts at Athens or the Boule, offering or accepting money for bribery, or forms an association for subversion of the democracy, or as a synegoros accepts money for private or public cases, there are to be *graphai* of them before the thesmothetai.' (Law quoted by Demosthenes 46. 26)

In the courts another possible kind of corruption was the bribery of witnesses. A man who gave false or illegal evidence was liable to prosecution by *dike* for false witness (*pseudomartyrion*), and the man who put him up to doing so could be prosecuted for *kakotekhniai* (see pages 244–5). The procedure of *graphe*, in which any volunteer could prosecute, was used for accusing a man of falsely testifying that a summons had been delivered (*pseudokleteia*; see page 238). To us it would seem natural to regard any kind of perjury by a witness as an offence against the court, obstructing the jurors' attempt to reach the right verdict. It is remarkable that the Athenians apparently regarded it as being, as a rule, an offence only against an individual affected by it and therefore needing only a *dike*; and it is further remarkable that they regarded false testimony about the delivery of a summons as an exception to that rule. Why that in particular was thought to need the *graphe* procedure is obscure; it is not clear that it harmed the community more than other false testimony, or that an individual harmed by it was any more in need of another person to initiate the prosecution for him.

Finally, there were the speakers in the Ekklesia itself. Telling lies in the Ekklesia was 'misleading the people', and could lead to *eisangelia*, as described in chapter XI. But it was also possible to take legal action against a speaker not for what he said but for not being a suitable person to speak at all. The law laid down that a citizen might not address the people if he had maltreated his parents, had failed to perform military service when required or had 'thrown away his shield' (see page 160), had been a prostitute, or had wasted inherited property. If such a person spoke in the Ekklesia, any other citizen could call on him to undergo a *dokimasia*. The *dokimasia* took the form of an ordinary trial in a court, and if the jury found that the orator's life was indeed disgraceful in any of the ways specified, he was disfranchised.[398] The surviving speech of Aiskhines *Against Timarkhos* belongs to such a case. When Timarkhos was speaking in the Ekklesia in 346, Aiskhines denounced him as a prostitute. At the *dokimasia* which followed Aiskhines delivered his speech for the prosecution and the jury gave their verdict against Timarkhos, who consequently was disfranchised and could not proceed with his own prosecution of Aiskhines for misconduct as an ambassador. The assumption underlying this law is striking.

'The legislator considered it impossible for the same man to be bad privately and good publicly, and thought that an orator ought not to come to the platform if he had given previous attention to his speech but not to his way of life. He believed that what was said by an honourable man, even if very clumsily and simply spoken, was useful to the hearers; but that what was said by a disgusting person, who had abused his own body despicably and devoured his ancestral property disgracefully, would not benefit the hearers even if it was spoken very well.' (Aiskhines 1. 30–1)

XI TREASON

TYRANNY AND SUBVERSION OF DEMOCRACY

The most drastic kind of treason is to overthrow the existing government and seize control of the state oneself. In Greek terms an absolute ruler was a 'tyrant', and there is some evidence that in the seventh and sixth centuries an attempt to set up a tyranny was an offence for which trials were held by the Areopagos and the penalty was outlawry (see pages 28–9).

In the time of the Peloponnesian War, when no tyrant had in fact been in power in Athens for almost a century, the Athenians were still afraid of tyranny. Aristophanes makes fun of their ungrounded fears of it, especially at the time of the religious scandals in 415, when rewards were offered for the capture or killing of men aiming at tyranny.[399] But the revolution in 411 showed that oligarchy was a greater threat than tyranny, and from then on 'subversion of the people' became the commoner form of words, although 'tyranny' did not disappear from the law. In 410, when democracy had just been restored, the following law was passed on the proposal of Demophantos.

'If anyone subverts the democracy at Athens, or holds any office when the democracy has been subverted, he shall be an enemy of the Athenians and shall be killed with impunity, and his property shall be confiscated and one-tenth of it shall belong to the Goddess; and he who kills or helps to plan the killing of such a man shall be pure and free from guilt. All Athenians shall swear over unblemished sacrifices by tribes and by demes to kill such a man. The oath shall be as follows: "I shall kill, by word and deed, by vote and by my own hand, if I can, anyone who subverts the democracy at Athens, and anyone who, when the democracy has been subverted, holds any office thereafter, and anyone who sets himself up to be tyrant or helps to set up the tyrant . . ." ' (Law quoted by Andokides 1. 96–7)

Here the main emphasis is on subversion of the democracy, though the setting up of a tyrant is mentioned too. The penalty is outlawry, just as it had been in the sixth century. The oath was doubtless taken by all Athenians in 410 only, not by later generations; but the law, inscribed on stone at the entrance to the Bouleuterion, where members of the Boule would see it every time they came to a meeting, remained in place in the fourth century, and there is no evidence that it was ever annulled.[400] But in 336 an additional law was passed on the proposal of Eukrates. The inscribed text has been found in the excavations in the Agora. After saying briefly that anyone who sets up a tyranny or subverts the democracy may be killed with impunity (which is just a recapitulation of the law of Demophantos) it is mainly concerned with the Areopagos: any Areopagite who attends a meeting when the democracy has been subverted is to suffer disfranchisement (*atimia*) and confiscation of property. Evidently there was in 336 some fear that the democracy might be subverted with the connivance of members of the Areopagos. But investigation of the reasons for that fear would require an analysis of the political circumstances of the period which cannot be attempted here.[401]

BETRAYAL

The English word 'treason' is vague: in Greek, overthrowing the government and seizing control of one's own country was one thing, but betrayal (*prodosia*), giving away one's own country or people to a foreign enemy, was a different crime, the subject of a different law. Betrayal was covered by the same law as theft of sacred property; it is not clear why these two offences were combined in one law, and possibly there was no reason except that the same penalty was considered appropriate for both. The law is reported for us by Xenophon.

> ' . . . this law, which applies to temple-robbers and traitors: if anyone either betrays the state or steals the sacred property, he is to be tried in a court and if he is condemned, he is not to be buried in Attika, and his property is to be confiscated.' (Xenophon *Hellenika* 1. 7. 22)

The wording seems odd: it forbids burial in Attika, but it does not say that the offender is to be put to death. For theft of sacred property we know from other sources that the death penalty was required by law (see page 149). Possibly it was in fact specified in the law quoted by Xenophon both for theft of sacred property and for betrayal, and Xenophon has not troubled to mention it because he thought it obvious. But the case of Themistokles suggests otherwise. Themistokles had already been ostracized from Athens and was living in Argos when, about the year 467, information from Sparta brought him under suspicion of betraying Greek interests to the Persians. He eluded men sent to arrest him, and a trial was held in Athens in his absence, at which he was pronounced guilty of betrayal. Thucydides confirms that, in consequence, it was not legal to bury him in Attika when he died some years later; but Thucydides does not say that he was condemned to death, and another historian, Idomeneus, stated explicitly that the penalty imposed was perpetual exile for Themistokles himself and his family, with confiscation of property. Plato too says that Themistokles was condemned to exile.[402] Plato and Idomeneus could have mistaken the actual upshot for the legal sentence. But it is a better interpretation to assume, in the absence of disproof, that Idomeneus and Plato are correct. If so, the law quoted by Xenophon specified only the ban on burial in Attika and the confiscation of property. Another law must have specified that thieves of sacred property were to be executed; for betrayal, however, there was no law requiring the death penalty, and that left the court free to decide whether death or exile should be imposed. With this offence there must, after all, have been many cases in which a man who had betrayed Athens to an enemy took refuge with that enemy and it was not in practice possible for the Athenians to execute him.

Another instance of this offence, perhaps contemporary with that of Themistokles or perhaps earlier, was that of Hipparkhos (son of Kharmos; in 487 he was the first man ever to be ostracized). He was accused of betrayal, fled before trial, and was condemned to death in his absence; and the Athenians melted down an image of him, making a flat surface on which to inscribe the names of traitors. We are told no details of his offence, but we can presume that the Persians were the enemy to whom he was accused of betraying Athenian interests.[403]

Betrayal was also the charge brought against several members of the oligarchic regime of the Four Hundred after that regime fell in 411. One of them, Phrynikhos, had already been assassinated, but a decree was passed that he should nevertheless be tried for betrayal. He was found guilty, his bones were dug up and cast out of Attika, the property which he had left was confiscated, his house was demolished, and the verdict and penalties were inscribed on bronze.[404] A separate trial was held for two others, Antiphon the orator and Arkheptolemos (Onomakles was to have been tried at the same time, but seems to have escaped), and the *Life of Antiphon* preserved among the works of Plutarch gives us the text of the decree of the Boule making arrangements for the trial, and also the text of the condemnation. The decree instructed the thesmothetai to arrange for the trial, and the strategoi and others to produce the defendants in court and present the case against them; the charge was to be betrayal, and the penalties, if they were found guilty, were to be in accordance with the existing law about traitors. And the condemnation did duly include prohibition of burial in Attika and confiscation of property (the penalties which the law, according to Xenophon, required), together with the penalties (presumably decided by the jury) of execution, demolition of their houses, and disfranchisement of their whole families. All this was to be inscribed on bronze beside the decisions about Phrynikhos. It is notable that these oligarchs were not prosecuted for subversion of the democracy. The text of the decree is clear (and must be preferred to Thucydides's vague phrase 'accused of helping to set up [the regime of the Four Hundred?]'): they were charged with betrayal because they had gone as envoys to Sparta to the detriment of Athens, they had travelled on an enemy ship, and they had set foot in enemy-occupied Dekeleia.[405] This confirms that, as far as the law was concerned, betrayal (*prodosia*) meant betrayal to a foreign enemy, in this case Sparta, and was a different offence from subversion of the Athenian constitution. The reason why Antiphon and Arkheptolemos were not accused of subversion of the democracy may have been simply that their trial (in the autumn of 411) was held under the regime of the Five Thousand, which included other men who had equally been involved in establishing oligarchic government. But another possible reason is that subversion of the democracy may not have been explicitly forbidden before the law of Demophantos was passed in 410 (see page 175): it may have seemed doubtful whether the regime of the Four Hundred could be called 'tyranny', which was what the older law forbade.

A general was liable to be prosecuted for betrayal if he was alleged to have allowed a foreign power to win a battle or gain some advantage, and several cases of this kind are known. So, for example, Anytos was prosecuted in 409 because he failed to prevent the Spartans from recapturing Pylos, Timotheos in 373 because he did not sail round the Peloponnese to stop the Spartan siege of Kerkyra, and Khabrias in 366 because he had allowed the Thebans to occupy Oropos.[406]

A supplement to the law about betrayal was made in 338. After the battle of Khaironeia, when the Macedonians were expected to invade

Attika, the Athenians passed a decree that anyone who fled from Attika should be held guilty of betrayal (see page 185). One such offender was summarily executed by the Areopagos (see page 191), but there was also at least one man who underwent a normal prosecution and trial on this charge: this was Leokrates, who seems actually to have left Athens before the decree was passed, taking his family to Rhodes and afterwards to Megara, where he stayed for some years. In 331/0 he returned to Athens, and Lykourgos prosecuted him for betrayal. The only surviving speech of Lykourgos is the one which he delivered in this case, containing extravagant denunciations of the treachery of a man who deserted his country in its hour of need. Aiskhines tells us the result: the votes were equal on both sides, and so Leokrates was acquitted. 'If one vote had been changed, he would have been expelled or put to death,' says Aiskhines (3. 252).

If that text is right (emendation has been proposed),[407] it confirms that at this period, as in the fifth century, either death or exile could be imposed as a penalty for betrayal. Deinarkhos too (1. 63) mentions a man exiled for this offence. Alternatively a mere fine was now possible; Demosthenes tells us (24. 127) that Melanopos, on conviction for betrayal, paid a fine of three talents. That shows that it was no longer a legal requirement that a man found guilty of this offence should have the whole of his property confiscated. The law about betrayal quoted by Xenophon must have been amended or repealed.

MISLEADING THE PEOPLE

Another offence, distinct from betrayal and from subversion of the democracy, was making a false promise to the Athenian people. The law stated that anyone who, making a promise, deceived the people or the Boule or a court was to be punished by death. 'The people' here means the Ekklesia, as is shown by the mention of the Boule and the courts as alternatives; the law was directed against those who caused a public body to make a wrong decision, by leading it to think that some benefit would result when in fact it would not. Demosthenes calls the law an ancient one, and it was probably under this law, or an earlier form of it, that Miltiades was prosecuted in 489. After the battle of Marathon he had promised the Athenians that he would enrich them if they put him in command of seventy ships. He took the ships to Paros, but his siege failed and he himself was injured. On his return to Athens he was prosecuted by Xanthippos for deceiving the Athenians.

He was too ill to make a speech, but he lay on a couch while his friends spoke in his defence. The precise verdict is not clear: Herodotos says that the people decided not to impose the death penalty but a fine of 50 talents; Plato says that the people did vote for the death penalty, but the prytanis (chairman) prevented it. In the law as Demosthenes stated it in the fourth century the penalty had to be death; either the law was different in 489, or the people were somehow persuaded to break it in this case. But it made little difference to Miltiades in the end, since he died soon afterwards from his wound; his son Kimon paid the fine.[408]

Yet another distinct offence was that of a speaker in the Ekklesia who said what he had been bribed by enemies of Athens to say. It was forbidden 'being an orator, to say what is not the best for the Athenian people, receiving money and gifts from the people's opponents'. This was the charge brought against Philokrates. In 346 he had spoken in favour of making the peace (subsequently named after him) with Philip, and proposed the decree to give effect to it; three years later Hypereides prosecuted him for giving wrong advice to the Athenian people because Philip had bribed him. He fled from Athens before the trial and was condemned to death in his absence.[409] A stranger case was that for which Hypereides composed his speech *For Euxenippos*. A dispute had arisen whether two of the Athenian tribes should be allowed to retain possession of a hill at Oropos (on the borders of Attika and Boiotia) which had formerly been sacred to the god Amphiaraos. The Athenian people instructed three citizens, one of whom was an elderly gentleman named Euxenippos, to sleep overnight in the god's temple to ascertain his will. They did so, and Euxenippos duly reported that he had had a dream, which he recounted, though we are not told what it was; probably it was able to be interpreted as meaning that the two tribes should keep the piece of land. Subsequently Polyeuktos prosecuted Euxenippos; the charge was that he had said what was not the best for the Athenian people because he had been bribed by the people's opponents. From the surviving speech of Hypereides for the defence it appears that Euxenippos was liable to be put to death if found guilty, and it seems likely that the death penalty was required by law for this offence. But the result of the case is not known.

An even vaguer offence was 'wronging the people'. This was mentioned in the decree of Kannonos, as reported by Xenophon.

'If anyone wrongs the Athenian people, he is to make his defence in chains at a meeting of the people. If he is found guilty of doing wrong, he is to die and be thrown into the pit [*usually emended to die by being thrown into the pit*], and his property is to be confiscated and one-tenth of it is to belong to the Goddess.' (Xenophon *Hellenika* 1. 7. 20)

References in Kratinos and Aristophanes indicate that it was in force at least from the 420s until the 390s.[410] But no case is known in which anyone was prosecuted specifically under this decree, and there is nothing to show what Kannonos meant by 'wronging the people'.

INFORMING ('MENYSIS')

In cases of treason, especially subversion of the democratic constitution and betrayal to an enemy, it was particularly important to detect the crime before it was carried out, because afterwards no remedy was likely to be practicable. That is why informants were encouraged to report this kind of crime directly to the Ekklesia or the Boule without going through any preliminaries with a magistrate which might cause delay.

The simplest way to proceed was the one generally called *menysis*, which just means 'informing'. Any person, whether man or woman, Athenian or foreigner, free or slave, could go to the Boule or the Ekklesia to reveal the name of a traitor or other serious criminal; it was then up to the Boule or the Ekklesia to decide what to do with the information, and the informer was not required to be the prosecutor in a trial or to take any other action. If, as might often be the situation in such cases, the informer was one member of a conspiracy who had decided to 'turn state's evidence', he could ask to be granted impunity (*adeia*) before he gave his information. A law existed in 415 that an informer was to have impunity if his information was true, but to be put to death if it was false; but in 400 or 399 Andokides (1. 20) spoke of that law as if it were no longer in force, and thereafter probably the terms of impunity were fixed for each informer by the decree of the Boule or the Ekklesia granting it. A slave who gave true information against his own master was normally given his freedom, but this also may have been not a legal requirement but a customary reward conferred by decree in individual cases.[411]

A good example of informing is provided by the affair of Agoratos in 405/4, described in the surviving speech against him (Lysias 13). A man named Theokritos went to a meeting of the Boule and gave information that some men were forming a conspiracy, apparently to take over the government; he would not give their names because he had sworn an oath of loyalty to the conspiracy, but he indicated that Agoratos would do so. The Boule sent some of its own members to arrest Agoratos, and eventually he was brought before another meeting of the Boule and gave a list of names. The men he named were arrested, but at the next meeting of the Ekklesia one of them, Menestratos, was brought into the meeting, was granted impunity by vote of the Ekklesia, and gave further names. The Ekklesia decreed that all the men denounced should be tried in a court with 2000 jurors, but in fact the oligarchic revolution prevented that, and they were eventually tried and condemned by the new oligarchic Boule.[412]

The fullest account of informers which we have is in the speech of Andokides *On the Mysteries*. The profanation of the Mysteries and the mutilation of the Hermai in 415 were religious offences and will therefore be considered in chapter XII (page 198), but in the present chapter we can take evidence from that speech to give a more complete picture of the use of informers. When the Hermai in Athens were found to have been mutilated, the Athenians were very alarmed. The Ekklesia authorized the Boule to take all necessary action to bring the offenders to justice, a team of investigators (*zetetai*) was appointed, and rewards were offered for information. Then a citizen named Pythonikos stood up at a meeting of the Ekklesia and declared that a slave, if granted impunity, would give information about profanation of the Myteries. The slave, named Andromakhos, was fetched; the Ekklesia voted impunity for him; and he declared that Alkibiades and nine other men, whom he listed, had profaned the Mysteries in a private house. Subsequently Teukros, a metic, asked the Boule for impunity, and when he had been given it he listed some men who had profaned the Mysteries and others who had mutilated the Hermai. Further lists were given by a woman named Agariste, a slave named Lydos, a man named Diokleides (his information turned out to be false and he was put to death for it), and Andokides himself. Several people claimed the rewards offered for information; the Ekklesia decreed that a *diadikasia* should be held in the court of the thesmothetai to decide between the claimants, and the rewards were eventually given to Andromakhos and Teukros.[413]

From all this we see how, if the Ekklesia was anxious to receive information about any serious crime, it could by decree appoint investigators and offer rewards, but it was equally possible without these for anyone to offer information to the Ekklesia or to the Boule. Other instances of informing are known, but they add nothing further to our knowledge of the procedure.[414]

'EISANGELIA'

When the Ekklesia or the Boule received information that someone had committed treason or another serious crime, the meeting had to decide what to do about it. They could, of course, decide to do nothing, if the information seemed obviously false or trivial. But if it seemed serious, several possibilities were open. The case could be referred to a court for trial. Or the Boule could hold a trial; but the Boule was not allowed to impose any heavier penalty than a fine of 500 drachmas, so that if it found that a heavier penalty was required it had then to pass the case on to a court or to the Ekklesia. The other possibility, adopted only for the most serious cases, was that the Ekklesia might try the case itself. The decision to follow one of these procedures was made by a normal decree (*psephisma*) of the Boule and the Ekklesia. The decree might also specify what penalty was to be imposed if the defendant was found guilty.

If the informer was an Athenian citizen, it would be normal for the same man to report that a crime had been committed, propose the decree that a trial be held, and act as prosecutor at the trial. The whole of this procedure, in a case initiated by giving information to the Ekklesia or the Boule, was called *eisangelia*. The literal meaning of this word, 'reporting', hardly differs from that of *menysis*, 'informing', and sometimes the two words (or the verbs *eisangellein* and *menyein*) were used as interchangeable synonyms for the act of giving information.[415] But in some cases, for example when the informer was a woman or a slave, the prosecutor was someone other than the informer; and then *eisangelia* could mean the prosecution only, as distinct from the giving of information. It is confusing that the Athenians also used the name *eisangelia* for several other kinds of prosecution: accusing an official of maladministration (see page 170), accusing a guardian of wronging an orphan (see page 94), and accusing an arbitrator of misconducting an arbitration (see page 210). Here we are concerned only with the kind of *eisangelia* which was used for treason and other serious offences.

Which other serious offences? It is plausible to assume that in the earlier period there was no legal restriction, and anyone could try making to the Ekklesia or the Boule any accusation to which he thought they would listen; but in practice they would be unwilling to listen unless the matter concerned the safety and welfare of the whole community, and they would not accept any case for which the law prescribed some other procedure. Some writers of later centuries, beginning with the rhetorician Kaikilios in the first century BC, say that *eisangelia* was a procedure used for new offences about which no law existed.[416] This may have been partly true in the fifth century, when it was possible to accuse someone by *eisangelia* for doing something which was clearly wrong, but which was not specifically forbidden by any law because it had never occurred to anyone that such a crime might be committed; the mutilation of the Hermai (see page 198) is an obvious example. Yet it was not the whole truth even in the fifth century; *eisangelia* was undoubtedly used for some offences about which laws did exist. One example is betrayal; there was a law specifying penalties for betrayal (see page 176), and yet *eisangelia* was the procedure always used for it. And the decree of Diopeithes (see page 200) in one breath laid down the law about atheism and made *eisangelia* the procedure for enforcing it. So we may say, more accurately than Kaikilios, that in the fifth century *eisangelia* was the procedure used, by law or by custom, to prosecute for the various kinds of treason and (after Diopeithes) for atheism, and could also be used for other offences not specified by law if the Boule and Ekklesia considered them serious enough.

But in the fourth century its scope was defined more strictly. The speech of Hypereides *For Euxenippos* quotes part of the law then in force about *eisangelia*, listing the offences for which that procedure was to be used.

> 'If anyone subverts the Athenian people, or attends a meeting anywhere or forms a group for subversion of the people, or if anyone betrays any city or ships or infantry or naval force, or, being an orator, says what is not the best for the Athenian people, receiving money and gifts from the people's opponents . . .'   (Law quoted by Hypereides *For Euxenippos* 7–8, 29)

From this we see that by the second half of the fourth century the three kinds of treason, described in the first three sections of this chapter (subversion of the democracy, betrayal, misleading the people), were listed together in one law which laid down that *eisangelia* was the legal procedure to be used for them. The date of this law is not known. It may well be that until the last decade of the fifth century there was no inscribed law specifying any procedure of prosecution for treason and it was just by custom that *eisangelia* was used, and that it was during the revision and reinscription of the laws in 410–403 (after which no uninscribed law could be enforced: see page 47) that the custom was turned into written law; but that cannot be proved.

Two further questions arise about the law as Hypereides preserves it. First, has he given us a complete list of the offences mentioned in it? His words imply that he has; in particular, he calls the clause about orators 'the last part of the law', which appears to mean that no more offences were listed after the ones which he mentions. However, we know from Demosthenes 49. 67 that in the fourth century *eisangelia* was the procedure prescribed by law if anyone making a promise deceived the people. But this is hardly a significant conflict of evidence. Anyone making a promise to the people would be likely to do so in a speech, and so could be called an orator. So the best explanation is that the clause about orators was indeed the last one, but Hypereides has not quoted it in full; the whole of it will probably have been '. . . or, being an orator, says what is not the best for the Athenian people, receiving money and gifts from the people's opponents, or making a promise deceives the people or the Boule or a court . . .'

Apart from this, we should accept that Hypereides has given us a complete list of the offences mentioned in the law about *eisangelia*. There is no evidence in the orators that it mentioned any others. However, Theophrastos is reported to have said in his *Laws*, now lost, that *eisangelia* was used also against anyone who went into the territory of the enemy, took up residence there, or fought on the enemy's side in war. These are various kinds of betrayal. Probably Theophrastos got them not from the law quoted by Hypereides but from the decree passed in 338 (see pages 178–9), which extended the scope of *eisangelia* by saying that anyone who fled from Attika should be held guilty of betrayal; Theophrastos's wording may well be a more accurate quotation of that decree than Lykourgos's 'those fleeing from risk on behalf of their country'.[417]

The other problem is: does the precision of the list of offences in the law quoted by Hypereides, supplemented by the decree of 338, mean that in the fourth century the *eisangelia* procedure could no longer be used for any other offences than these? Or was it still possible, as in earlier times, to use it for a new offence about which no law existed? Modern scholars have given different answers to this question,[418] but my own view is that, once the law quoted by Hypereides was passed, the offences listed in it were the only ones for which *eisangelia* to the Boule and Ekklesia was permitted. The main grounds for this view are in the speeches of Hypereides. In the Euxenippos case Hypereides takes pains to argue that, whereas the law says '. . . being an orator, says what is not the best for the Athenian people . . .', Euxenippos was not an orator when he recounted his dream and therefore was not guilty of the offence. This implies that in an *eisangelia* case a man was not guilty unless he had done one of the things listed in the law about *eisangelia*. No doubt it could be disputed whether Euxenippos was an orator or not; but that would not have been worth disputing if it had been permissible to bring an *eisangelia* against Euxenippos even if his offence was not one listed in the law. The speech of Hypereides *For Lykophron* is more fragmentary and the details of the case are less clear, but it appears that Lykophron was accused by Ariston by *eisangelia* of subverting the democracy; it was alleged that he had seduced a married woman and thus had undermined the marriage customs of Athens. It seems strange to call such an act subversion of the democracy. The reason for calling it so must have been that an *eisangelia* could not be brought unless the charge was one of those listed in the law about *eisangelia*. Thus Ariston, if he wanted to proceed by *eisangelia*, had to exercise his ingenuity to fit Lykophron's act under one of the heads of the law.

So we may conclude that the purpose of the law quoted by Hypereides was to restrict the use of *eisangelia* to treason. The cases of Euxenippos and Lykophron illustrate the tendency of prosecutors to attempt to use this procedure for bringing cases which were not really cases of treason to the attention of the Ekklesia and Boule. By the time of Aristotle there was a rule that the only meeting of the Ekklesia at which an *eisangelia* could be initiated was the principal (*kyria*) meeting in each prytany; and, at some date probably between 333 and 330, prosecutors in *eisangeliai* were made subject to the fine (imposed in most other kinds of public case: see page 64) of 1000 drachmas if they failed to get one-fifth of the votes in the trial.[419] All these changes should be seen as attempts to prevent the waste of the time of the Ekklesia and Boule on *eisangeliai* brought for trivial reasons.

THE TRIAL OF THE ARGINOUSAI GENERALS

One notorious trial was that of the strategoi who had commanded the Athenian fleet at the battle of Arginousai in 406. It closely resembled an *eisangelia* for treason, but no ancient author actually calls it an *eisangelia*, and a question arises whether the procedure followed was really legal at all.

The Athenian force had won the battle, but twenty-five of their ships had been lost. Most of the surviving sailors from those ships had been left to drown, and a dispute arose whether that was the fault of the strategoi commanding the fleet, or the fault of the trierarchs whom the strategoi had instructed to rescue the men, or whether the rescue had simply been made impossible by a storm.

The course of events after that is reasonably clear from Xenophon's account in *Hellenika* 1. 7. The first legal step taken was that the Athenians dismissed the eight strategoi concerned; this must have been a vote of deposition (*apokheirotonia*: see page 169) in the Ekklesia, and the fact that other men were immediately appointed to fill two of the vacancies shows that this deposition was not just a suspension which would end if the men were acquitted in a trial. Two of the eight deposed strategoi did not return to Athens at all, but the other six did; and the next legal step was that one of them, Erasinides, was prosecuted by Arkhedemos and tried in a court for embezzlement of public money which had come into his hands in the Hellespont. The fact that this case came to trial before anything more was done about the other strategoi tends to support the view that prosecution was not an automatic consequence of deposition. The court sent Erasinides to prison; this was a usual penalty for not paying money owed to the state.

Next there was a meeting of the Boule at which the strategoi spoke about the battle and the storm which followed it. The Boule had the function of supervising administration (see pages 169–70), and although it is difficult to find other clear instances it is likely that it had authority to require officials to report to it on their actions. If it considered an official guilty of maladministration, it could impose a fine (up to 500 drachmas) or refer him to a court for trial. But on this occasion it took a step which was more unusual, but still legally proper: it resolved to refer the matter to the Ekklesia. Meanwhile it sent to prison the other five deposed strategoi who were in Athens (in addition to Erasinides, who was in prison already); this presumably was not a penalty but 'remand in custody', a precaution to prevent flight from Athens.

When the Ekklesia met, the matter came before it as one placed on the agenda by the Boule, arising out of the Boule's supervision of officials (not as an *eisangelia* to the Ekklesia by an individual on a charge of treason). A large number of citizens spoke: some attacked the deposed strategoi for failure to rescue the sailors from the sunk ships; the strategoi each spoke briefly in their own defence, blaming the storm; others who had been at the battle spoke vouching for the severity of the storm. All this was, legally, a debate in the Ekklesia rather than a trial. Probably some specific proposition had been made, but we do not know its terms, and the debate lasted so long that it became too dark to count a show of hands. So the meeting agreed not to take a vote now, but to defer the matter to a later meeting, at which the Boule was to bring forward a proposal about how the men should be tried.

The next meeting was held some time later, after the Apatouria festival. One member of the Boule, Kallixenos, persuaded the Boule to accept the following proposal and put it before the Ekklesia.

'Since they have heard the accusers of the strategoi and the strategoi's defence at the previous meeting, all the Athenians are to make a decision by voting by tribes. Two urns are to be set up for each tribe. For each tribe a herald is to proclaim that anyone who considers that the strategoi are guilty, in not having picked up the men victorious in the sea-battle, is to cast his vote into the first urn; anyone who considers that they are not, into the second. If they are found guilty, they are to be punished by death and handed over to the Eleven and their property is to be confiscated and one-tenth of it is to belong to the Goddess.' (Quoted by Xenophon *Hellenika* 1. 7. 9–10)

But when Kallixenos's proposal was put before the Ekklesia, Euryptolemos and others stated their intention of bringing against him a prosecution for making an illegal proposal (*graphe paranomon*: see page 50). The consequence of this would be that the proposal could not take effect unless Kallixenos was first tried and acquitted on that charge. Uproar followed. There were shouts that it would be intolerable if the people were not allowed to do what they wished. One speaker suggested that Euryptolemos and his supporters should be tried by the same vote as the strategoi, and they felt compelled to withdraw their threat of a *graphe paranomon*. Some of the prytaneis presiding at the meeting (especially Sokrates, who by chance was one of them) still demurred at putting an illegal proposal to the vote. But in the end, after another speech by Euryptolemos, a vote was taken to choose between two alternatives: a proposal by Euryptolemos that the strategoi should each be tried separately in accordance with the decree of Kannonos, which laid down a procedure for those accused of 'wronging the people' (see pages 180–1), and the proposal by Kallixenos that a single vote should be taken about them all. The proposal of Kallixenos was passed after a recount. The people then voted, in accordance with the procedure laid down by it, to condemn the eight deposed strategoi; and the six who were present in Athens were executed.

The legal question arising from all this is whether the proposal of Kallixenos was, as Euryptolemos and Sokrates alleged, contrary to law. Euryptolemos maintained that the strategoi ought to have a whole-day trial, and he may have pointed out that at the previous meeting of the Ekklesia the strategoi had not been able to make speeches of the length permitted by law in whole-day trials;[420] but it seems fairly clear, from Plato as well as from Xenophon, that the thing which he mainly emphasized as being illegal was not the inadequacy of the hearing given to the accused men, but the giving of a single verdict for them all instead of a separate verdict for each.[421] Was there in fact a law requiring a separate vote for each defendant in a trial? We have no other evidence that there was, and it is noticeable that Euryptolemos, in the speech attributed to him by Xenophon, does not quote or refer to any written law on the point. This silence is not conclusive, but it may well be that the practice of voting separately about each defendant when several were accused in one trial was simply the normal procedure and had never been put down in writing. In 406 Euryptolemos could have argued that even an unwritten law should be observed; it was not until 403/2 that the law was made that no unwritten law should be enforced.

Except for the shortness of the defendants' speeches and the giving of a collective verdict, there is no good reason to suppose that there was any legal impropriety in the procedure followed in this case. The case was unusual, in that an investigation by the Boule of the strategoi's performance of their duties led on to a hearing and condemnation by the Ekklesia. But the Boule and Ekklesia undoubtedly had the right to decide that the case was one in which it was appropriate for the Ekklesia to give the verdict. The reason why they did so decide was that the accusation was virtually one of treason.

EXECUTION ORDERED BY THE BOULE

A few cases are known in which the Boule ordered (or it was proposed that the Boule should order) someone's execution. These cases have been found puzzling, because there is also evidence that the Boule, at least by the fourth century, was not allowed to impose any penalty more severe than a fine of 500 drachmas.[422] One of them occurred shortly after the amnesty of 403/2 (see page 47): a man attempted to bring a prosecution for some offence committed before that date, and Arkhinos persuaded the Boule to make an example of him by executing him without trial.[423] Other cases concerned aliens: a Kean was condemned to death by the Boule for killing the Athenian proxenos in Keos; and some members of the Boule proposed execution without trial for a Bosporan who had provided finance in Athens for a cargo on a Delian ship, and for some metics accused of hoarding grain, though in neither of these two cases was the proposal accepted.[424]

It is likely that in some of these cases the Boule did not really have legal authority to order execution. But it seems unlikely that execution could have been proposed if the Boule never had authority to give such an order in any circumstances. Presumably it was possible to send a man off for immediate execution if he was considered to be outside the protection of Athenian law. It has been suggested by Hansen that the Boule had authority to execute a 'wrongdoer' (*kakourgos*), but it may be more accurate to say that a man could be put to death without trial if he was an 'enemy' (*polemios*). Thus the law of Demophantos (quoted on page 175) includes the words '. . . he shall be an enemy of the Athenians and shall be killed with impunity'. So this may have been a possible means of punishing a man for an act hostile to Athens, but the examples which we have are not really sufficient to make the legal basis clear.[425]

REPORT ('APOPHASIS') FROM THE AREOPAGOS

A further procedure was introduced by a law which must have been made around the middle of the fourth century, though we have neither its text nor its date. The council of the Areopagos, whose functions had for the last hundred years been limited to homicide trials and a very few others, was now enabled to investigate other offences. If the Ekklesia considered that there was reason to think that some crime had been committed but that there was not enough evidence for a trial, the matter could be referred to the Areopagos for investigation. It was also possible for the council of the Areopagos to decide on its own initiative to investigate some matter. In either case it made a report (*apophasis*) of its findings to the Ekklesia. On the basis of this report the Ekklesia decided whether any person should be prosecuted. If so, it passed a decree about the details of the trial; it presumably specified the charge which was to be made, the persons who were to act as prosecutors, the number of jurors, and (if these were not already clear from the nature of the charge) the magistrate who was to bring the case into court and the penalty which should be imposed if the defendant was found guilty.[426]

The best-known instance of this procedure is the one which arose out of the Harpalos affair: Demosthenes proposed in the Ekklesia a decree that the disappearance of half of the money brought by Harpalos to Athens should be investigated by the Areopagos, but the Areopagos reported against himself, and he was then tried and found guilty of taking a huge bribe (see pages 172-3). An earlier case concerned a man named Antiphon – not the orator, but a man in Demosthenes's time who had for some reason been removed from the citizen roll. Either aggrieved at this or because he was bribed, he promised Philip of Macedon (or so Demosthenes alleges) that he would set fire to the docks at Peiraieus. Demosthenes caught him and brought him into the Ekklesia, but after debate the Ekklesia released him. The Areopagos then investigated the matter and made a report to the Ekklesia, after which Antiphon was tried and put to death. This evidently is a case in which the Areopagos took its own decision to make an investigation and report, not ordered by the Ekklesia.[427]

It is not known whether the law about *apophasis* specified particular kinds of offence which the Areopagos could investigate. Some of the offences reported by it to the Ekklesia were quite trivial ones committed by its own members; for example, there was the Areopagite who cheated a ferryman of his fare.[428] But perhaps there was a separate law about Areopagites who committed offences, requiring them to be expelled from the Areopagos. Otherwise we hear of *apophasis* only in connection with serious offences against the state, including betrayal and consorting with exiles in foreign territory as well as the offences of Demosthenes and Antiphon already mentioned.[429] It is likely that in practice this procedure was used only for offences similar to treason, and it thus became an alternative to *eisangelia*. But that does not necessarily mean that the law forbade its use for other offences.

Quite distinct from the law about *apophasis* was a decree passed, on the proposal of Demosthenes, at the time of the battle of Khaironeia in 338, empowering the Areopagos to punish lawbreakers. In accordance with this the Areopagos arrested and executed at least one Athenian who was attempting to leave the country. But this was an emergency measure to prevent treason at a time when an enemy invasion was expected, and it did not become part of the permanent code of laws.[430]

XII RELIGION

SACRED LAW

Athenian religion had many rules. Its emphasis was more on practice than on conscience. The aim was to do the things which would please the gods, in the hope of getting their help, and to avoid anything which would annoy them and provoke their vengeance. And their likes and dislikes were, apparently, quite complicated. They were formulated in elaborate rules, mainly about sacrifices and other rituals which were to be performed by certain persons in certain ways at certain times; details cannot be given here, but may be found in books on Athenian religion.

These laws were believed to have been made by gods, not by men. Sometimes new ones were obtained from sources thought to be divinely inspired, especially the Delphic oracle. But most sacred laws had no remembered origin and were just ancestral traditions (*patria*). Many of them were inscribed on stone by the end of the fifth century, but even then others remained unwritten, and comprehensive knowledge of them was possessed only by a few experts, each of whom was supposed to pass on the knowledge to his successor. One might have expected any priest to be regarded as an expert on the cult whose rituals it was his duty to perform, but it is not certain that this was true of all priests and cults. For example, one of the most important Athenian cults was that of the two Eleusinian goddesses, Demeter and Kore, which included the secret ritual of the Mysteries. This cult was controlled by the two aristocratic families named Eumolpidai and Kerykes, who provided the two chief priests of it, the hierophant ('shower of the sacred') and dadoukhos ('torch-bearer') respectively; but it was only the Eumolpidai who gave authoritative statements of sacred law about it, and on one occasion (in 400 or 399) an objection was made when Kallias, who belonged to the Kerykes and was the dadoukhos, tried to usurp this function.[431]

Probably the Eumolpidai expounded laws only about the Eleusinian cult. But there also existed religious officials called exegetai ('expounders'); perhaps they could expound all sacred laws, or perhaps just those sacred laws which did not concern a particular priest or temple. They are mentioned four times in the literature of the fourth century. The earliest mention is this one in Plato, referring to the year 399 or a little earlier.

> 'When we were farming in Naxos, he was a labourer on our farm there. He got drunk, lost his temper with one of our slaves, and killed him. So my father bound him hand and foot, threw him into a ditch, and sent a man to Athens to ask the exegetes what should be done.' (Plato *Euthyphron* 4c)

In all the four passages what happens is that someone asks 'the exegetes' (singular in three of the instances; plural, 'the exegetai', in the other) to state the correct religious procedure in an unusual situation concerning death or purification.[432] On the basis of this evidence we cannot say when exegetai were first appointed, nor how they were appointed, nor how many there were, nor how much of the sacred law they expounded in the fourth century; it is unsafe to use (as J. H. Oliver does in his book on this subject) inscriptions of the Hellenistic Age as evidence for the earlier period.[433]

There is no reason to think that either the Eumolpidai or the exegetai had any powers of enforcement. Although one Demosthenic passage (22. 27) indicates the possibility of requesting the Eumolpidai to judge whether a person had acted impiously, that does not show they could impose a penalty. Where private problems were concerned, the question of enforcement would be unlikely to arise. A man who enquired of the exegetai about the proper ritual to be performed on some occasion by himself in his own household would do so with the intention of following their instructions; or if he neglected them and risked incurring the gods' hostility, that was his own affair. But it was a different matter if an infringement concerned a public ceremony or shrine; for then the gods, if offended, were thought likely to show their hostility to the Athenian people generally, unless the people placated the gods by punishing the offending individual.

For this reason a person could be brought to trial for a religious offence. In such trials the Eumolpidai, exegetai, and other priests had no standing; the trials were conducted by secular magistrates, usually the basileus, with secular juries. (A minor exception is that, if a case concerned the secret rituals of the Mysteries, men who had not been initiated in the Mysteries were excluded from the jury.[434]) The jury would need to take account of any relevant sacred law, and indeed on some occasion in the middle of the fifth century Perikles told a jury that they should enforce the unwritten laws expounded by the Eumolpidai.[435] After 403/2 the law that no uninscribed law was to be enforced by the courts (see page 47) must have applied to sacred law too, but perhaps by then most sacred law which was likely to concern the courts had in fact been inscribed.

Some offences connected with religion have already been mentioned in previous chapters: homicide, which was thought to give rise to religious pollution (see page 110); destruction of sacred olive-trees (see page 135); theft from a temple (see page 149). In this chapter we are concerned with offences concerning the performance of religious ceremonies and the vaguer offence of impiety.

FESTIVALS

Offences in connection with certain festivals were dealt with by the procedure called *probole* (a word which literally just means 'putting forward', sc. to the Ekklesia). At least this was so in the fourth century: our information comes from the speech *Against Meidias* (Demosthenes 21), composed in 347/6, and at one point Demosthenes remarks that one of the relevant laws did not exist in the time of Alkibiades some seventy years before, but we cannot say what the rules were in the fifth century. Demosthenes mentions several laws and quotes two of them (there is no sufficient reason to reject the genuineness of these texts), from which we see that there were separate laws about different festivals – possibly because different festivals had different rules, but more probably because the scope of the *probole* procedure was only gradually extended to the various festivals. By 347/6 it was in use for at least the following festivals: the great Dionysia, the Dionysia at Peiraieus, the Lenaia, the Thargelia, and the Eleusinian Mysteries.[436]

The procedure was that anyone wishing to prosecute for an offence in connection with a festival notified the prytaneis (the fifty members of the Boule responsible for arranging meetings of the Boule and the Ekklesia), who had to place it on the agenda for the Boule and the Ekklesia on the day after the festival. (One phrase in the first law quoted by Demosthenes, 'those which have not been paid', implies that a prosecution need not be brought to the Ekklesia if it was agreed in the Boule that a small fine was sufficient penalty; but not all scholars agree that the phrase is genuine.) In the Ekklesia the prosecutor and the defendant each made a speech, and the citizens voted for one or the other. But – and this was the peculiarity of the procedure – this vote had no effect, except that it was prejudicial (in the strict sense of that word). If the prosecutor wished to take the matter further, there had still to be a trial with an ordinary jury in the court of the thesmothetai. Neither the prosecutor nor the jury was bound by the result of the voting in the Ekklesia. But no doubt it did in practice carry much weight with the prosecutor, in deciding whether to proceed to a trial, and with the jurors, in reaching their verdict. Presumably the purpose of the hearing in the Ekklesia was, in the absence of any public official to decide whether a prosecution was worth while (like, for example, the procurator-fiscal in Scotland), to enable the citizens generally to express their approval of it.

Any 'wrong action concerning the festival' could be the subject of a *probole*; this expression was not defined in the law, and it was for the Ekklesia and subsequently the jury to decide whether the defendant's behaviour should be so described. In addition the law stated that at certain festivals no one might seize money or other property from another person, even if it was something (such as an overdue debt) which he was otherwise legally entitled to seize; if he did so, he was subject to *probole*. Presumably the Athenians had found by experience that creditors would often hope to track down their debtors at a festival which a large part of the population attended, and that their activities, though they formed no part of the festival, were liable to disturb its smooth conduct. (One can imagine the effect of a creditor scanning the rows of the audience in the theatre, spotting his debtor, and challenging him while the performance of a tragedy was going on.)

Demosthenes 21. 175–80 gives several examples of the use of *probole*. In one case a Karian complained that a Thespian to whom he owed money caught hold of him during the Eleusinian Mysteries. It is interesting that both men involved in this *probole* were non-Athenians. In another case a man complained that the arkhon's paredros ('assessor') had manhandled him in the theatre at the Dionysia. In a third case a man named Ktesikles was riding in a procession at a festival and, catching sight of someone he did not like, struck him with his whip. The man brought a *probole* against him. Ktesikles seems to have defended himself by saying that he was drunk at the time, and perhaps it was regarded as excusable to be drunk at a festival. But the jury decided that he had acted 'from *hybris*, not from wine, . . . treating free men as slaves', and he was condemned to death.

But the case which we know most about is that of Demosthenes and Meidias, for which the surviving speech was written. In the spring of 348 Demosthenes was a khoregos for a men's dithyrambic chorus at the Dionysia. Meidias, having a grudge against him, made various attempts to obstruct the chorus's preparation for the contest and prevent its success, and finally on the day of the performance came up to Demosthenes in the theatre and punched him in the face. On the day after the festival Demosthenes proceeded against Meidias by *probole*. Each spoke in the Ekklesia, and the citizens voted against Meidias. Demosthenes describes, perhaps with some exaggeration, the scene in the Ekklesia when some of Meidias's rich friends tried to persuade Demosthenes not to take the case on to a trial.

'You were all so furious and angry and indignant that, when Neoptolemos and Mnesarkhides and Philippides and one of those very rich men started pleading with me and with you, you shouted out not to let him go; and when Blepaios the banker came up to me, you yelled "This is it!" so loudly, thinking I was going to accept money from him, that in my fright at the noise you were making, and trying to evade his grasp, I let my cloak fall off, and in my short tunic I was nearly nude.' (Demosthenes 21. 215–16)

The speech which we have is the one composed by Demosthenes for delivery at the ensuing trial of Meidias. In it he emphasizes tremendously the awfulness of Meidias's crime, declares that it would have been appropriate to condemn Meidias for either *hybris* or impiety (which incidentally shows us that a *probole* for an offence concerning a festival was legally distinct from a prosecution for impiety or any other offence), and prides himself that no threat or bribe has induced him to give up the prosecution of which the Athenians in the Ekklesia showed such overwhelming approval. The truth was different. The speech, which remains in an unfinished condition, was never delivered. The anticlimax of the affair is revealed to us by Aiskhines.

'What need is there to mention now . . . that business about Meidias, and the punch which [Demosthenes] got in the orkhestra when he was a khoregos, and how he sold for thirty mnai both the assault on himself and the vote which the people gave against Meidias in the precinct of Dionysos?' (Aiskhines 3. 51–2)

The fact that the people had voted against Meidias in the Ekklesia did not compel Demosthenes to take his prosecution to a trial, and he preferred to accept a substantial bribe and drop the case. The *probole* procedure appears to be one of those procedures which were designed to make up for a lack of public prosecutors by encouraging individuals to prosecute for offences which concerned the general public; but the case of Meidias shows that it did not always work.

IMPIETY

Whereas the procedure of *probole* for an offence against religion could be used only in connection with certain festivals, the procedure of *graphe* could be used for any impiety (*asebeia*) on any occasion.

We have brief information about several cases in the fourth century which provide examples of behaviour regarded by juries as impiety. Arkhias, who was the hierophant of the Eleusinian Mysteries, was convicted because on the day of the festival of the Haloa, as a personal favour to a woman he knew, he carried out a sacrifice for her at Eleusis. This was simply an infringement of two rules of sacred law: the sacrifice ought to have been performed by the priestess, not by the hierophant, and sacrifices were not allowed on the day of the Haloa.[437] In a case in 376/5 several Delians were convicted of impiety because they chased the Athenian administrators (Amphiktyones) out of the temple of Apollo at Delos and hit them; they were condemned to exile and heavy fines (10,000 drachmas each). Since the Athenians controlled Delos at that time, the case was probably tried in Athens under Athenian law, and it shows that violent conduct in a temple or towards officials performing religious duties could be regarded as impiety.[438] In a third case a Lemnian woman named Theoris was condemned to death for impiety because she used magic ('drugs and incantations'); but we cannot tell whether she was convicted because she used magic at all, or only because she used it for some particular impious purpose.[439] Also condemned to death was a priestess named Ninos; she too is said to have made potions, but her chief offence seems to have been an attempt to form a new religious sect or a ritual in honour of a new god.[440] In another case a man was prosecuted by Androtion for impiety because he had associated (by going into the same house) with his nephew Diodoros, whom Androtion alleged to be a parricide (and therefore polluted: see page 110). The jurors acquitted him, but this was probably because they did not believe that Diodoros was a parricide, and does not make clear whether they thought that association with a killer amounted to impiety.[441]

Earlier and more notorious than any of these cases were the religious scandals of the year 415. Shortly before the Athenian expeditionary force was due to sail for Sicily, a large number of the images of Hermes which stood in streets and public places in Athens were found to have been mutilated during the night. The perpetrators appear to have been a group of men who wanted to stop the expedition; they evidently had little religious respect themselves for the Hermai, but hoped that the Athenian people generally would be afraid to undertake the expedition if they thought that the god of travellers had been offended. There was great public alarm, and while the matter was being investigated another kind of irreligious behaviour came to light: a number of men, including Alkibiades the general, were found to have been amusing themselves and their friends on various occasions by performing parodies of the Eleusinian Mysteries. The offence in this was not just that parodying any religious ceremony implied contempt for it, but that this particular ritual was a secret one and the frivolous performances had given the secrets away to some uninitiated people. Some of the offenders were arrested and executed; others, including Alkibiades, escaped by going into exile. Much of this is described by Andokides in his speech *On the Mysteries*, and the charge brought against Alkibiades is quoted by Plutarch in his *Life of Alkibiades* 22; from these it is clear that the prosecutions for mutilation of the Hermai and for profanation of the Mysteries were not brought by *graphe* but by *eisangelia* (see page 184). But Andokides, who was implicated but escaped trial by giving evidence against others, later found himself subjected to a decree, proposed by Isotimides, excluding from holy places those who had committed impiety and admitted it; and Andokides himself some years later is said to have initiated a prosecution for impiety against Arkhippos on the ground that he had mutilated one of the Hermai.[442] This confirms that (as we could confidently have guessed anyway) the mutilation and profanation were both regarded as instances of impiety.

But there are still several problems about the legal definition of impiety and the procedure used for it. First there is the question of intention: was a person guilty of impiety if he accidentally or in ignorance contravened a sacred law, or did the word *asebeia* necessarily imply an attitude of mind which was contemptuous of the gods? In this connection the story that Aiskhylos the tragic dramatist was tried is interesting. He was accused of impiety because he revealed some secrets of the Mysteries in one of his plays, but he was acquitted when he pointed out that he had not been initiated in the Mysteries and therefore did not know that what he had put into his play resembled them.[443] That suggests that an act was not impious if the doer was unaware that he was breaking any religious rule; but just the opposite is suggested by Andokides's accusers' allegation that he had incurred a penalty by placing a suppliant-branch on the altar of the Eleusinion during the Mysteries, not knowing that there was a law against it.[444] On this matter Andokides is a more reliable source than the anecdote about Aiskhylos, and it is preferable to accept that in Athenian law an act could be regarded as impious even if the doer did not know that it was so when he committed it.

Then there is a problem about the type of prosecution used for impiety. In the fourth century it was *graphe*, but there is no fifth-century case of impiety in which the procedure is definitely known to have been *graphe*. The procedure used against the profaners of the Mysteries in 415 was *eisangelia*,[445] which was also the procedure specified in the decree of Diopeithes about atheism (see page 200). Does that mean that *eisangelia* was the only method of prosecution for impiety at that period, and that the use of *graphe* for this offence was an innovation made not long before 400? No; it is unlikely that until then every minor case of impiety was allowed to take up the time of the Boule and the Ekklesia. It is better to believe that *graphe* was the normal procedure for impiety in the fifth century as in the fourth, but *eisangelia* was also possible for any offence which seemed to be specially serious until the introduction of the law restricting the offences for which this procedure could be used (see pages 184–6).

The final problem concerns the period after 403/2, when the law was made that no uninscribed law was to be enforced (see page 47). It has been suggested that this meant that no one thereafter could be prosecuted for impiety unless he was accused of breaking a law specifying that some particular act or behaviour was required or was forbidden.[446] But there is no proof that this was so, and it seems unlikely that the Athenians would have considered that an act could not be impious if no law-maker had thought of forbidding it. My guess is that the law about impiety, which is not preserved, was probably similar to the law about *hybris* (quoted on page 129) and said something like 'If anyone commits impiety, let anyone who wishes submit a *graphe* . . . ' without offering any definition of impiety. If the prosecutor could point to a sacred law which had been contravened, that would be good evidence that impiety had been committed; otherwise it would be for the jury to decide whether what the defendant had done was impiety or not.

ATHEISM

Because ordinary Athenians saw religion primarily as a matter of performing the right acts and avoiding wrong acts, it is likely (though evidence is lacking) that in earlier times it was only for irreligious deeds, not words, that prosecutions for impiety were brought. A man who thought and said something unorthodox about the gods may well have been regarded as harmless, provided that his opinion did not lead to unorthodox actions. (In this connection it is interesting that the authors and actors of Old Comedy seem to have been able to say what they liked about the gods without fear of the law, and even to bring them on to the stage as comic characters behaving in stupid or cowardly or other despicable ways. However, the satirical treatment of gods may have been a tradition of comedy at dramatic festivals, and should not be used as evidence that similar mockery of the gods would have been acceptable on other occasions.)

A change occurred in the second half of the fifth century. This is not the place to discuss the 'enlightenment' which reached Athens in the age of Perikles, and on which other books have been written. For the present purpose the essential point is that there was some decline in traditional religious belief, and those who held to the traditional religion began to see atheism as a threat. In the law this development is marked by the decree of Diopeithes. Its exact date is uncertain, but it must be within the 430s. It laid down that those who did not believe in the gods or gave instruction about astronomy should be subject to *eisangelia*.[447] The combination of these two offences looks bizarre to modern eyes, but it is clear that the offenders whom Diopeithes had primarily in mind were those like the philosopher-scientist Anaxagoras, who declared that the sun, so far from being a god, was a hot stone. This decree was the first attempt in Athens, as far as we know, to extend the scope of legal action from impious behaviour to atheistic speech and thought.

Anaxagoras is in fact said to have been prosecuted, but the details of his trial are doubtful. According to one account, he was prosecuted by Kleon and defended by Perikles, and was condemned to exile from Athens and a fine of five talents. In another account he was prosecuted by Thucydides (the politician, son of Melesias), fled from Athens to avoid trial, and was condemned to death in his absence; in another he was present when condemned to death, and while he was being held in prison awaiting execution Perikles persuaded the Athenians to let him off.[448] Another philosopher said to have been prosecuted is Protagoras, who wrote a book beginning 'Concerning the gods I am unable to know either that they exist or that they do not exist . . .' The Athenians condemned him to exile, and also collected up copies of his book and burned them in the Agora – the earliest recorded instance of official book-burning.[449] Although our evidence does not make the legal procedure clear, and one cannot be quite sure that the trials were held at all,[450] I regard it as probable that both Anaxagoras and Protagoras were prosecuted by *eisangelia* in accordance with the decree of Diopeithes. Then there was Diagoras of Melos, who is said to have aroused hostility by disparaging talk about the Mysteries in 415/4 (soon after their profanation by Alkibiades and his friends). He fled from Athens, and the Athenians issued a proclamation offering a reward of one talent to anyone who killed him, two talents to anyone who brought him back alive. But there is no evidence that he was ever caught or tried.[451]

The decree of Diopeithes may have lapsed in 403 when the code of laws had been reinscribed (see pages 46–7), and the prosecution of Sokrates in 399 seems to have differed legally from the cases of Anaxagoras and Protagoras. It was not brought by *eisangelia* but by the ordinary procedure of *graphe* for impiety. The charge was:

'The following *graphe* was brought and the oath taken by Meletos son of Meletos of Pithos against Sokrates son of Sophroniskos of Alopeke: Sokrates is guilty of not recognizing the gods whom the state recognizes and introducing other new divinities; he is also guilty of corrupting the young.' (Quoted by Diogenes Laertios 2. 40)

Other books have been written about the trial of Sokrates, and it needs only brief treatment here. After Meletos's speech, supporting speeches for the prosecution were made by the politicians Anytos and Lykon. Sokrates replied in his own words, having rejected a speech written for him by Lysias on the ground that it was 'beautiful' and therefore inappropriate for him. (Plato and Xenophon have each written for us an *Apology of Sokrates* which purports to be a record of Sokrates's speech. The two are very different from each other, and therefore cannot both be accurate reports. Perhaps neither is even intended to be an accurate report; they may rather be idealized versions, giving what Plato and Xenophon thought Sokrates should or might have said.) It is not known whether anyone spoke in support of Sokrates; according to one anecdote the young Plato attempted to speak but was shouted down by the jury. When the vote came, Sokrates was found guilty; there is a discrepancy of testimony about the numbers, but probably either 280 or 281 jurors (out of 500 or 501) voted against him. Then came the assessment of the penalty. The prosecutor proposed death. Sokrates facetiously suggested that he deserved free meals for life in the Prytaneion, like other outstanding benefactors of Athens, but his friends persuaded him to propose a moderate fine; different authorities give different figures. The jury voted for the heavier penalty, and thus he was condemned to death. In the voting on the penalty the number of votes against Sokrates was 80 more than in the voting on the verdict.[452]

It is not known what evidence and arguments the prosecutors brought forward in their speeches, but from all that we know of Sokrates it seems unlikely that they can have adduced any impious actions committed by him. They must have relied mainly on verbal utterances, on what Sokrates had said to his young followers and to other people. If so, this may have been the first case in which a *graphe* for impiety was brought for impious thought and speech, rather than impious behaviour. However, there were undoubtedly many Athenians who thought that Sokrates's influence on Alkibiades, Kritias, and others had been indirectly responsible for the political troubles of recent years and especially the oligarchic regime in 404. If in fact the reasons why the prosecutors brought the case, and many of the jurors voted for conviction, were political, that was simply a misuse of the procedure, and the case does not show us what the concept of impiety normally meant in Athenian law.

Part Three: Legal Proceedings

XIII ARBITRATION

PRIVATE ARBITRATION

In modern times it is notorious that people without large financial resources are generally best advised to settle disputes out of court; even if one is sure that right is on one's side, the risk and expense involved in legal proceedings are often too great to make them worth while. Legal proceedings in ancient Athens were much less expensive, but the procedure of trial by jury could still be troublesome and time-consuming. Since the days when an individual king had simply given his judgements, the administration of justice had been made more and more elaborate in order to obtain just verdicts in the most important and difficult cases. But simple cases might not need an elaborate procedure. If two men could just refer their dispute to a third man whom both agreed to be impartial, and were both willing to abide by his decision, that would often be enough.

Arbitration of this sort could be privately arranged; this must have been common in Athens at all periods. One example, fictional but revealing, is one of the best-known scenes in New Comedy. It is the scene in Menander's *Arbitration* from which the play as a whole takes its name. Daos has found a baby, which he has handed over to Syriskos. Now Syriskos claims that the ornaments found with the baby ought to be handed over too.

> *Syriskos:* You're not doing what's right!
> *Daos:* Mind your own business, you wretch! You've no right to keep what's not yours!
> *Syriskos:* We must get someone to arbitrate about it.
> *Daos:* Certainly; let's get a decision.
> *Syriskos:* Well, who?
> *Daos:* Anyone suits me. But it serves me right; why did I offer you a share?
> *Syriskos:* Will you agree to have that man as judge?
> *Daos:* Just as you like.
> *Syriskos:* Excuse me, sir. Could you spare us a few moments?

Smikrines: You? What for?

Syriskos: We're having an argument about something.

Smikrines: What's that got to do with me?

Syriskos: We're looking for someone to decide it, a fair judge. If you're not busy, will you settle it for us?

Smikrines: You'll come to a bad end! Walking around in leather jackets, making law speeches!

Syriskos: Well, still, it's quite a small matter, easy to understand. Do us a favour, sir. Please don't think it doesn't matter. On every occasion justice ought to prevail everywhere. That's something which every passer-by should see to. It's a duty of life, common to everyone.

Daos (aside): A fair orator I've got mixed up with! Why did I offer him a share?

Smikrines: Well, tell me, will you abide by the judgement I give?

Syriskos: Certainly.

Smikrines: I'll hear you; why shouldn't I? (*To Daos*) You speak first, you who've said nothing.

(Menander *Epitrepontes* 218–39)

In this case Smikrines eventually decides in favour of Syriskos, and Daos, though annoyed at losing the ornaments, sulkily accepts the decision. But obviously, in an arbitration arranged informally at a moment's notice, he might easily have refused to accept it; and what could Syriskos or Smikrines have done about that? To avoid this abortive result in arbitrations in real life, a law was made to regulate them, laying down conditions which made an arbitrator's judgement binding. It is not known when the law was made, but there certainly were legally binding arbitrations before 404.[453] A surviving text which purports to be the law about arbitration is probably not genuine.[454] But it is clear from other evidence that, before an arbitration began, there had to be an agreement (which could be in writing, though there is no evidence that it had to be so) saying who was to arbitrate (it could be either one man or more) and what the question was; and that the arbitrator had to take an oath (presumably to the effect that he would decide justly) before giving his judgement. If one of the disputants had already initiated a prosecution of the other, the agreement to submit the dispute to arbitration was notified to the appropriate magistrate, who would accept it as sufficient reason for dropping the prosecution.[455]

But even a written agreement was sometimes not enough to make an arbitration effective in practice. One such agreement is described in the speech *Against Apatourios* (Demosthenes 33). A dispute about a loan between two Byzantine merchants in Athens, named Apatourios and Parmenon, is described by an Athenian friend of Parmenon.

'They were persuaded by the bystanders to go to arbitration, and they entrusted the case, under a written agreement, to one arbitrator nominated by them both – Phokritos, a fellow-citizen of theirs – and each of them nominated one other: Apatourios named Aristokles of Oe, and Parmenon named me. In the agreement they agreed that if the three of us were unanimous, that decision was binding on them; otherwise they must abide by the decision of two. On making this agreement, they provided sureties for each other: Apatourios's was Aristokles, Parmenon's was Arkhippos of Myrrhinous. And at first they were going to deposit the agreement with Phokritos, but then Phokritos told them to deposit it with someone else, and so they deposited it with Aristokles. . . .

'When Apatourios saw that Phokritos and I were of the same opinion, and realized we were going to give our decision against him, he wanted to stop the arbitration, and he made an attempt to destroy the agreement in collaboration with the man who held it. He proceeded to claim that as far as he was concerned Aristokles was the arbitrator, and he said Phokritos and I had no authority to do anything except conduct negotiations. Parmenon was very indignant at this statement, and demanded that Aristokles should produce the agreement; it was easy enough to prove, he said, if there was any fiddling about with the document, since it was in his own slave's handwriting. But Aristokles, after consenting to produce the agreement, has never produced it openly to this day, but on the day which was fixed he turned up at the temple of Hephaistos and made the excuse that his slave, while waiting for him, had fallen asleep and lost the document. (The man who arranged that was Eryxias, the physician from Peiraieus, who is a friend of Aristokles.) . . .

'So after that the arbitration was at a standstill, because the agreement had disappeared and there was a dispute between the arbitrators; and when they tried to write a fresh agreement, they quarrelled about that, Apatourios wanting Aristokles only, and Parmenon all the three original arbitrators. And when a fresh agreement had not been made, and the original one had disappeared,

the man who had caused its disappearance was shameless enough to say he would declare the result of the arbitration by himself! Parmenon called witnesses and forbade Aristokles to declare the result against him without his colleagues, contrary to the agreement . . .'
(Demosthenes 33. 14–19)

From this and other instances we see that private arbitration was sometimes less than satisfactory. A common stumbling-block was the choice of an arbitrator. In a privately arranged arbitration the disputants chose their arbitrators from among their own relatives or friends; but if each disputant refused to accept an arbitrator suggested by his opponent, the arbitration could not proceed. So there was a need for 'public' arbitration, in which an arbitrator, having authority to give a decision without the need to hold a full-scale trial by jury, was appointed by state authority.

DEME AND TRIBE JUDGES

The Athenian system of public arbitration developed out of a system of district judges. Some deme judges (*dikastai kata demous*) had been appointed by the tyrant Peisistratos in the middle of the sixth century, to save farmers' time by hearing their disputes in the districts where they lived instead of requiring them to travel to the city; but these appointments lapsed, we do not know when. In 453/2 deme judges were appointed afresh. There were thirty of them, and they went on circuit around Attika. It has been suggested that there was one for each *trittys* or group of demes, but at this period there is no evidence about the method of appointment, the organization of hearings, or the kinds of dispute which they were authorized to hear.[456]

At the end of the fifth century (in 403/2 or very soon after) the number of these judges was raised from thirty to forty, four picked by lot from each of the ten tribes (*phylai*). Henceforth, they were often just called the Forty; or each group of four was named after its tribe, for example 'the judges for Hippothontis'. Sometimes they were still called deme judges, even though they no longer travelled around Attika. I shall call them tribe judges.[457]

In the fourth century the tribe judges were the magistrates responsible for most private cases (*dikai*), excluding those private cases which were dealt with by the arkhon (such as inheritance cases), the thesmothetai (such as mercantile cases), or other magistrates. Anyone who wished to bring a case which fell within the jurisdiction of the tribe judges had to make application to the four judges for the tribe to which the defendant belonged. (Or if the defendant was a metic or proxenos and consequently did not belong to any of the tribes, he made it to the polemarch, and the polemarch drew lots to distribute such cases each to a tribe.) If the amount of money involved in the case was not more than ten drachmas, the four tribe judges just decided it on their own authority. Otherwise they passed it on to an arbitrator. This was not a matter of choice either by the disputants or by the tribe judges; reference to an arbitrator was automatic.[458]

PUBLIC ARBITRATION

Public arbitrators were instituted in 399, shortly after the forty tribe judges superseded the thirty deme judges.[459] They functioned only in connection with the tribe judges. At one time many scholars thought that some types of case which were brought into court by the arkhon, the thesmothetai, or other magistrates were also subject to public arbitration; but it is now generally accepted that public arbitrators dealt with no cases except those for which the tribe judges were responsible. Two types of case which caused particular difficulty to scholars were those concerning guardianship and registration in a deme. Guardianship cases (see page 95) were submitted to public arbitration, and yet, it used to be thought, the magistrate in charge must have been the arkhon because inheritance was involved; but in fact there is no evidence that the arkhon handled guardianship cases, and the references to arbitrators should be taken as proof that the tribe judges were responsible.[460] In registration cases, a distinction should be made between a young man's appeal against rejection at his *dokimasia* (see page 69), which was brought into court by the thesmothetai and was not subject to public arbitration, and prosecution of a deme for wrongful deletion of a name from their existing list of members, for which the references to public arbitration in the speech *For Euphiletos* (Isaios 12) should probably be taken as evidence that the tribe judges were responsible (though an alternative view is that they merely show the spuriousness of that speech).[461] So it seems best to maintain that it was only in the tribe judges' cases that a public arbitrator was appointed.

All male Athenian citizens served as arbitrators in their sixtieth year, which was the year that marked the end of their liability for military service. To be more exact, it was the forty-second year from a man's registration in a deme as an adult citizen; if it is correct that his registration took place at the beginning of the calendar year in which his eighteenth birthday fell (see page 69), his year of service as an arbitrator was the calendar year in which his fifty-ninth birthday fell. The only exceptions permitted were men who happened to hold some public office for that year, or who were abroad. Apart from these, all in the appropriate age-group had to attend regularly to have cases for arbitration allocated to them by lot. A complete list of the names of the arbitrators for the year 325/4 happens to be preserved in an inscription. It contains 103 names. This is smaller than one might expect for the total number of citizens in their sixtieth year. But the number would inevitably vary from one year to another, and 103 does not seem impossibly small for a below-average year; so it may not be necessary to resort to the hypothesis that citizens in the lowest property-class (*thetes*) were excluded from service as arbitrators, as has been suggested.[462]

Thus a public arbitrator, like arkhons and most other magistrates, was an ordinary citizen of no special intelligence or ability, though of course his age meant that he did have some experience of life. When prosecuting Meidias for slander, says Demosthenes (21. 83), 'I got Straton of Phaleron as arbitrator, a poor man, who took no interest in public affairs, but in other respects not bad, in fact very respectable.'

Each arbitration was held in some public place, where anyone interested could watch and listen to the proceedings.[463] The arbitrator heard the arguments and evidence produced by the prosecutor and the defendant, and tried if possible to bring about a reconciliation. This could take a number of meetings on different days. If no reconciliation was achieved, he fixed in advance a day on which he would give his judgement. If either disputant wished the date to be postponed, he could make a written objection to it (*paragraphe*; this is a different type of *paragraphe* from the one described in chapter XIV) supported by an oath that he could not attend (*hypomosia*) because of illness or because of absence from Attika. If the arbitrator accepted the objection, he postponed the date; if he thought it unacceptable, he gave his judgement on the date originally fixed, despite the absence of one of the disputants. If a man had a weak case, it must have been tempting to apply for postponement even when it was not really needed. In two surviving speeches Meidias and Theophemos are alleged or implied by their prosecutors to have done this because they had no confidence in their own innocence; but perhaps prosecutors would say this anyway, even when the grounds for postponement were actually good.[464]

When the arbitrator gave his judgement, he immediately reported it to the four tribe judges from whom the case had come. Normally this completed his duties in the case. For his services he received from the prosecutor a fee of one drachma (called *parastasis*). A disputant who applied for postponement of the date of the arbitrator's judgement, in the way described in the last paragraph, had to pay the arbitrator another drachma.[465] The sum seems small, but is perhaps not grossly out of proportion to the three obols (half a drachma) received by a juror.

APPEAL AND ANNULMENT OF PUBLIC ARBITRATION

If both disputants accepted the arbitrator's judgement, it was final. But either could appeal against it. This was an important difference between public and private arbitration. In private arbitration both disputants agreed voluntarily to submit their dispute to an arbitrator selected by themselves, and so it was reasonable that they were then required by law to accept his judgement as final, having the same validity as a jury's verdict. In public arbitration they were compelled by law to submit their case to an arbitrator who was not of their own choosing, and they still retained the right to have a trial by jury afterwards if they wanted one.

If either of them did appeal, the four tribe judges had to bring the case into court. The statements of witnesses and other evidence produced at the arbitration were put into jars (one jar for the prosecutor, one for the defendant) and sealed up until the day of the trial, and no evidence could be produced at the trial which had not been produced at the arbitration.[466] The purpose of this rule was presumably to get disputants to take the arbitration procedure seriously; otherwise, a man might often have shirked the trouble of presenting his case properly at the arbitration, believing that he could win his case anyway on appeal to a jury, and so the object of reducing the number of trials by jury might have been defeated.

Besides the possibility of appeal to a jury, two other methods of getting an arbitrator's judgement invalidated were available in cases to which they were appropriate. If one of the disputants had applied for postponement of the arbitrator's judgement, in the way already described, and the arbitrator had rejected the application in his absence and had given judgement against him in the case as 'deserted' (*eremos*), he could within ten days make an application to the four tribe judges, supported by another oath that his attendance had been prevented by illness or absence from Attika. If this application was accepted, the case was 'non-existent' (*me ousa*) and went afresh to arbitration.[467]

The other possibility was that the disputant against whom the arbitrator gave his judgement might claim that the arbitrator had treated him unjustly by conducting the arbitration in an improper manner. In this case he made his accusation (*eisangelia*) to the whole body of fifty-nine-year-olds who were arbitrators that year, at any of the ordinary meetings which they attended to have cases allotted to them for arbitration. If they voted against the accused arbitrator, he could appeal to a jury. The penalty for an arbitrator convicted of this offence was the heavy one of total disfranchisement. Presumably the conviction meant that the arbitrator's judgement in the original case was invalidated, and a new arbitrator would have to be appointed for it.[468]

All this is illustrated by Demosthenes's account of his prosecution of Meidias for slander, for which Straton was the arbitrator.

'When the day for judgement arrived, and all the legal possibilities were now exhausted, *hypomosiai* and *paragraphai*, and there was nothing else left, Straton first asked me to agree to adjournment of the arbitration, then to put it off to the following day; finally, since I would not agree and Meidias did not appear, and it was getting late, he gave judgement against him. Then, when it was already evening and getting dark, Meidias arrived at the magistrates' office, and found the magistrates leaving and Straton already going away, having handed in the deserted case, as I have been told by one of the people who were there. At first he had some success in persuading him to change his judgement from condemnation to acquittal, and the magistrates to change the record; and he offered them fifty drachmas. But when they got annoyed with him, and he failed to persuade either of them, he went away uttering threats and abuse, and – did what? Notice the nasty way he behaved. In his application against the existence of the arbitration he didn't take the oath, but he let the condemnation become final and was reported as having failed to take the oath; and, wanting his intention to be overlooked, he waited for the arbitrators' last day,[469] when some of the arbitrators came and some didn't; he persuaded the president to take a vote, contrary to all the laws; and without putting down the name of a single summons-witness, accusing in a deserted case, when nobody was there, he expelled and disfranchised the arbitrator. And now one Athenian, just because Meidias was convicted in a deserted case, has lost all his rights in the state and become completely disfranchised! Prosecuting Meidias for an offence, or being an arbitrator for him, or even walking down the same street, it seems, is not safe.'

(Demosthenes 21. 84–7)

Thus Demosthenes says that, when Straton gave judgement against Meidias in his absence, Meidias could just have applied for 'non-existent case'; but instead he abandoned (by offering no *hypomosia*) the application which he began for 'non-existent case', and followed the other procedure, making an accusation against the arbitrator (on the arbitrators' last day in office, when attendance was slack), with much direr consequences for Straton. No doubt Demosthenes's account is biased. Perhaps Straton really had transgressed the proper procedure for an arbitration. The fact that Demosthenes does not mention an appeal by Straton to a jury may be significant; perhaps Straton either did not appeal because he was obviously guilty or, if he did appeal, was found guilty by the jury. But in any case the account shows how an arbitrator was subject to opposing pressures, and was liable to suffer severely if he did the wrong thing. The appointment was no sinecure.

XIV BARRING LEGAL ACTION

'DIAMARTYRIA'

The more complex a state's legal procedure becomes, the greater the possibility that a prosecutor may try to follow the wrong procedure for a particular case; perhaps just by mistake, or perhaps deliberately, because he thinks that this procedure will give him some kind of advantage. So it becomes necessary to have some recognized method by which a defendant can object before a trial is held if he claims that there is something wrong with the way in which he is being prosecuted. This is a different matter from claiming to be not guilty; it is a claim that the question whether a person is guilty or not should be decided only in the proper legal manner.

In Athens the first and most obvious way of objecting was simply to make the objection to the magistrate to whom the prosecutor gave the charge. Any charge or claim had to be made to a particular magistrate. If it was made to the wrong magistrate or in the wrong way, the magistrate (whether he noticed this for himself or had it pointed out to him by the defendant) could simply refuse to accept it. However, there were two reasons why this method of objection was sometimes inadequate. The first was that the magistrate might himself get the legal procedure wrong, either from ignorance or from favouritism towards one of the disputants; for magistrates appointed by lot might happen to be stupid or corrupt or both. The second was that the correctness of the procedure might depend on some fact which was in dispute. For example, certain types of charge had to be made to the arkhon or the tribe judges if the defendant was an Athenian citizen but to the polemarch if he was not; but if the defendant claimed to be a citizen and the prosecutor denied it, how was the polemarch to decide whether he should accept the case?

Some attempts to get round this second type of difficulty were made by a procedure called *diamartyria*. *Diamartyria* was a formal assertion of a fact by a witness who was in a position to know it. The witness might state, for example, that a man was a member of a certain deme, or the legitimate son of a certain father; and this might enable the magistrate to decide whether he should accept the case or not. The historical development of *diamartyria* is obscure, but it is less obscure now than it used to be, thanks to a classic study by the most distinguished of all French students of Athenian law, the late Louis Gernet.[470] Gernet argues that, even though no surviving text mentions *diamartyria* before the closing years of the fifth century, it was really a much older procedure; it had archaic features which cannot have originated as late as the age of the Attic orators and the democratic juries. Some details of his inferences may be open to doubt, but he is surely right to regard *diamartyria* as primitive. Formal assertion seems out of tune with the dialectical age of Sokrates.

For an assertion, even if formal, may still be untrue. An opponent who challenges it needs to have a recognized procedure for doing so. A procedure did come into use (probably at a later stage of the historical development) for challenging a *diamartyria*: it consisted of prosecuting the witness. When a disputant got a witness to make a *diamartyria* in support of his claim before a magistrate, his opponent could formally object (*episkeptesthai*) to the witness's statement immediately, and then proceed to bring against him an ordinary *dike* for false witness (*pseudomartyrion*). On receiving the objection the magistrate would delay his decision about the admissibility of the original case until the false witness case had been decided; but if the objector failed to proceed with his prosecution for false witness (presumably within a limited time, but we do not know how long), the magistrate would assume that the *diamartyria* was true and act accordingly.

That is what happened in both the recorded cases in which *diamartyria* was used in the closing years of the fifth century. One is described in the speech *Against Pankleon* (Lysias 23. 13–14). Aristodikos wished to prosecute Pankleon for something (it is not known what). Believing that Pankleon was not an Athenian citizen, he made his application to the polemarch. Pankleon objected that he was a Plataian (at this period Plataians were Athenian citizens: see page 71), so that the case should not be accepted by the polemarch but by some other magistrate. Aristodikos resorted to *diamartyria*: he produced a witness who stated that Pankleon was not a Plataian. Pankleon challenged the witness, but subsequently did not prosecute him; so the polemarch accepted the case, and Aristodikos eventually won it. The other case is mentioned in the speech *Against Kallimakhos* (Isokrates 18. 11). Kallimakhos wished to prosecute the speaker (whose name is not known) for taking 10,000 drachmas from him unjustly. The speaker claimed that this dispute had already been settled by private arbitration, which made it illegal to reopen it (see page 204); proceeding by *diamartyria*, he produced a witness to state this. Kallimakhos did not attempt to prosecute the witness, but dropped the case. These two examples show that *diamartyria* could be used either by the prosecutor or by the defendant, and that an assertion made in this way was accepted by the magistrate as true unless the witness who made it was successfully prosecuted for false witness.

'PARAGRAPHE'

But the procedure of *diamartyria*, open to rebuttal by the device of prosecuting the witness, though it may have worked effectively in some cases, cannot have been always satisfactory. The ground of objection to a prosecution would not always be a question of fact, but sometimes a question of legal procedure; and what is needed to settle disagreement about legal procedure is usually a reasoned argument rather than a formal assertion by a witness. So we find that at the end of the fifth century a new procedure for objection began to be used, called *paragraphe*. It too has been the subject of an important modern study, this one by the most distinguished living German student of Athenian law, H. J. Wolff, under the title *Die attische Paragraphe*.

By luck we possess the text of what the speaker says (and there is no reason to disbelieve him) is the first speech ever delivered in a *paragraphe* case. It is the Isokratean speech already mentioned, *Against Kallimakhos*, delivered in 400. It begins like this, with a reference to the restoration of democracy by the counter-revolution based on Peiraieus in 403 and the amnesty which followed.

'If other people had already had a *paragraphe* trial of this sort, I should begin my speech from the actual facts. But as it is, I must speak first about the law governing our appearance in court, so that you may understand the matters in dispute before you vote, and so that none of you may wonder why I, who am the defendant, am speaking before the prosecutor.

'After your return to Athens from Peiraieus, when you saw that some citizens were ready to make accusations for their own advantage and were trying to destroy the agreements, you wanted to stop them, and to show everyone that the agreements were not made under compulsion but because you thought them beneficial to the state. So, on the proposal of Arkhinos, you made a law that, if any-

one brought a case in contravention of the oaths, the defendant was
to be permitted to bring a *paragraphe*; the magistrates were to bring
that to trial first; the first speaker was to be the man who brought the
paragraphe; and whichever side lost was to be liable to pay one obol
per drachma. Thus men who dared to recall past wrongs would not
only be shown to have broken their oaths and be liable to divine
punishment, but would also suffer an immediate penalty.'

(Isokrates 18. 1–3)

In this passage 'you' means not just the present jury but the people
of Athens. When the civil war ended in 403, citizens of all parties
agreed not to take legal action against one another for offences committed in the civil war or under the oligarchic regime, and every
citizen swore an oath, 'I shall not recall past wrongs . . .'; further
oaths were sworn by the Boule and by jurors.[471] It was to enforce this
agreement that Arkhinos proposed the *paragraphe* procedure.

Paragraphe probably means 'prosecution in opposition', 'counter-
prosecution'; and the procedure was essentially a separate trial in which
the original prosecutor was himself prosecuted for bringing a prosecution in a way forbidden by law. Thus it was logical that the order
in which the disputants spoke was now reversed, because the man who
was the defendant in the original case was the prosecutor in the
paragraphe trial. The original case was postponed until the *paragraphe*
case was decided; the result of the *paragraphe* trial settled whether the
original case should proceed or not. (If it did proceed, its trial was held
at a later date, not on the same day as the *paragraphe* trial; this is
indicated by Demosthenes 36. 2, where the speaker denies that the postponement of the trial of the original case was his and Phormion's
motive in bringing a *paragraphe*. The view formerly held by Paoli and
others, that the *paragraphe* and the original case were decided by a
single trial, has been decisively refuted by Wolff's detailed study.[472]) In
addition, whoever lost the *paragraphe* case had to pay a penalty of
one-sixth of the amount of money or property in dispute (*epobelia*, one
obol per drachma). The magistrate to whom the original prosecution
was brought would also be responsible for bringing the *paragraphe* case
to court. (That seems to be implied by 'the magistrates . . .' in the
passage just quoted from Isokrates.) Thus any of the magistrates who
held ordinary trials might have to hold a *paragraphe* trial; and if the
original case was of a type which went from the tribe judges to a public
arbitrator, the *paragraphe* case would likewise go to a public arbitrator,

from whose decision the loser could appeal to a jury in the usual way.[473]

The opening stages of the dispute between Kallimakhos and his opponent have already been described (pages 213–14). When the speaker of the surviving speech presented a *diamartyria*, claiming that the dispute had already been settled by private arbitration, Kallimakhos did not prosecute the witness, but dropped the case. Later, however, as is related in section 12 of the speech, he made his accusation afresh. Presumably he thought he now had, for some reason, a better prospect than before of convincing a jury that the dispute had not been settled by private arbitration; the reason for bringing a fresh prosecution instead of proceeding with the old one by prosecuting the witness may have been that meanwhile a new year (400/399) had begun. But this time his opponent, instead of repeating the previous *diamartyria*, used the new *paragraphe* procedure; he claimed that the occasion when he was alleged to have taken money from Kallimakhos was before the end of the civil war, so that prosecution for this offence contravened the amnesty. The speech which we have is his speech in the *paragraphe* trial, accusing Kallimakhos of illegal prosecution. This change in the procedure used by the speaker suggests that the *paragraphe* procedure was instituted in 400, between Kallimakhos's first and second attempts at prosecution.

The speech *Against Pankleon* (Lysias 23) is another early *paragraphe* speech, also delivered in 400/399.[474] The speaker wished to prosecute Pankleon; for what offence is not known. Like Aristodikos (see page 213) he believed that Pankleon was not an Athenian citizen, and therefore made his application to the polemarch. Pankleon claimed that he was in fact a Plataian, so that the case was not within the competence of the polemarch; and he brought a *paragraphe* accusing his opponent of prosecuting him in the wrong way. The surviving speech is his opponent's defence in the *paragraphe* trial. It is interesting that the word used in the speech to refer to the procedure is not *paragraphe* but *antigraphe*. This does not mean that *antigraphe* was a different procedure from *paragraphe*; it just shows that, because the procedure was new, there was not yet a consensus about what its precise name should be.[475]

In the previous case Aristodikos had used a *diamartyria* against Pankleon. So here again, as in the speech *Against Kallimakhos*, we see *paragraphe* being used in circumstances in which *diamartyria* had been used earlier; the new procedure has superseded the old one. Yet Pankleon's case, unlike Kallimakhos's, has nothing to do with the amnesty for which the *paragraphe* procedure was originally instituted.

What appears to have happened is that within a few months of its institution the new procedure was found to be so satisfactory that its use was extended to other types of case. To this date presumably belongs a law mentioned in Demosthenes 37. 33, authorizing the use of *paragraphe* against a prosecution submitted to a magistrate who was not the right magistrate to bring that type of case into court. Pankleon must have been one of the first to take advantage of that law.

The Demosthenic corpus includes a group of seven speeches (nos 32–38) written for *paragraphe* cases, which provide further examples of circumstances in which *paragraphe* was used in the fourth century. In three of these speeches (nos 36–38) the speaker is objecting by *paragraphe* that a prosecution is inadmissible because the prosecutor has previously absolved his opponent; a law is quoted saying that no cases are to be admitted for offences which a person has 'released or discharged'.[476] In one of them another ground of objection is that a law prohibits cases arising from guardianship after five years have elapsed since the guardianship ended.[477] The other four speeches in the group (nos 32–35) concern mercantile loans: the mercantile laws allowed prosecution in Athens to recover a loan secured on cargo travelling to or from the Athenian market, but not if the cargo had no such connection with Athens, and not if there was no written agreement about the loan (see page 232), so that in those circumstances an attempted prosecution could be blocked by *paragraphe*. In one of these speeches, *Against Lakritos*, the borrower has died and the lender is trying to recover his money from the borrower's brother, who is objecting to the prosecution by *paragraphe* on the ground that he is not his brother's heir.

Thus we see that *paragraphe* was used to block prosecution in a number of cases in which the defendant claimed either that the case was of a type not allowed by law, or that it was of a type for which a different procedure was required, or that it was a case which had already been decided by some other means (such as private arbitration, or absolution by the prosecutor himself). After the original law instituting the procedure for use against prosecutions which contravened the amnesty of 403, there may have been several further laws at different dates authorizing its use against prosecutions of other kinds.

'DIAMARTYRIA' IN THE FOURTH CENTURY

Yet the old procedure of *diamartyria* did not disappear entirely. There was one type of private case in which *paragraphe* could hardly be used, because there was no prosecution. This was a *diadikasia* in which there were several claimants for an inheritance. The claimants were contending against one another; yet no one of them was the prosecutor or the defendant. Now, the law was that, if a man died leaving one or more legitimate living sons, the inheritance must go to the sons; no one else could claim it, and so there could be no *diadikasia*. But suppose other men did attempt to make claims: how should the sons stop them? *Paragraphe* would have been an awkward weapon to use against several separate persons, each possibly requiring a separate trial. What was needed was simply a legal declaration that legitimate sons were living, to settle once for all that no other claim was admissible. For this purpose *diamartyria* remained the more suitable procedure. The sons could get a witness (usually a close relative) to testify that they were legitimate sons of the deceased. Anyone who wished to challenge this statement could prosecute for false witness; otherwise no further claim to the inheritance was possible. Three surviving speeches of Isaios (nos 2, 3, 6) were written for false witness trials arising out of *diamartyriai* concerning inheritances. So also was the speech *Against Leokhares* (Demosthenes 44) – an odd case, for Leokhares, claiming to be a legitimate son, made his *diamartyria* himself, as his own witness; it is surprising that that was acceptable, but his opponent does seem to concede that it was legally permitted.[478]

It is not clear to what extent *diamartyria* continued in use in the fourth century for any kind of case other than a *diadikasia* for an inheritance. The lexicographer Harpokration in his entry under *diamartyria*, referring to lost speeches of Isaios and Hypereides, mentions its use in connection with cases concerning the status of a freedman or metic, a *dike apostasiou* (see page 82) and a *graphe aprostasiou* (see page 78). There is no other evidence that it was ever used for a *graphe* or any other public case. On the other hand, there is no evidence at all that the *paragraphe* procedure was ever used for a public case. One would suppose that the Athenians would have found it useful in every kind of case, public or private, to have a procedure, whether *paragraphe* or *diamartyria*, for objecting to a prosecution brought in the wrong way or in circumstances in which prosecution was forbidden by law; and so possibly the arrangement may have been that the *paragraphe* procedure, after it was introduced in 400, was used for private cases other than *diadikasiai*, while the *diamartyria* procedure remained available for *diadikasiai* and public cases. But the evidence is not sufficient to show that the distinction was in fact so neat.[479]

'PARAGRAPHE' AND THE ROLE OF THE JURY

Since *diamartyria* and *paragraphe* were both methods of preventing a case from coming to trial, a man who used either of them could be alleged by his opponent to have no confidence in the justice of his own case. The speaker of Isaios 7. 3 tries to make a favourable impression on a jury by saying that, though he could have employed *diamartyria*, he has refrained from doing so, in order to give an opportunity for his claim to be fairly considered by a jury. Surviving speeches for *paragraphe* trials are never confined to legal argument about the admissibility of a case; they all include discussion of the rights and wrongs of the case itself, as the man bringing the *paragraphe* maintains that its purpose is not, and his opponent that it is, merely to avoid trial of a weak case.

But, despite the comments of speakers who happen to have their own motives for disparaging *paragraphe*, there is no real evidence that it was not an efficient procedure for deciding the kinds of dispute for which it was used. And its introduction at the beginning of the fourth century was a further important step in the development of democratic justice in Athens. In the fifth century it had become normal for important legal cases to be judged by juries of the Athenian people; it was anomalous that the authority to admit or not to admit a case for trial by a jury remained largely in the hands of magistrates. The institution of *paragraphe* diminished this anomaly. It transferred to the democratic juries the responsibility for deciding whether a prosecution was admissible. Henceforth the Athenian people not only judged cases; they also judged whether cases were to be judged.

xv FOREIGNERS, MERCHANTS, AND THE LEGAL CALENDAR

TREATY CASES ('DIKAI APO SYMBOLON')

Greek cities were fairly self-contained, and many Athenians probably never left Attika except on military or naval campaigns. Holidays abroad were not yet fashionable, and even under the Athenian democracy not many citizens went abroad as ambassadors or official representatives. But traders, at least, visited other states frequently; so it inevitably happened sometimes that a dispute arose between an Athenian and a foreigner.

Suppose, for example, a dispute between an Athenian and a citizen of Naxos: the Athenian has lent a sum of money to the Naxian; the Naxian claims to have repaid all that he owed, but the Athenian claims that he has not received the full amount; so the Athenian wishes to prosecute the Naxian for debt. If they are both in Athens, naturally the Athenian makes his accusation to the authorities in Athens; if they are both in Naxos, naturally he makes it to the authorities in Naxos. If the Athenian is in Athens but the Naxian has gone home to Naxos, it would not be much use taking legal proceedings in Athens which the Naxian might just ignore, and so naturally the Athenian goes to Naxos and makes his accusation there. If the prosecution is brought in Athens, the Athenian magistrates and jury try the case according to Athenian law and procedure, for they can hardly be expected to be familiar with Naxian law; conversely Naxian law and procedure are naturally followed if the case is tried in Naxos.

But this arrangement may seem unsatisfactory if on some relevant point there is a substantial difference between Athenian law and Naxian law; if, for example, circumstances have arisen which excuse the debtor from payment under Naxian law but not under Athenian law, the Naxian will feel cheated if the case is tried under Athenian law and the Athenian will feel cheated if it is tried under Naxian law. To meet this difficulty it was common for a state to make a formal treaty (the neuter plural noun *symbola*) with another state, laying down the law and procedure to be followed in legal cases between citizens of the two states. This treaty would become part of the law of both states. Fragments survive of several fourth-century treaties of this sort, inscribed on stone, including one between Athens and Troizen and another between Athens and Stymphalos.[480] The offences mentioned include homicide and physical injury, though the fragments are too small to make clear any of the rules or procedures laid down; presumably they were some sort of compromise between the existing laws of Athens and of the other state concerned. Other inscriptions, including some fifth-century ones, contain references to a treaty, or to cases arising under treaties, using the feminine plural noun *symbolai*.[481] All the evidence has recently been discussed by P. Gauthier in his book entitled *Symbola*. He suggests that *symbolai* is the word for an agreement admitting aliens to an Athenian court, where Athenian law was applied, whereas *symbola* means a treaty specifying different legal procedures and penalties; but the scantiness of the inscriptions and literary references leave this and other points doubtful.

No doubt Athens had such treaties with many states. But not with all; there was none between Athens and Macedon, for example, before Philip proposed one in the middle of the fourth century, and then Hegesippos in the speech *On Halonnesos* opposed it, saying that Athenians and Macedonians in the past had always prosecuted one another quite satisfactorily without it. This passage proves that the lack of a treaty did not prevent legal proceedings between citizens of different states.[482]

THE POLEMARCH AND THE XENODIKAI

Some aspects of the position of aliens in Athenian courts have already been mentioned, including the fact that an alien defendant could be required to provide, in the presence of the polemarch, sureties to guarantee his appearance for trial (see page 76). It is clear that the polemarch had special responsibilities in connection with aliens, and it seems likely (though there is no explicit evidence on the point) that in early times he was the magistrate responsible for bringing to court any case brought in Athens in which either the prosecutor or the defendant was not Athenian. It is possible that homicide cases were an exception to this rule: in the fourth century prosecutions for the killing of an alien (which would normally be brought by the deceased's family, who would naturally be aliens too) were held at the Palladion under the presidency of the basileus (see page 117); and although there is no evidence for this at any earlier period, the Athenians were conservative about their homicide law and it may well be that the basileus had always conducted homicide trials for aliens as well as for citizens. Apart from this, however, it seems reasonable to accept that at one period the polemarch took all aliens' cases.

But by the middle of the fifth century this was no longer so. There are several surviving fifth-century decrees which confer on foreigners the right of bringing cases to the polemarch – generally on individual foreigners who are being honoured for services to Athens,[483] but there is also a well-known inscription of an Athenian decree which confers this right on all citizens of Phaselis (for disputes with Athenians arising at Athens) and mentions in passing that the citizens of Khios already have it.[484] The fact that the right of bringing cases to the polemarch was conferred on some aliens as a privilege proves that aliens generally, if they wished to bring a prosecution in Athens, had to go to some other magistrate. This can hardly have been any of the magistrates who dealt with Athenian citizens' cases (for it is unlikely that citizens and un-privileged aliens would be treated alike, when privileged aliens were distinguished from them), but some other magistrate or magistrates; and in fact we know that there did exist magistrates called xenodikai ('judges of aliens'). They are the magistrates who appear in the sur-viving fragments of fourth-century legal treaties between Athens and other states, and two other inscriptions prove that they already existed in the 440s.[485] Although there is no other evidence about them, it is plausible to suppose that at some time in the first half of the fifth century, when the growth of the Athenian navy and trade brought Athenians into more frequent contact with foreigners, prosecutions by and of aliens in Athens became too numerous for the polemarch to deal with them all, and so it was decided that he should deal only with certain aliens' cases, while new magistrates called xenodikai were cre-ated to deal with the rest. The cases kept by the polemarch doubtless included all those in which a metic or a proxenos (see page 79) was either the prosecutor or the defendant (for we know that he still dealt with some cases for metics and proxenoi in the fourth century), as well as those involving foreigners who had been given the right of bringing cases to him by special decree – in fact, all cases involving an alien who had any kind of special status in Athens. For some reason trial before the polemarch was preferable, but we do not know why.

The fifth-century decrees giving to certain aliens the privilege of trial before the polemarch clearly imply that the privilege extended to all cases in which those aliens were involved, whether as prosecutors or as defendants. But later evidence shows some cases involving aliens coming before magistrates other than the polemarch and the xenodikai, and it is clear that the scope of these magistrates' jurisdiction was subjected to further limitations.

First, a well-known decree laying down regulations for Khalkis in the Athenian Empire orders that the most serious legal cases involving Khalkidians should be referred to the Eliaia of the thesmothetai in Athens. This piece of evidence is discussed on page 226; here it is enough to say that it proves that some trials involving aliens went to the thesmothetai in the second half of the fifth century. But it is possible that this was an exceptional rule, applying to Khalkidians only, because the Athenians were particularly concerned to exercise close control over Khalkis.

By the fourth century, however, this tendency had gone further. Several instances are known of a *graphe* in which an alien was involved, either as the prosecutor or as the defendant, going to the thesmothetai, just as if it had involved citizens only.[486] And Aiskhines mentions (1. 158) that an alien accused of failing to pay a sum of money owed to an orphan was brought before the arkhon, which was the normal procedure for *eisangelia* for maltreatment of an orphan. Probably, then, all public cases involving aliens followed the same procedure as public cases involving citizens. Yet the fifth-century decrees giving privileged aliens the right of trial before the polemarch do not make any exception for public cases, but seems to mean all cases, whether public or private. So probably a change was made late in the fifth century or early in the fourth: public cases involving aliens were taken out of the hands of the polemarch and the xenodikai, and henceforth followed the same procedure as public cases involving citizens. Perhaps the Athenians decided that an offence against the community (which was the subject of a public case) was equally serious whoever had committed it. Only one kind of public case remained the responsibility of the polemarch: this was a *graphe aprostasiou* (see page 78), in which the defendant was invariably an alien.[487]

The arrangements for private cases for aliens in the fourth century are more obscure. From *AP* 58 we learn that the polemarch drew lots to allocate to the tribe judges of a particular tribe a private case in which the defendant was a metic or proxenos, not belonging to any tribe (see page 207). So the tribe judges, not the polemarch, were then the magistrates responsible for cases in which the defendant was a metic – and perhaps we may assume also those in which the prosecutor was a metic, though *AP* does not say that explicitly – if they were cases of the kinds for which the tribe judges were responsible when they involved citizens only. *AP* goes on to say that the polemarch brought into court for metics the kinds of case which the arkhon brought into court for citizens (that means family and inheritance cases), and also cases concerning the status of metics and freedmen (*apostasiou* and *aprostasiou*: see pages 78 and 82). That leaves an unexplained residue, since there were some private cases which, when they involved citizens, went to the thesmothetai (such as cases concerning mines), the agoranomoi (cases for damage to goods in the Agora), or other magistrates. My guess is, though there is no evidence to prove it, that by Aristotle's time all such cases involving metics went to the same magistrates as when they involved citizens, and that *AP*'s list of the polemarch's cases is a complete one for that period. If that is right, the decrease in the polemarch's functions since the fifth century is a mark of the decrease in distinctions made between citizens and metics.

The mention of the xenodikai in the fragments of legal treaties of the first half of the fourth century indicates that they still existed and took some part in treaty cases at that time.[488] Presumably they continued to be responsible for private cases involving aliens who were not metics or proxenoi, until the system was changed in the middle of the century by the introduction of the mercantile laws (discussed later in this chapter).

THE ATHENIAN EMPIRE

The sharpest increase in the number of trials in Athens involving non-Athenians, leading to the institution of the xenodikai, may have been due to the transformation of the Delian League into the Athenian Empire in the middle of the fifth century. When 'the allies' became 'the cities which the Athenians rule', one of the results was that citizens of the allied cities were sometimes required to travel to Athens for trials. Not for all trials: many treaty cases continued as before,[489] even though this sometimes meant that an Athenian was prosecuted in a subject-ally city where resentment of Athenian imperialism might prejudice the judges or jurors against him. Thucydides makes the Athenians boast rather indignantly of their moderation in this respect, in a difficult sentence of which the correct interpretation must be something like: 'Although we submit to being at some disadvantage in treaty cases with the allies, while making the laws impartial for trials held in Athens, yet we are regarded as litigious!'[490] All the same, it was

notorious that the Athenians compelled a considerable number of trials
to be held in Athens.[491]

Such trials were of several types. First, cases concerning the tribute
which the subject-allies were compelled to pay to Athens were naturally
tried in Athens. A decree proposed by Kleinias to improve the system
of collecting tribute includes clauses laying down a legal procedure for
prosecution of any Athenian or ally alleged to have committed an
offence concerning the tribute; if the lost parts of the inscription have
been restored correctly, any Athenian or ally who wished could make
such an accusation by *graphe* to the Boule, which, if it thought the
accusation true, passed the case on to the Eliaia for trial.[492] Another
decree, dated to 426, provides for the appointment of epimeletai
('supervisors') to bring to court prosecutions by *graphe* of anyone
accused of interfering with the collection of tribute.[493] On at least two
of the occasions when the amounts of tribute payable by various cities
were reassessed, Athenian juries of 1000 or 1500 jurors were convened
to try appeals against assessments, and eisagogeis ('introducers', not to
be confused with the fourth-century magistrates of the same name,
mentioned on page 233) were appointed to deal with them.[494] Those
who disapprove of imperialism will of course believe that the Athenians were wrong to compel tribute to be paid to them at all. But, if it
is once accepted that they did demand tribute, it is natural that they
did not allow the allies to decide for themselves how much they
should pay; what is remarkable is that complaints and disputes were
not just rejected or suppressed by force or by imperial command, but
were submitted to the consideration of a jury.

Secondly, if an Athenian wished to prosecute a citizen of a subject-
ally city by *graphe* (perhaps only for certain offences; our evidence is
too scanty to show how far the rule extended), the trial was held in
Athens. The defendant had to travel to Athens, and if he was found
guilty the Athenian judgement could then be enforced against him in
his own city. In Aristophanes's *Birds* one of the characters is a pompous
government inspector, who comes from Athens to inspect the new
city of Cloudcuckooland, which is comically treated throughout the
scene as if it were a subject-ally of Athens. Peisthetairos hits him, and
he yells 'I summon Peisthetairos for *hybris*, to appear in the month of
Mounikhion!' (*Birds* 1046–7). The procedure for prosecution for *hybris*
was *graphe*, and it appears that Peisthetairos is required to travel to
Athens for trial. Later in the play a sycophant appears. He is keen to
have wings, which will be a great advantage to him in his prosecu-

tions (which would commonly be *graphai*, since private cases were not open to volunteer prosecutors): he will be able to deliver a summons to a non-Athenian in one of the islands, then fly to Athens to get a trial and conviction before the defendant can reach Athens to defend himself, and then fly back to the island to execute the judgement by confiscating the convicted man's property before he can return from Athens.[495] The scene culminates in slapstick farce; but the comic effect would be largely lost if it were not true in fact that non-Athenians in the islands were required to travel to Athens when they were prosecuted by Athenians by *graphe*.

Even when a citizen of a subject-ally city was being prosecuted by one of his own fellow-citizens, the Athenians sometimes insisted on having some control over the trial. The earliest hint of this is in an Athenian decree of perhaps the year 453/2, laying down regulations for the city of Erythrai on the coast of Asia Minor. Part of the decree specifies penalties for homicide and other offences, apparently implying that trials for these offences will be held in Erythrai; but at one point the members of the Boule of Erythrai are required to swear an oath which includes the words 'I shall not receive back any of the exiles . . . who have taken refuge with the Medes, without the concurrence of the Athenian Boule and people, nor shall I expel any of those who remain, without the concurrence of the Athenian Boule and people.'[496] This seems to mean that there had been a pro-Persian revolution in Erythrai, which the Athenians had suppressed; and now the Athenians reserved the right to insist on punishment of any of the revolutionaries who tried to return to Erythrai, and to veto any attempt to impose the penalty of exile on Erythraians who had supported Athens. Thus the purpose of interfering with Erythraian jurisdiction was political, to support the pro-Athenian regime.

Later, in the decree laying down regulations for Khalkis in Euboia, the Athenians went further: 'Trials [*euthynai*, probably not here restricted to trials of ex-magistrates] for Khalkidians against Khalkidians are to be held in Khalkis, just as in Athens for Athenians, except for exile and death and disfranchisement; concerning these there is to be reference to Athens, to the Eliaia of the thesmothetai.'[497] This means that a court in Khalkis was not permitted to impose any of the three most severe penalties; if any of these penalties was thought necessary, the case had to be referred to Athens, where it was heard afresh – and not just in the court of the xenodikai, where a petty dispute between an Athenian and a foreigner would be heard at this period, but in the court of the thesmothetai, which was the court for many of the most important types of case. It probably means that the Athenians wished to have control over all cases which might have serious political implications; perhaps one might even say, to ensure the acquittal of Khalkidians who supported Athens and the condemnation of Khalkidians who opposed Athens.

This rule may well have become general throughout the Athenian Empire. Decrees about Miletos and Samos seem also to have specified that certain Milesian or Samian offenders were to go to Athens for trial and were liable to the penalty of death or exile or disfranchisement with confiscation of property, though the inscriptions of both these decrees are fragmentary and the details are uncertain.[498] The anonymous writer nicknamed 'the Old Oligarch' says that the Athenians 'disfranchise and confiscate their property and exile and execute' the kind of people likely to oppose them in the subject-ally cities.[499] And a speaker in about 415 remarks 'Not even a city is permitted to punish anyone by death without the concurrence of the Athenians'; 'a city' is vague, but it probably means that the rule applied to all or most cities in the Athenian Empire.[500] A few individuals, presumably champions of Athens in their own cities, were given a specially privileged position: without the concurrence of the Athenian people no penalty of any sort could be imposed on them.[501] These obstacles to punishing pro-Athenians in the subject-ally cities by legal methods might have goaded the more fanatical anti-Athenians to take the law into their own hands by surreptitious murder; and so there was also a rule that, if an Athenian or any of certain named non-Athenians (supporters of Athens, clearly) was killed and the killer was not brought to justice (or perhaps even if he was brought to justice; details of the rule are uncertain), the city where the murder occurred had itself to pay to Athens a fine of five talents, a very large sum.[502]

All this indicates that in the second half of the fifth century the Athenians did interfere a good deal in the jurisdiction of cities in the Athenian Empire. The primary motive was no doubt to keep political control over them. But 'the Old Oligarch', in the longest surviving contemporary comment on the matter, suggests that there were economic and social motives too.

'Another respect in which the Athenian people are regarded as ill-advised is their practice of compelling the allies to travel to Athens for trials. But others reply to this criticism by calculating the benefits

which the Athenian people gain by this: first, obtaining pay throughout the year from court fees; secondly, while staying at home,
without any sea-voyaging, they control the allied cities, acquitting
the democrats and condemning their opponents in the law-courts;
whereas, if each state held its trials at home, hostility to Athens
would have made them condemn those of their own citizens who
were friendliest to the Athenian people. Besides, the Athenian people
get the following gains from having trials at Athens for the allies.
First, the state gets more from the one-per-cent tax at Peiraieus; next,
anyone who keeps lodgings does better; next, so does anyone who
has a vehicle or a slave for hire; next, heralds do better as a result of
the allies' visits. Besides, if the allies did not come for trials, they
would respect only those Athenians who travel, the strategoi and
trierarchs and ambassadors; but as it is, every one of the allies is
compelled to be subservient to the Athenian people, realizing that
when he comes to Athens the judges before whom he must prosecute
and be prosecuted are none other than the people, because that is the
law at Athens; and he is compelled to plead in the law-courts, and
shake the hand of any juror going in. This makes the allies more the
slaves of the Athenian people.' ([Xenophon] *Athenaion Politeia*
1. 16–18)

The Athenian Empire came to an end in 405. In 378/7 the Athenians
formed a new league, generally known now as the Second Athenian
Confederacy, but it may not have involved as much variation from
normal judicial practice as the earlier Empire did. It did involve some:
the decree which formally established it makes reference to trials held
by the congress of the Confederacy (or, less probably, by a separate
court set up by the Confederacy);[503] and another decree, if the fragments are correctly restored, indicates that an Athenian prosecuted in
any of the cities on the island of Keos for any matter involving more
than a sum of 100 drachmas had the right to be tried in an Athenian
court.[504] But there is not enough evidence to show how extensive this
kind of control was in the Second Athenian Confederacy.

THE LEGAL CALENDAR AND THE NAUTODIKAI

It is in connection with cases arising in the Athenian Empire in the
second half of the fifth century that we see the first signs of an attempt
to construct a legal calendar. The fragmentary decree laying down

regulations for Miletos seems clearly to have specified not only that certain trials should be held in Athens, but also that they should be in certain months: Anthesterion and Elaphebolion (approximately February and March) are named, and the name of another month may have been lost before these two.[505] The decree proposed by Kleinias about the collection of tribute refers at one point to the possibility of prosecution by *graphe* in a month ending in -lion, but the first letters are lost: it may have been Gamelion or Elaphebolion or Thargelion.[506] Another inscription is also relevant, though it refers not to a subject-ally but to a cleruchy (an overseas settlement of Athenian citizens) at Hestiaia (in northern Euboia) in 445 or soon after. It gives the decree laying down the organization of trials in the new settlement. The cleruchs were to have their own courts in Hestiaia for some kinds of case, but other kinds (the part of the inscription saying which kinds is not preserved, but presumably they were the most serious) were to be referred to Athens and brought to court by the nautodikai in a certain month; the name of the month is not preserved.[507]

Two passages of Aristophanes parody the practice of holding trials in a particular month. One is the scene of *Birds* already quoted, in which the inspector from Athens, visiting Cloudcuckooland, summons Peisthetairos for *hybris*, to appear in the month of Mounikhion. The other is a fragment referring to a case between the Dead and the Living: it is a treaty case (*apo symbolon*), and the month for such cases, both *dikai* and *graphai*, is Maimakterion. If it is true that treaty cases were regularly tried in Maimakterion, that may be why another comic dramatist called that month 'a judicial month'.[508]

This evidence is not enough to make clear how the Athenians chose the month or months for particular classes of trial. But all the cases concerned are ones which involve people travelling to Athens from overseas. They are the people for whom it would be a hardship to have to wait in Athens for a long time for their cases to come on. Possibly the Athenians allotted different months to different cities, or to different types of city (cleruchies, subject-allies, cities having treaties with Athens), so that the citizens of each place, if involved in disputes with Athenians, knew at what time of year they must arrange to be in Athens.

The decree about Hestiaia is the earliest evidence for the existence of the magistrates called nautodikai. The word means 'judges of sailors', and their primary function was presumably to bring to court cases involving Athenians who travelled by sea, either because they lived overseas (in a cleruchy such as Hestiaia) or because they travelled as mariners or merchants.[509] One piece of evidence connecting the nautodikai with merchants is a difficult sentence in a speech of the 390s (Lysias 17). The speaker relates that he tried to bring against some other Athenians in the ordinary way a case for recovery of some land and a house which he claimed to be his; they objected by *paragraphe* that they were merchants, and this meant that he could not continue with his original prosecution. Instead he brought a fresh case before the nauto-dikai in Gamelion of the following year; at the time of the text which we have, the nautodikai had not yet pronounced a verdict. This seems to confirm that if a case involved merchants it was the nautodikai, in-stead of other magistrates, who received it. But does the reference to Gamelion mean that they received merchants' cases in that month only; was it a legal requirement or merely his own procrastination which caused the prosecutor to wait until that month? And does the word which I have translated 'pronounced a verdict' mean that the nautodikai themselves decided cases without reference to a jury (which might make for quicker trials), or only that they presided over a court and formally announced the jury's verdict? Our information is not sufficient to answer these questions.[510]

There is also some evidence that in the fifth century the nautodikai brought to court cases in which a man was prosecuted for masquerading as an Athenian citizen (*xenia*: see page 70), but the interpretation of the evidence is disputed, and it is not clear how this activity fitted in with the nautodikai's other functions.[511]

Although the surviving evidence about the nautodikai and the xeno-dikai is scanty, that does not prove that they were unimportant (be-cause fifth-century evidence about legal procedure is so sparse anyway). It seems reasonable to conjecture that both were brought into existence because in the fifth century the growth of Athenian maritime enterprise and of the Athenian Empire caused a big increase in the number of trials in Athens involving either non-Athenians or Athenians who spent much of their time away from Athens; and these kinds of person needed courts and magistrates who worked in accordance with some kind of calendar, so that prosecutors and defendants knew when to arrange to be in Athens for their trials. But the nautodikai and the xenodikai were not just instruments of imperialism: that they were found to be useful for other purposes is proved by the fact that, though the Empire disintegrated in 405, they continued in existence into the fourth century.

But in the first half of the fourth century there are signs of dissatisfaction with the nautodikai. In the 390s there is the speaker already mentioned (Lysias 17. 5) who complained that the nautodikai had not yet pronounced a verdict in his case. Some forty years later we find Xenophon, in his treatise on Athenian revenues (*Poroi* 3. 3), saying that Athens is an excellent city for commerce, except in one respect: 'If only someone offered prizes to the magistrates of the market, for the man who settled disputes the most justly and the most quickly, so that a merchant wishing to sail away was not prevented from doing so, that would make trading far more popular and pleasant.' This is probably a reference to the nautodikai; perhaps to the xenodikai too, since Xenophon is referring to non-Athenian merchants as well as Athenian ones. An increasing demand by business men for speed and efficiency may have been the chief reason for a drastic reform which was made in the middle of the fourth century. The date of the change must be between 355, which is the earliest date when Xenophon's treatise can have been written, and 342, when the new system is mentioned in the speech *On Halonnesos* (Demosthenes 7. 12).

The nautodikai and the xenodikai were swept away. Legal treaties between Athens and other states, and cases arising from them, became a responsibility of the thesmothetai.[512] But cases involving foreign merchants and ship-masters (and these must have been the great majority of cases arising between Athenians and foreigners) were now classed with cases involving Athenian merchants and ship-masters as 'mercantile cases' (*dikai emporikai*). 'Ship-master' (*naukleros*) means a man commanding a merchant ship; he might own it himself, or he might be the owner's employee or servant. 'Merchant' (*emporos*) means a man who buys goods in one city to sell in another; he would usually travel as a passenger on the ship transporting his goods. Or a man could convey his own goods on his own ship, being ship-master and merchant simultaneously. A merchant would often borrow capital to enable him to buy larger quantities of goods, using the goods as security for the loan. To judge from our limited evidence, it was this kind of loan which most often gave rise to disputes.

Under the new legislation, called 'the mercantile laws', cases involving merchants and ship-masters were brought before the thesmothetai.[513] The cases were monthly (*emmenoi*) from Boedromion to Mounikhion (approximately September to April), as we are told by

Demosthenes 33. 23, but the interpretation of this passage has given modern scholars some difficulty. It used to be thought that 'monthly' meant that judgement was given within one month from the bringing of the case, but an American lawyer and scholar, Edward E. Cohen, has shown in his book *Ancient Athenian Maritime Courts* that the correct interpretation is that applications to bring cases were accepted every month. We may infer that previously a cause of complaint had been that merchants and ship-masters often had to wait in Athens for more than a month before they could begin legal proceedings. This would be particularly annoying to them during the summer, and the reason for not holding their cases in the four summer months must be that at that time of year they would want to make the most of the good sailing weather and not be detained in Athens by a prosecutor. That the passage does mean that outside the specified months there were no trials of mercantile cases at all, not that there were trials but they were not monthly, is shown by a reference later in the speech (33. 26) to the time 'when trials were on'. Some scholars have gone so far as to emend the text in 33. 23 to read 'from Mounikhion to Boedromion', but that is wrong, because there is no reason why mercantile cases should have been completely banned throughout the winter.[514]

For a case to be brought by this procedure, the ground of prosecution had to be that an agreement, embodied in a written contract, existed between the disputants which, the prosecutor alleged, the defendant had failed to fulfil. The agreement must either have been made in the Athenian market (*emporion*: see pages 157–8) or concern a voyage to or from the Athenian market.[515] A particular penalty (though we do not know what it was) was specified for a ship-master or merchant who in an agreement undertook to sail to a particular port and then did not do so.[516] If the court decided in a case brought by this procedure that a man should pay some amount, he could be imprisoned until he paid it.[517] But if a man was considered to have prosecuted a ship-master or merchant without justification, he could himself be prosecuted as a sycophant by *endeixis* and *apagoge*.[518]

The chief purpose of these arrangements must have been to enable merchants and ship-masters to obtain justice promptly, without being deprived of their livelihood for months at a time by having to wait in Athens for a trial. The idea of accepting cases every month (very likely on the same day each month) seems to have been a success, for it was extended to other types of case. Not that it was a completely new idea: when Strepsiades in Aristophanes's *Clouds* is afraid of being prosecuted by his creditors on the last day of the month, that may well indicate that even in the fifth century cases for debt were accepted on that day every month; and the law that the arkhon must accept claims for inheritances in every month except Skirophorion may also be an early one.[519] But it is in the second half of the fourth century that we find a whole group of cases organized on this basis. Cases concerning the purchase of tax-collecting rights, for which the apodektai were the magistrates responsible, and cases concerning mines (*dikai metallikai*), which were brought before the thesmothetai, were made 'monthly' in this sense.[520] About this time (perhaps not until the 330s) five new magistrates, the eisagogeis ('introducers', not to be confused with the fifth-century magistrates of the same name, mentioned on page 225) were instituted to take over most other financial cases and bring them to court every month, including banking and trierarchic cases and various kinds of claim for payment of a loan or of a dowry. Evidently it was in financial matters that speedy justice was thought to be particularly desirable. But cases of battery and claims for slaves and draught animals were also included among the monthly cases of the eisagogeis.[521]

One interesting feature of the mercantile laws is the insistence on written contracts. It is a sign that the use of written documents had by now become normal in commercial affairs.[522] And the information which we find in speeches in the Demosthenic corpus about particular mercantile loans shows that the conditions of such loans were often so complicated that a written statement of them was really necessary. A loan could be secured on a ship, or on the slaves who formed its crew, or on the cargo, or on some part of the cargo; the borrower could be required to purchase certain kinds of goods in a certain port, take them to a certain other port, or to any of several specified ports, sell the goods there, use the money to buy certain other kinds of goods, and so on, before finally repaying the loan with interest; and there would be special clauses to say what repayment, if any, should be made if the ship was wrecked (all the contracts about which we have information specified that no repayment was required in this case; thus a loan could serve as a kind of insurance for the merchant) or if part of the cargo was thrown overboard to lighten the ship in a storm.[523] When a dispute arose about a loan of this sort, it would have taken a very long time to sort out the rights and wrongs of the case if the only available evidence had been people's recollections (or fabrications) of what had been orally agreed several months before. Producing a written document could cut short a long argument, and so the insistence on written contracts in the new mercantile laws should be seen as one of the means by which trials were speeded up. The purpose of the rule allowing a man to be imprisoned until he paid what he owed was also, of course, speed; it would not have been much use to a merchant or ship-master to get a prompt trial and verdict in his favour if he had then had to wait a long time in Athens for his opponent to pay up, and so he needed a means of inducing the debtor to pay quickly.

But the most remarkable thing in the new mercantile laws is that there was no distinction between Athenians and aliens. 'Aren't the laws and justice concerning mercantile cases the same for all of us?' asks rhetorically the speaker of the speech *Against Lakritos* (Demosthenes 35. 45). He is an Athenian; his opponent is a Phaselite. He makes some very rude remarks about the dishonesty of Phaselites, rather as the English sometimes say rude things about the Welsh or vice versa. But he never suggests that Phaselites should be subject to some different legal procedure; on the contrary, he implies that they should be treated just like Athenians. In the course of this speech (35. 10–13) a contract is quoted, giving the detailed conditions of a loan made by one Athenian and one Karystian to two Phaselites; the witnesses to the document are two Athenians and one Boiotian. In the speech *Against Phormion* one of the persons involved is a ship-master named Lampis, who is said to be a slave of Dion; yet he makes loans and gives evidence before an arbitrator, and there is no suggestion that his legal rights in the affair are less than those of the other men concerned.[524] 'Travelling about the world and spending my time in the market have made me familiar with most of the men who sail the sea,' says another speaker (Demosthenes 33. 5). Greek merchants in the fourth century were becoming a cosmopolitan community, in which the old distinctions of citizenship and nationality were unimportant. The new Athenian mercantile laws recognized this fact, and were an important step towards the unity of the Greek world.

TRIAL AND PUNISHMENT

In this final chapter a number of points mentioned separately in earlier chapters are brought together with other information to give a general account of the procedure used in the time of Demosthenes to decide a case. Before coming to the more usual kind of case in which the initiative of accusing someone else was taken by an individual in his personal capacity, we may first look at cases in which a magistrate took action officially.

A magistrate had authority to impose a fine for various kinds of minor offence connected with his own sphere of activity. Demosthenes mentions (21. 179) that the arkhon and his paredroi ('assessors'), who had the responsibility for organizing the festival of the Dionysia, could impose fines on persons who behaved in an improper or disorderly manner at the festival; and we have the text of a law of the year 421/0, quoted in the next paragraph, giving similar authority to the hieropoioi ('sacrificers') to impose a fine for disorderly behaviour at the procession for the festival of the Hephaistia. Doubtless all officials responsible for organizing festivals were given this authority. Another law (probably genuine, even though it may be misplaced in the text of Aiskhines 1. 35) lays down that the proedroi ('chairmen'), who were the officials who presided over meetings of the Boule and Ekklesia in the fourth century, may impose a fine on a speaker who speaks irrelevantly or abusively or disrupts the proceedings in other specified ways. There was also a law authorizing any official to fine anyone who abused him in his office;[525] and Aiskhines remarks (3. 27) that Demosthenes, while holding the office of teikhopoios ('wall builder'), imposed fines 'like the other magistrates'. So it is clear enough that the authority of magistrates to impose fines was not something exceptional, granted only to a few magistrates in particular circumstances. It was a general principle that a man appointed to an office was not only required to perform various functions but was also entitled to punish anyone who hindered him from performing them.

The relevant part of the law about the Hephaistia specifies a limit to the fine which the hieropoioi may impose on their own authority.

'The hieropoioi are to see to it that the procession is conducted as well as possible; and if anyone does anything disorderly, they are to have authority themselves to impose a penalty up to fifty drachmas and delete him from the procession list. If anyone deserves a greater penalty, they are to impose as high a fine as they think fit and bring him to the arkhon's court.' (*IG* i² 84. 26–30)

Likewise, the law about order at meetings of the Boule and Ekklesia authorizes the chairmen to impose a fine up to fifty drachmas, but requires them to bring to trial in the Boule or Ekklesia anyone who deserves a greater penalty; and a law about orphans and heiresses authorizes the arkhon to impose a fine 'according to the fixed rate', but requires him to bring to the Eliaia anyone who deserves a greater penalty.[526] It is probably safe to infer that all fines imposed by officials on their own authority were limited to fifty drachmas. In such a case no trial would be held. However, if the man on whom the fine was imposed considered himself unjustly treated, he still had two ways of getting his case heard: he could fail to pay the fine and then state his case if prosecuted by *endeixis* or *apographe* as a debtor to the state (see pages 165–6), or he could make a complaint at the magistrate's *euthyna* (see page 171).

One type of magistrates could impose on their own authority other types of penalty besides fines: strategoi (generals) in the field.

'When they are in command, they have authority to imprison a man guilty of indiscipline and to proclaim him and to impose a fine; but they do not often impose a fine.' (*AP* 61. 2)

In this passage the reading and interpretation of the word here translated 'proclaim' are doubtful, but the main point is clear: to maintain discipline in the face of the enemy the threat of a fine is unsuitable and inadequate. Naturally military commanders have powers of close arrest. Civilian officials (including strategoi, when not on military expeditions) were limited to fines. Their power to punish was, all the same, considerable. Fifty drachmas was a substantial sum. The power of an Athenian official to impose a penalty was much more than the authority of a modern policeman or traffic warden to impose spot fines for infringements of car-parking regulations.

Even so, there must have been some cases in which a magistrate wished to impose a heavier penalty than a fine of fifty drachmas. It is clear that he then had to have the case tried in a court by a jury, and we can assume that the trial procedure was much the same as in a case in which the prosecutor was a private individual (as described later in this chapter). The only puzzle arises from the fact that, at least in some cases, the magistrates bringing the prosecution must have been the same as the magistrates presiding over the court. Lysias 14. 21 implies that the strategoi, who were the magistrates presiding over trials for desertion from the army, were free to speak either for or against the defendant. Possibly the procedure was that one strategos presided while another strategos spoke for the prosecution or defence. But it is also possible that the Athenians did not see a need to keep the two functions apart, and allowed the same magistrate to be both chairman and prosecutor.

INITIATION BY A PRIVATE INDIVIDUAL

More often a case was initiated not by a magistrate but by a private individual, who had to start by getting his opponent to appear before the appropriate magistrate so that he could make his complaint or accusation. If he did not know which magistrate was the right one, he had to consult either the inscribed texts of the laws or a more knowledgeable person (such as a speech-writer) who could advise him.

In the time of Demosthenes and Aristotle the main categories were these. The arkhon took cases concerning relationships between members of Athenian families, including disputes about inheritance, and also cases concerning certain religious festivals, including the Dionysia. The basileus took most cases concerning religion or homicide. The polemarch took cases concerning the status or families of metics. The thesmothetai took a wide range of cases, including many kinds of public case, mercantile cases, and cases coming under legal treaties with other states (*dikai apo symbolon*). The Eleven took most cases of 'wrongdoers' (*kakourgoi*) and others who were arrested and held in prison before trial. Military, financial, and market officials took cases concerning the activities for which they were responsible. The eisagogeis took various kinds of monthly case. Other kinds of private case were taken by the forty tribe judges.[527]

Charges would not be accepted by all these magistrates every day. Various dates were appointed for the reception of various kinds of charge, though few of the dates are known to us. For some kinds of charge there was a day in every month (see pages 231-3), but for other kinds the days for charges must have been less frequent than that. A homicide case could not be initiated at any time in the last three months of the year (see page 118); an *antidosis* could be initiated on only one day of the year (see page 162). At the other extreme, it must have been possible to arrest a *kakourgos* and deliver him over to the Eleven, thus initiating an *apagoge* case, on any day of the year.

Once the prosecutor knew which magistrate would accept the kind of charge he wished to make, and on what day, his next task was usually to get his opponent to appear before the magistrate on that day. This meant issuing a summons. A summons was oral, not written, and it was delivered by the prosecutor himself, not by any public official. He simply went to his opponent and said 'I summon you to appear before magistrate X on day Y for the offence Z'. But his summons, to be valid, had to be witnessed; otherwise a defendant might have failed to appear before the magistrate and then have claimed that he had never been summoned. One summons witness (*kleter*) seems to have been enough in the 420s,[528] but in the late fifth century and in the fourth two were required.[529] So a man going to issue a summons would take with him one or two friends who would be able to testify, if necessary, that the summons had been issued. Testifying falsely to a summons (*pseudokleteia*) was an offence for which the offender could be prosecuted by *graphe* before the thesmothetai; the penalty was fixed by the jury, but if a man was convicted of this offence three times he was disfranchised automatically.[530]

Although in most legal matters in which a child or a woman was involved the *kyrios* (see page 84) acted on his or her behalf, it was possible for a woman to issue a summons herself.[531]

There were some kinds of case for which a summons was not necessary. In cases of *apagoge* or *ephegesis* (see page 148) the defendant, instead of being merely summoned, was arrested and put in prison. *Endeixis* could also involve arrest and imprisonment (see page 75); there seems to be no evidence to show whether a prosecutor by *endeixis* who decided that arrest was not needed had to issue a summons instead. An *eisangelia* could be initiated in the Ekklesia or the Boule without any previous summons, though the prytaneis who had charge of the meeting, if they knew of the *eisangelia* in advance, might take steps to see that the man to be accused was present. No summons would be needed for accusing an arbitrator by *eisangelia* at a meeting of arbitrators (see page 210) or for accusing an official at his *dokimasia* (see pages 167-9), since on those occasions the accused man was expected to be present anyway. In a homicide case the first step was a proclamation ordering the defendant 'to keep away from the things laid down by law' (see page 111) and there is no evidence to show whether a summons was needed in addition. In a claim for an inheritance there was no defendant and therefore no summons (except when a new claimant came forward to challenge an heir to whom the inheritance had already been awarded), but at the principal (*kyria*) meeting of the Ekklesia each month all such claims which had been made were read out, to alert anyone who might wish to make a counter-claim (see page 102).

When the appropriate day arrived, the prosecutor or claimant gave the magistrate a statement of his charge or claim. By the time of Demosthenes it was always submitted in writing, not only in a *graphe* but in private cases too. Some examples of charges have already been quoted (pages 150-1 and 201).

Besides giving in his charge the prosecutor had also, in many cases, to pay a fee. In some kinds of case in which the prosecutor claimed money from his opponent, he had to pay a fee called *prytaneia* (3 drachmas if the sum claimed was over 100 and not more than 1000 drachmas, 30 drachmas if the sum claimed was over 1000 drachmas); but if he won the case, his convicted opponent had to refund to him the amount he had paid in *prytaneia*, besides paying the debt or other money owed.[532] In some other cases, both private and public, he paid a fee called *parastasis*, the amount of which is not known.[533] In a case which went to a public arbitrator the prosecutor had to pay a fee of one drachma, also called *parastasis*, to the arbitrator (see page 209). In other kinds of case no fee was payable.[534] But we are not in a position to say why fees were charged in some cases and not in others.

If the defendant was an alien, he could be required to provide sureties to guarantee that he would remain in Athens for trial; that is, men (they probably had to be Athenians) who undertook to pay an agreed amount if he did not appear for trial. If he could not provide sureties, he was liable to be kept in prison until the trial.[535]

In most cases the chief duty of a magistrate receiving a charge, before taking it to a court for trial, was to hold a preliminary inquiry, called *anakrisis*. So, on a day when charges were submitted and the prosecutor and defendant in each case appeared before him for the first time, he had to fix a date for an *anakrisis* for each case. He probably used lot to allocate the various dates to the individual cases; at least, that seems the most plausible explanation of the fact that a phrase commonly used to refer to the initiation of a case is one which literally means 'get a case by lot' (*lankhanein diken*). If the magistrate allotted to you a date for *anakrisis*, that meant that you had successfully initiated proceedings.

PRELIMINARY PROCEEDINGS

When a magistrate had received a charge, it was posted on a notice-board in the Agora, near the statues of the eponymous heroes of the ten tribes.[536] If it was a charge of homicide, the basileus made a proclamation ordering the defendant 'to keep away from the things laid down by law' (see page 111).

Then came the magistrate's preliminary inquiry, the *anakrisis*. Historically this occasion was probably the direct descendant of the hearing at which in earlier centuries the king or arkhon had decided the case. Even in the fourth century it was still possible in certain cases for the magistrate to give a verdict at this stage. It is known that the forty tribe judges and the apodektai had authority to decide disputes about small sums of money, not exceeding ten drachmas,[537] and perhaps this authority was possessed by all magistrates who dealt with financial cases. But with these minor exceptions magistrates no longer gave verdicts in the fourth century.

What then did happen at the *anakrisis*? The proceedings must have begun with the reading out of the charge which the prosecutor had submitted to the magistrate. The defendant would be asked whether he admitted it, and if he denied it he would submit a formal statement to that effect.[538] If the case was a claim for an inheritance, any number of rival claimants might present themselves at the *anakrisis*, having seen the notice in the Agora or heard in the Ekklesia that the inheritance was to be adjudicated; each of them had to submit a statement of the grounds of his claim and, in some cases at least, he had also to pay as a deposit (*parakatabole*) a sum equal to one-tenth of the value of the property which he claimed.[539] Then each disputant or claimant swore an oath (generally called *antomosia*) that the charge or denial or claim which he had submitted was true.[540] But when an heir was being prosecuted for a debt allegedly owed by his deceased relative, he had only to swear that it did not seem (*dokein*) to him to be owed.[541]

An alternative possibility was that the defendant might claim that the case was inadmissible because it was of a type which was not allowed by law or for which a different procedure was required, or that it was a case which had already been decided. A claim of this sort was a *paragraphe*, and it prevented the case from proceeding until the *paragraphe* had been decided (see pages 214–17). Likewise in an inheritance case, if one claimant submitted a *diamartyria* asserting that he was the legitimate son of the deceased man, no other claims could be admitted by the magistrate; a *diamartyria* could be set aside only if the witness who gave it was successfully prosecuted for false witness (see pages 212–14 and 217–18).

The main part of the *anakrisis* was interrogation: the magistrate put questions to the disputants or claimants, and they could also put questions to each other. This would give each of them a clearer idea of what the other was alleging and what were the exact points in dispute, and it would help them to decide how it would be best to present their arguments in the trial and what supporting evidence would be needed.

We have in a speech of Isaios some account of an *anakrisis* held by the arkhon. The case was a claim to inherit the estate left by Euktemon, whose sons were all believed to be dead, but at the inquiry some relatives came forward with a *diamartyria* asserting that two boys were legitimate sons of Euktemon by a second wife. The account, besides giving instances of questions asked at an *anakrisis*, shows that a *diamartyria* did not stop the proceedings until questions had been asked to check its validity, that there was a law requiring that questions should be answered, and that if necessary the inquiry could be adjourned to give time for the answers to be ascertained.

'When the inquiries were held before the arkhon, and they paid a deposit on behalf of these boys, as being legitimate sons of Euktemon, on being asked by us who was their mother and whose daughter she was, they were not able to say, although we protested and the arkhon told them to answer in accordance with the law. To think, gentlemen, that they made a claim and *diamartyria* as on behalf of legitimate sons, and yet were not able to say who was the mother or any of the relatives! Well, on that day they made the excuse that she was a Lemnian, and procured a postponement. Later, on arriving for the inquiry, before even being asked, they immediately said that the mother was Kallippe, and that she was the daughter of Pistoxenos, as if it were enough just to produce the name of Pistoxenos. When we asked who he was, and whether he was living or not, they said he had died in Sicily on military service . . .' (Isaios 6. 12–13)

When the *anakrisis* was finished and the issues in dispute were clear, a date for the trial would be fixed. But there were some kinds of case in which the procedure was different. Cases which came before the tribe judges were passed on to a public arbitrator (see page 207); this may mean that the tribe judges held only a brief *anakrisis* and left most of the investigation to the arbitrator. In homicide cases the basileus, instead of an *anakrisis*, held three *prodikasiai* in separate months (see page 118); it is not clear whether a *prodikasia* differed very much from an *anakrisis*. There is no evidence that any *anakrisis* was held for a *probole* or an *eisangelia* which came before the Ekklesia or the Boule, and it may be that in these procedures the preliminary consideration of the case by the Ekklesia or the Boule was felt to make it unnecessary.

EVIDENCE

Before the trial came on, each litigant had to get together the evidence which he wished to present to the jury. If the case was one which went to a public arbitrator, all evidence had to be presented at the arbitration and none could be added at a later stage (see page 209). Otherwise it was enough to have the evidence ready in time for the trial.

One important kind of evidence was laws, which were evidence of what conduct was right or wrong. If a litigant wished to adduce the text of a law or decree, it was he himself, not any court official, who was responsible for obtaining a copy of it and taking it to the court. We do not hear of any procedure for checking that the text which he brought was accurate, but a law prescribed death as the penalty for anyone found to have presented a non-existent law.[542] (In a *graphe paranomon* the allegedly illegal decree and the laws with which it allegedly conflicted were written out on a board.[543] But in this case perhaps those documents were regarded as adjuncts to the charge, not merely as supporting evidence.) Other kinds of documentary evidence could also be produced, such as a will or a contract.

Evidence of facts was provided mainly by witnesses who stated what they knew. In the earlier period a witness gave evidence orally in court: the speaker who called him would put questions to him, or invite him to say what he knew of the matter or to confirm what the speaker had said.[544] But in the fourth century it became the rule that a written statement of a witness's evidence, made out in advance, was read out to the court by the clerk, and the witness simply confirmed that the statement read out was correct. (The verbal formula used for this confirmation is unknown; it may or may not have included an oath.) The reason for the change is not known; it may have been to save time, or to make the evidence easier to follow. The date is not known either; Calhoun argues that 378/7 was the year in which written statements were made compulsory, both for a charge and for a witness's testimony, but this cannot be proved.[545]

Certain kinds of evidence were not admissible. First, a litigant could not be his own witness; that is, he could not submit a written statement of what he himself had seen and have it read out as evidence. Secondly, hearsay evidence (testimony that someone had heard someone else say that a fact was so) was not allowed, except that it was allowed to report what had been said by a person now dead. If a witness was ill or abroad, his written statement could still be used if other people were able to testify that he had confirmed it.[546] The evidence of a disfranchised citizen could not be used, even though he might be present in the court.[547] Women and children seem never to have given evidence, though it is not clear whether that was because a law forbade them to do so or just because it was considered socially improper for them to speak in a public court. There must in practice have been some cases in which the testimony of a disfranchised citizen or a woman or a child would have made all the difference; it is remarkable that the Athenians were prepared to deprive litigants and juries of relevant evidence, rather than have evidence given by a person whom they considered, for reasons quite unconnected with the case, to be an unsuitable person to speak in court.

But provided that a man was not disqualified from appearing as a witness, a litigant was legally entitled to insist that he should do so. He could summon a man to appear as a witness, whether at a trial or at a public arbitration, and if the man did not turn up at the right time and place he could prosecute him for failure to testify (*lipomartyrion*).[548] If he did turn up, the litigant could produce a statement of evidence (*martyria*) written by himself, which he wished the witness to confirm, and insist that the witness should either confirm it or take an oath to the contrary; presumably this oath to the contrary could be either that the facts were not as stated or simply that he knew nothing about the matter. If he would neither confirm the statement nor take the oath to the contrary, the litigant could make a formal pronouncement of summons (*kleteuein*); the details are not known, but the consequence seems to have been that the recalcitrant witness had to pay a fine of

1000 drachmas.[549] Another possible course was the one followed by Apollodoros: he brought a case for damage against Antiphanes, alleging that by his failure to testify he had caused Apollodoros to lose the money which he ought to have recovered from Timotheos (see page 150).

If a witness did testify as requested by a litigant, the opposing litigant might maintain that the evidence was false. He could then bring a case for false witness (*pseudomartyrion*). Andokides remarked that sometimes men had given evidence which led to the execution of defendants, and then had been convicted of false witness when it was too late to be any use to the victims.[550] That seems to imply that a case could be brought by someone other than the victim, and thus that the procedure used was *graphe*, and could be initiated some time after the end of the trial in which the allegedly false evidence was given. Possibly Andokides had in mind an occasion in the middle of the fifth century when the Hellenotamiai (treasurers of the Athenian Empire) were condemned to death for embezzlement; after all but one, named Sosias, had been executed, fresh evidence came to light showing that they were innocent, and so Sosias alone was saved.[551]

But by the time of Demosthenes a different procedure was used: the opposing litigant himself had to make a formal objection (*episkeptesthai*), signifying his intention to bring a *dike* for false witness, before the jury voted in the trial.[552] The jury then proceeded to vote for the verdict and (when required) the penalty; but the procedure after that is not entirely clear, and seems to have differed in different cases. If the penalty imposed was merely a payment of money, the defendant apparently had to pay it; and if in due course he succeeded in winning his prosecution for false witness, the convicted witness would be required to compensate him. But if the penalty imposed in the original case was death (or, one may guess, anything else but a financial payment), it was not carried out until the trial for false witness had been held; if the witness was found guilty of giving false evidence, the verdict and penalty in the original case presumably lapsed. Sometimes a new trial of the original case was then held. That certainly happened when the case was a *diadikasia* for claiming an inheritance. If we can trust a scholiast's citation from Theophrastos, a new trial was allowed only when the original case had been about an inheritance, or masquerading as a citizen (*xenia*), or another case of false witness; but it is not known whether a new trial was always held in such cases, nor why it was not allowed in other cases.[553]

A case of false witness could also be brought against anyone who gave evidence of a kind which was not allowed, such as hearsay evidence.[554] A man who was found guilty of false witness on three different occasions was automatically disfranchised; for this reason, a man who had been found guilty of false witness twice was exempted from the rule that a man could be compelled to testify – an interestingly humane exemption.[555] A litigant who brought forward a witness to give false or illegal evidence was also liable to prosecution; his offence was called *kakotekhniai*.[556]

A special rule governed the testimony of slaves: they could not appear in court, but a statement which a slave, male or female, had made under torture (*basanos*) could be produced in court as evidence. The reason for this rule must have been that a slave who knew anything material would frequently belong to one of the litigants, and so would be afraid to say anything contrary to his owner's interests, unless the pressure put on him to reveal the truth was even greater than the punishment for revealing it which he could expect from his owner. But a slave was a valuable piece of property, which might be damaged by torture, and so could not be tortured without the owner's consent. Consequently we often find challenges on this subject in forensic speeches: one speaker challenges his opponent to allow his slave to be tortured, and interprets a refusal as an indication that the opponent knows that his slave's evidence would be against him; another speaker offers his own slave to his opponent for torture, and interprets a failure to take up the offer as an indication that the opponent knows that the slave's evidence would be in the speaker's favour.

'Since I knew, men of the jury, that immediately after the trial Onetor had received the goods from Aphobos's house and taken over all his and my property, and since I was well aware that the woman was living with Aphobos, I asked Onetor to hand over three slave-women, who knew that the woman was living with Aphobos and that the goods were in their hands, so that there might be not only allegations but *basanoi* on the subject. But when I made that challenge, and everyone present declared that what I said was right, he refused to have recourse to that test. As if there were any clearer proof on such subjects than *basanoi* and witnesses' statements, he neither produced witnesses that he had paid over the dowry, nor handed over for *basanos* the women who knew the truth, to show that his sister was not living with Aphobos; and, because I made this request, in a very overbearing and abusive manner he refused to let me talk to him. Could anyone be more obstinate than that, or more deliberately pretend not to know the right thing to do? (*To the clerk of the court*) Take the actual challenge and read it out. (*The challenge is read.*) Now, you consider *basanos* the most reliable of all tests both in private and in public affairs. Wherever slaves and free men are present and facts have to be found, you do not use the statements of the free witnesses, but you seek to discover the truth by applying *basanos* to the slaves. Quite properly, men of the jury, since witnesses have sometimes been found not to have given true evidence, whereas no statements made as a result of *basanos* have ever been proved to be untrue.' (Demosthenes 30. 35–7)

This passage is one of many in which orators praise a practice which is one of the most startling features of Athenian life and society. To torture a person as a punishment for an offence is logical, even if undesirable; to torture a person to make him confess an offence of his own or of an accomplice is understandable, though deplorable; but to torture an innocent man or woman in order to check the truth of information about someone else's offence appears to us an act of wanton and purposeless barbarity. It conflicts with the humanity which we are accustomed to regard as characteristic of the Athenians. And it is not even an effective way of discovering facts, since it induces the witness to say what the torturer desires rather than what is actually the truth.[557]

The challenger could make his challenge orally in front of witnesses, but perhaps more often it was put in writing. It would state which slaves he wished to be questioned and what they were to be asked; it could also state what method of torture would be used and who was to inflict it, and it could include an undertaking to pay the owner for any permanent damage to the slave.[558] Often the challenge was refused. But we should not assume that it was never accepted. The statement made by some modern scholars that no instance is known in which a slave was in fact tortured is misleading, since there are three fairly clear cases in which an investigation authorized by the Boule or the Ekklesia involved the torture of witnesses.[559] (These were probably all slaves. There is some evidence that free aliens could also be tortured as witnesses, but it is not clear in what circumstances this was possible;[560] more often aliens appeared as ordinary witnesses, without torture.[561] Cases are also known in which an alien accused of a serious offence was tortured, whether to extract a confession or as a punishment.[562] But torture of Athenian citizens was forbidden by law.[563])

If a slave was questioned under torture, presumably what he said was written down and could then be read out in court like the evidence of any other witness, except that others who had been present at the questioning, not the slave himself, would attend at the trial to confirm that the document read out was an accurate record of what he had said. But if a challenge to use a slave's evidence obtained under torture had been rejected, the challenger might have the text of his challenge read out in court as evidence in his own favour, as in the passage of Demosthenes already quoted.

Another kind of challenge which could be used as evidence was a challenge to take an oath. A litigant would propose that he and his opponent should each take a solemn oath in a temple that his own statement, on some point which was in dispute, was true. If the opponent did not agree to do this, the challenger could have the terms of his challenge read out at the trial as evidence that his opponent did not really believe in his own case.[564]

Finally, there was the possibility of producing real evidence, an object for the jury to see with their own eyes. The real evidence could even be a person. When Pantainetos complained of the violent activities of Nikoboulos's slave, Nikoboulos produced the slave in court to let the jurors see what a feeble creature he was.[565] A more spectacular instance occurred in a homicide trial described in Isokrates 18. 52–4. Kallimakhos and his brother-in-law had a dispute with Kratinos over the ownership of a piece of land. The quarrel led to blows, and afterwards Kallimakhos and his brother-in-law declared that a slave-woman of theirs had died from wounds inflicted by Kratinos. They prosecuted him for homicide. Kratinos produced in court the best possible item of evidence in his defence: the slave herself, alive, whom Kallimakhos and his brother-in-law had secretly hidden away.

THE TRIAL

When a trial was held by the Ekklesia or the Boule for a case brought by *eisangelia* or *probole*, no doubt those bodies followed their own normal procedures. The Areopagos and the other homicide courts also had special features of procedure (see pages 118–20). Here I describe only the trial procedure of the ordinary courts; a list of their known names has already been given (see pages 35–6).

On the day fixed for the trial the litigants, with their witnesses and supporters, went to the court of the magistrate who had received the case. The general public could stand round the outside of the enclosure which formed the court proper, to listen.[566] The magistrate presided, and the jury was in attendance, selected as already described (see pages 35–40). The jurors did not need to take an oath, since they had taken one at the beginning of the year (see page 44), but the magistrate selected by lot one juror to supervise the water-clock, four to supervise the voting, and five to supervise the payment of the jury at the end of the day.[567] The case (or the first case, if several were due for trial in one court on the same day) was then called, and the charge was read out by the clerk of the court.[568]

If either of the litigants was unable to attend because of illness or absence abroad, he could send a friend to swear an oath (*hypomosia*) to that effect; if the other litigant opposed postponement, the jury voted to decide whether to postpone the case or to give a verdict in favour of the litigant who was present.[569] It is interesting that postponement was not regarded as a merely administrative matter, to be decided by the magistrate, but as a question for the jury, because it would favour one litigant or the other; a man with a weak case might try making excuses to get it put off as long as possible.

'The comic dramatists call a rough case "a Skyrian case", because men evading a trial used to make the excuse that they were away in Skyros or Lemnos.' (Polydeukes 8. 81)

If the jury decided that the excuse given for absence was unacceptable, or if no excuse was offered, the case was automatically decided against the litigant who was absent; and if he was the defendant, the penalty required by law or proposed by the prosecutor was automatically imposed. If the absent litigant was the prosecutor and the case was a public one, he became liable to a fine of 1000 drachmas and he forfeited the right to bring prosecutions of the same type in future, unless the case was an *eisangelia* (see page 64). A case decided against either litigant in his absence was said to be 'deserted' (*eremos*); and if within two months he showed that he had had a good reason for absence, a fresh trial was held.[570] But more often the reason for absence will have been that the litigant knew he would lose the case anyway. A man who expected to be condemned to death would naturally prefer to flee from Athens before the trial, as did, for example, Alkibiades and others accused of profanation of the Mysteries or mutilation of the Hermai (see page 198).

If the litigants were present, the case proceeded at once with the speeches. As in homicide cases (see page 119), there were several kinds of private case in which there is evidence that each litigant made two speeches (in the order: prosecutor, defendant, prosecutor, defendant), and it may be that this was the rule in all private cases.[571] This arrangement gave the prosecutor a chance to answer in his second speech some of the arguments put forward by the defendant, while still leaving the defendant with the last word. But Demosthenes in his speech *On the False Embassy* (19. 213) mentions that he will have no second speech in that trial, and it seems likely that in public cases, in which the speeches could be longer (see next paragraph), only one speech on each side was allowed. In a claim for an inheritance each claimant spoke twice, according to Demosthenes 43. 8; yet *AP* 67. 2 mentions *diadikasiai* for which there was no second speech. Either the rule about this was changed during the fourth century, or it was different for different sorts of claim.

The speeches were limited to a certain length of time, the same for both sides, measured by a water-clock (*klepsydra*). This was a large pot or pail, having at the bottom a small hole which could be plugged. It was filled with water, and when a speech began the plug was removed; the speaker had to stop when the water had all run out. The pot (or another of the same size) was then filled for the opposing speaker. Pots of different sizes were used to give different lengths of speech for different kinds of case. For private cases *AP* 67 gives some figures: if the sum at issue was more than 5000 drachmas, the amount of water allowed was 10 khoes for the first speech and 3 khoes for the second; if between 5000 and 1000 drachmas, 7 khoes and 2 khoes; if less than 1000 drachmas, 5 khoes and 2 khoes; in a *diadikasia* in which there was no second speech, 6 khoes were allowed for the one speech. Elsewhere we read that each claimant for an inheritance had 1 amphoreus (12 khoes) for his first speech and 3 khoes for his second. *AP* says (if the reading of the papyrus is correct) that four private cases were tried in one court in one day, and that the speakers took an oath to keep to the point. Only one public case was tried in one court on one day; a total of 11 amphoreis was allowed, of which one-third (44 khoes) was for the prosecutor, one-third was for the defendant, and one-third for the speeches about the assessment of the penalty if the defendant was found guilty. This was called a 'measured through' (*diamemetremene*) day.[572]

One water-clock has been found in the Agora excavations; it holds 2 khoes and the water takes 6 minutes to run out. Thus one may convert *AP*'s amounts of water to modern measurements of time by allowing 3 minutes for 1 khous. However, this equation may be unreliable. It all depends on the exact size of the plug-hole. The surviving water-clock seems, from its inscription, to have belonged to the Antiokhis tribe, and it may be unsafe to take for granted that the ones belonging to the law-courts had plug-holes of the same size.[573]

Evidence was presented in the course of a speech. The laws, witnesses' statements, and other documents which the speaker wished the jury to hear were read out by the clerk of the court. In private cases the water-clock was plugged while the clerk was speaking, so that the documents did not count against the speaker's allowance of time, but they did so count in a 'measured through' day.[574] A speaker could put questions to his opponent, and the opponent was required to answer, but there is no reason to suppose that the water was stopped for that.[575]

Each litigant had to speak for himself: he could not, as in a modern court, sit through the case in silence while a lawyer spoke for him. It was not that any inscribed law existed requiring him to speak, but rather that no Athenian jury would have voted for a man who said nothing. However, if he had little confidence in his own legal knowledge or oratorical ability, he could get someone else to compose his speech. It is clear that it was a common practice in the fourth century to get a speech written by a speech-writer (*logographos*), and a recent suggestion that speech-writers did not usually write complete speeches but merely acted as consultants is not altogether convincing.[576] Many of the surviving speeches attributed to Antiphon, Lysias, Isokrates, Isaios, and Demosthenes are written for delivery by someone else. It is not known for certain whether speeches were read out in court, or were learned by heart and recited from memory, but the latter is more likely. Probably it made a much more favourable impression on a jury if a speaker gave the appearance of saying simply what he himself knew about the case, without any elaborate preparation or assistance. No doubt some speakers diverged from their written text, either accidentally or deliberately, and some texts were altered for the benefit of readers after the trial was over. So we can never be sure that a text which we have is an exact record of the speech which was actually delivered. But since the composition and delivery of speeches was not the subject of any law, it need not be discussed further here. Readers may consult M. Lavency's *Aspects de la logographie judiciaire attique*.

Another possible source of assistance was a supporting speaker. A litigant could stop speaking before his time-limit was up and ask someone else, or several others, to speak in his support, within the time allowed him by the water-clock. In certain cases it was appropriate even to give the greater part of the time to a supporting speaker. Thus, when Aiskhines prosecuted Ktesiphon for proposing an illegal decree about Demosthenes (see page 51), most of what he said was really an attack on Demosthenes rather than on Ktesiphon, and it was quite suitable for Ktesiphon in defence to speak only briefly himself and leave most of his time for Demosthenes's supporting speech (viz. the speech *On the Crown*, though the actual speech in court cannot have been as long as the preserved written text). The most extreme instance known to us is the speech *For Phormion*. Phormion had started life as a slave, and although he became a banker and an Athenian citizen he seems to have been virtually incapable of making a speech to an Athenian jury. He must have uttered only a few words and then called on his supporting speaker, since the preserved text begins as follows.

> 'Phormion's inexperience of speaking, and his inability, you have all seen for yourselves, men of Athens. It is necessary for us, his friends, to say and explain to you what he has repeatedly told us ...'
>
> (Demosthenes 36. 1)

But supporting speakers were expected to be relatives or friends who spoke because of their personal connection with the litigant. To speak in court for a fee, like a modern lawyer, was not merely disreputable but an offence, for which a prosecution by *graphe* could be brought.[577]

There could be supporting speakers for the prosecution as well as for the defence; and in an *eisangelia*, when the Boule and the Ekklesia decreed that a trial should be held, they often appointed a number of men to speak for the prosecution, sometimes as many as ten.[578] Likewise there were ten men to present the case against a magistrate whose accounts were unsatisfactory (see pages 170–1). The same name, *synegoros* (literally 'joint speaker'), was used for all these kinds of speaker.[579]

Besides supporting speakers, a litigant could have with him in court supporters who did not speak. These could even include his own children; it became notorious, and a subject of Aristophanic satire, that a guilty man was sometimes let off by soft-hearted jurors for the sake of his weeping children.[580]

When the speeches were finished the jury proceeded to vote immediately. One of the most important differences between an Athenian trial and most modern trials is that in Athens no judge or other neutral person gave any directions or advice or summing-up to the jury, nor did the jury hold any formal discussion. Every juror had to make up his own mind, not only on the facts but also on questions of law and equity, solely from the speeches and evidence presented by the rival litigants.

In the fifth century each juror had one vote. It was a pebble (*psephos*) or a mussel-shell which he brought with him to the court. There were two urns, one for condemnation and one for acquittal; the jurors filed past them, passing the urn for condemnation first and the urn for acquittal second. Each urn had a wicker-work funnel to assist secrecy; the juror could put his clenched hand into the funnel of each urn, so that no one could see into which one he dropped his vote.[581]

In the fourth century bronze votes were used. They are described in *AP* 68, and some have been found in the Agora excavations. Each was a disc with a shaft or tube through the middle; a hollow tube indicated a vote for the prosecution, a solid tube for the defence. The juror no longer provided his own vote, as in the fifth century, but at the end of the speeches in the trial he was given one vote with a hollow tube and one with a solid tube. There were two urns, a bronze urn for valid votes and a wooden urn for invalid votes. Each juror put one of his votes into each urn; by holding the votes with his fingers over the ends of the tubes he could conceal from onlookers which vote he put into which urn. When all had voted, the votes in the bronze urn were counted. The majority of votes decided the verdict; an equal number of votes for each side meant acquittal.[582] In a *diadikasia* for an inheritance, when there might be more than two claimants, there was a separate urn for each competing claim, though two persons who claimed to share an inheritance (because they both had the same relationship to the deceased) shared an urn; each juror just placed a vote in one urn.[583]

In a public case, if the prosecutor obtained less than one-fifth of the votes, he had to pay a fine of 1000 drachmas and he forfeited the right to bring prosecutions of the same type in future, unless the case was an *eisangelia* (see page 64). In some private cases in which the prosecutor had claimed a sum of money from the defendant, on losing the case he had to pay to the defendant one-sixth of the amount which he had claimed (*epobelia*, one obol per drachma). Demosthenes faced this risk when he prosecuted his guardian Aphobos in 364/3 for making away with his inheritance, but Kallimakhos did not when he claimed 10,000 drachmas in 400/399, even though *epobelia* was payable in a *diamartyria* or a *paragraphe* at that period. Either the law was changed between those dates or *epobelia* was payable only on some financial claims and not all. It is also uncertain whether it was payable on every acquittal or only when the prosecutor failed to get one-fifth of the votes. (We cannot assume that the rule about this in a financial claim was the same as for *epobelia* in a *diamartyria* or a *paragraphe*.) The latter seems more reasonable, since the purpose of imposing fines on an unsuccessful prosecutor must have been to discourage prosecutions which had no hope of succeeding and which would waste the court's and the defendant's time.[584]

These fines automatically became payable by the unsuccessful prosecutor and did not require further proceedings at the trial. But if the jury's verdict was in favour of the prosecution, the question of imposing a penalty on the defendant or an award to the prosecutor arose. In some public cases the penalty for the offence was fixed by law, but in others the jury had to decide it. Likewise, in some private cases a verdict for the prosecution meant simply that, for example, an item of property of which the ownership had been disputed was now awarded to the prosecutor, while in other private cases, such as a case of battery, the jury had to decide the amount of damages or compensation to be paid to the victim. In a modern trial, even when the verdict is given by a jury, the penalty is generally decided by a professional judge; so here is another respect in which the Athenians gave to ordinary citizens a task which we give to experts.

The large Athenian jury could not discuss a range of possible penalties; it could merely vote to choose between alternatives which had been proposed. The procedure, therefore, was, in any trial in which assessment (*timesis*) of a penalty or compensation was required, that the successful prosecutor proposed a penalty, the unsuccessful defendant proposed another (naturally a lighter) penalty, and the jurors voted for one or the other; no compromise between the proposals was possible. It must often have been very hard to judge how severe a proposal to make, and especially worrying for the defendant; he would want the penalty to be as light as possible, but if the proposal which he made was too lenient the jury would vote for the prosecutor's proposal instead. When Sokrates was found guilty of impiety (see page 202), one reason why so many jurors voted for the death penalty may well have been that they thought that Sokrates, in making his alternative proposal, did not take a sufficiently serious view of his offence.

The prosecutor and the defendant each made another speech putting forward his proposed penalty or compensation. *AP* 69. 2 says that the limit for each of these speeches was half a khous of water, though in public cases the statement of Aiskhines 3. 197 that one-third of the day was used for assessing the penalty seems to imply a much longer time. As in the earlier part of the trial, at this stage too a litigant could if he wished give part of his time to a supporting speaker.[585] In the fifth century each juror had a tablet smeared with wax; a long line drawn in the wax was a vote for the heavier penalty and a short line for the lighter. In the fourth century this cumbrous method was abandoned and voting on the penalty was conducted in the same way as voting on the verdict. When the result of the voting had been announced, the trial was complete; and when all the day's trials in their court were finished, the jurors were paid for their day's work.[586]

PENALTIES

For some offences the penalty was fixed by law, but otherwise there seem to have been no limits; a litigant was free to propose any penalty he thought suitable, however unusual. When Sokrates suggested that he deserved free meals for life (see page 202), no doubt it would have been silly to put that forward as his proposed penalty, but it would not have been illegal. However, in practice only certain kinds of penalty were imposed.

The severest was death. Execution was supervised by the Eleven and carried out by a professional executioner, who was known euphemistically as 'the public man' (*demios*, not necessarily meaning that he was a publicly owned slave). Normally it was carried out immediately after the trial. But there were no executions during the annual voyage of the sacred ship from Athens to Delos; this was the reason why Sokrates had a period in prison between condemnation and execution, since his trial happened to be held at just that time and the return of the ship to Athens had to be awaited.[587]

Three methods of execution are known. First there was the chasm or pit, into which condemned men were thrown. In early times they were probably thrown down alive, so as to be killed by the fall or left to die at the bottom. That seems to be what happened to the envoys from the Persian king Dareios in 490. But at a later period it may have become customary to put the criminal to death first by some other means and use the pit merely as an ignominious place of burial; that is what

Xenophon's text implies, if not emended (see page 181). The fifth-century word was *barathron*, which probably means a natural chasm, though its location is uncertain. In the fourth century we find *orygma*, which should mean an excavated pit. It should not be assumed that both words refer to the same cavity, and the *orygma* may never have been anything other than a receptacle for the dead bodies of criminals. It does not seem likely that precipitation was still used as a method of execution in the fourth century.[588]

A second method was the board (*tympanon*): the condemned man was fastened to an upright wooden board by five iron bands around his neck, wrists, and ankles secured by nails. He either died from exposure and starvation or perhaps was strangled by the iron collar. This method was used for persons condemned to death for homicide, and also for traitors and thieves.[589] A third method was poisoning by a drink of hemlock. The death of Sokrates in this way is well known from one of the most famous descriptive passages in Greek literature, the end of Plato's *Phaidon*, though Plato was not an eyewitness and his account may be largely due to artistic imagination.[590] The Thirty in 404/3 ordered a number of men to drink hemlock,[591] but there is not much evidence for its use for execution (as distinct from suicide). It is still not clear when it came into use and to what extent it superseded other methods. It is remarkable that neither hanging nor decapitation seems to have been used.

Exile was another severe penalty, since a man arriving without resources in a strange city might find it hard to be accepted there. This penalty was imposed for unintentional homicide (see page 120) and sometimes for treason (see pages 176–9), but we do not hear of its use for other offences. (Ostracism, which meant banishment for ten years only, was not a penalty for an offence and is not relevant here.) Condemnation of an absent man to death (see page 119) or outlawry (see page 73) must have been similar in effect to exile, since a man who had suffered any of these was liable to be put to death if he showed himself in Attika. But one difference was that, as long as he remained outside Attika, an exile retained some protection under Athenian law, whereas an outlaw did not; thus anyone who killed or harassed an Athenian exile outside Attika and then came into Attika himself could be prosecuted in Athens for that offence.[592]

The penalties of death, outlawry, and exile could be augmented by one or more of several additional penalties: confiscation of one's property, demolition of one's house, loss of the right to be buried in

Attika on death, and disfranchisement of one's descendants. Cases of betrayal provide some instances (see pages 176–9). The procedure by which confiscation of property was carried out in such cases was a variety of *apographe* (see page 166). The demarch of the condemned man's deme was required to produce a list of his property.[593] If anyone else intervened with a counter-claim to some part of the property, there was a trial (a *diadikasia*); and then the property which was adjudged to the state was offered for sale by the poletai. In such cases it sometimes happened that relatives or friends of the condemned man surreptitiously took possession of some of his property to save it from confiscation and keep it for themselves. If this was discovered, anyone who wished could proceed against them by *apographe*, listing the items of property which he alleged were being wrongfully withheld from the state. For example, when Ergokles the general was condemned to death and confiscation of property, he was believed to possess more than 30 talents, but after his execution this money could not be found. So someone alleged that Philokrates, who had served as Ergokles's treasurer, had it, and proceeded by *apographe* to demand the confiscation of Philokrates's property; the surviving speech *Against Philokrates* (Lysias 29) was composed for that trial.

Enslavement was a penalty imposed on an alien who resided in Athens without being registered as a metic or paying the metics' tax (see pages 76–8), and on an alien, whether he was a metic or not, who exercised any of the privileges of a citizen (see page 70) or cohabited with a citizen as husband or wife (see page 87). In these cases the method of carrying out the penalty was that the poletai offered the offender for sale. Slightly different was the case of the freedman who failed to fulfil his obligations to his former owner; he simply became the slave of his former owner again (see page 82). A man captured in war became his ransomer's slave unless he repaid the amount of the ransom; but, with that exception, we never hear of an Athenian enslaved in Athens in the fifth and fourth centuries, though it had been commoner in earlier times (see pages 79–80).[594]

Citizens, however, could suffer the rather less serious penalty of disfranchisement (*atimia*), meaning loss of the privileges of Athenian public life, or of some of them (see pages 74–5). This penalty too was sometimes, though not always, accompanied by confiscation of property.

Imprisonment was less often used as a penalty than in modern times. The Eleven had charge of the prison, and they kept there men who were being held under arrest until trial (by the procedures of *apagoge, ephegesis* and *endeixis*: see pages 75, 120, 148) and men who had been condemned to death or enslavement and were awaiting execution or sale (such as Sokrates before the return of the sacred ship from Delos); but that was a different matter from imprisonment imposed by a court as the penalty for an offence. Different again was the requirement that a man condemned to pay a fine should be kept in prison until he paid it. That was the rule when a fine was imposed for *hybris*, or for failing to observe the restrictions of disfranchisement, or in a mercantile case; and in any case in which the litigants proposed penalties a proposal for a fine could include that stipulation.[595] The Boule also had some power to imprison a man who had not paid a debt owed to the state (see pages 166–7). One must also distinguish the period of five days' confinement in the stocks which could be imposed for theft (see page 148), since Demosthenes 24. 114 indicates that that took place not in the prison but in some open place where everyone could see the offender. None of those things is quite like the modern use of a term of imprisonment as, in itself, the entire penalty for an offence. But, despite a dearth of known instances, it is clear from general statements that imprisonment was one of the forms of punishment which a litigant could propose.[596]

Although slaves were beaten by their owners, there is no evidence that flogging or other physical maltreatment was ever imposed as a legal penalty on free men, apart from the rule that a man could do whatever he wished to a seducer of one of the women in his family (see pages 124–5).When orators speak of a penalty inflicted on the body (*soma*), they do not generally mean what we call corporal punishment, but death or exile or disfranchisement, contrasted with a financial penalty.

Financial penalties must in practice have been much the commonest. In public cases any fine which was imposed went to the state, except that half of the fine in a *phasis* (see page 159) and three-quarters of the amount confiscated in an *apographe* (see page 166) went to the successful prosecutor. If a man sentenced to pay a fine to the state did not pay it, he was liable to the various penalties which fell upon debtors to the state (see page 166). In a private case a losing defendant would usually be required to pay a sum of money to the successful prosecutor; in English we call this damages or compensation rather than a fine, though there is no distinct word for it in Greek. In a case of violence, the losing defendant had to pay compensation to the prosecutor and a fine to the state as well (see pages 124, 148). In a case of disputed ownership of money or property, the penalty for the loser of course was that he had to hand over the item in dispute. If the loser of a case failed to hand over the money or property which was awarded to his opponent, he could have a *dike exoules* brought against him (see page 153); and in mercantile cases he could be kept in prison until he paid (see page 232).

PARDON AND AMNESTY

A verdict and penalty imposed by a jury were normally final, except when a litigant was able to request a new trial on the ground that he had been unavoidably absent from the previous trial (see page 248) or that he had shown that false evidence was given at it (see page 244). A person exiled for unintentional homicide could be pardoned by the family of the person whom he had killed (see page 120). Otherwise retrials and appeals against a jury's decision (as distinct from appeals *to* a jury against the decision of a public arbitrator) were not allowed.[597]

But there was one body which had the power, if it wished, to annul a decision of a jury of the Athenian people: the Athenian people itself. In 403 the Ekklesia made laws saying that any verdict given under the regime of the Thirty was invalid, but that those given in the time of the democracy were valid; this shows that it considered that it, as the sovereign body, had authority to pronounce on the validity or invalidity of juries' verdicts.[598] Towards the end of the Peloponnesian War, at a time when efforts were being made to set aside past quarrels and unite the Athenians and any possible allies against Sparta, there were several occasions when the Ekklesia passed decrees to annul verdicts or penalties. Possibly we should discount the decree passed in 411 that Alkibiades and others, who had been condemned to death in their absence in 415 for profanation of the Mysteries and mutilation of the Hermai (see page 198), should be allowed to return to Athens; for at that time the regime of the Five Thousand was in control, and regular democratic procedures may not have been followed.[599] But full democracy had been restored by the time when Dorieus, a Rhodian athlete who had been condemned to death in Athens in his absence, apparently for some kind of opposition to the pro-Athenian regime in Rhodes, and had fled to Thourioi in Italy, was captured while in command of two Thourian ships; he was brought to Athens, but the Ekklesia on seeing him thought it a pity that a man of such athletic prowess should be brought so low, and released him.[600] In 405 there was a much wider amnesty: the decree of Patrokleides annulled all disfranchisement and overdue debts to the state.[601]

But after 403 the Athenians seem deliberately to have made the annulment of juries' decisions more difficult. This was the time when a clear distinction was made between laws and decrees (see pages 46–9). Thus the law that verdicts given under democratic rule were valid could not be overruled by a decree, but only by a new law. Other laws laid down that no law could be made about an individual, nor about releasing persons from disfranchisement or from payments owed to the state, unless six thousand Athenians voted in favour in a secret ballot.[602] (This form of words is ambiguous, but it probably means that at least six thousand votes had to be cast, the majority being in favour, rather than that there had to be six thousand favourable votes.) So a jury's verdict could be set aside only if a large number of Athenians went through a special voting procedure for that purpose. A few cases are known in which that may have been done, but not one in which it certainly was.[603] It is reasonable to infer that in the fourth century the Athenians felt a high degree of satisfaction with the working of their legal system.

NOTES

The following books are referred to by the author's surname and one or two significant words of the title.

Bonner, R. J. and Smith, G. *The Administration of Justice from Homer to Aristotle* (1930-8)

Cohen, E. E. *Ancient Athenian Maritime Courts* (1973)

Finley, M. I. *Studies in Land and Credit in Ancient Athens* (1951)

Gauthier, P. *Symbola* (1972)

Gernet, L. *Droit et société dans la Grèce ancienne* (1955)

Gomme, A. W. with Andrewes, A. and Dover, K. J. *A Historical Commentary on Thucydides* (1945-70)

Hansen, M. H. *Apagoge, Endeixis and Ephegesis against Kakourgoi, Atimoi and Pheugontes* (1976)

—*Eisangelia* (1975)

Harrison, A. R. W. *The Law of Athens* (1968-71)

Hignett, C. *A History of the Athenian Constitution* (1952)

Kränzlein, A. *Eigentum und Besitz im griechischen Recht* (1963)

Lacey, W. K. *The Family in Classical Greece* (1968)

Lipsius, J. H. *Das attische Recht und Rechtsverfahren* (1905-15)

MacDowell, D. M. *Andokides: On the Mysteries* (1962)

—*Aristophanes: Wasps* (1971)

—*Athenian Homicide Law* (1963)

Meiggs, R. *The Athenian Empire* (1972)

Ostwald, M. *Nomos and the Beginnings of the Athenian Democracy* (1969)

Paoli, U. E. *Altri studi di diritto greco e romano* (1976)

Rhodes, P. J. *The Athenian Boule* (1972)

Ruschenbusch, E. *Untersuchungen zur Geschichte des athenischen Strafrechts* (1968)

Stroud, R. S. *Drakon's Law on Homicide* (1968)

Thompson, H. A. and Wycherley, R. E. *The Agora of Athens* (The Athenian Agora xiv, 1972)

Wade-Gery, H. T. *Essays in Greek History* (1958)

Wilamowitz-Moellendorff, U. von. *Aristoteles und Athen* (1893)

Wolff, H. J. *Die attische Paragraphe* (1966)

Wyse, W. *The Speeches of Isaeus* (1904)

CHAPTER I

1 *Odyssey* 16.97–8, 1.298–300.
2 *Odyssey* 21.15–30.
3 *Odyssey* 3.244–5, *Iliad* 2.205–6, 9. 98–9; cf. H. Lloyd-Jones *The Justice of Zeus* (1971) 6–7.
4 Cf. M. Gagarin in *CP* 68 (1973) 81–94.
5 Cf. P. Walcot *Greek Peasants* (1970) 100–5.
6 Cf. H. J. Wolff in *Traditio* 4 (1946) 59–62.
7 *Odyssey* 7.66–74, 11.186.
8 Cf. Bonner and Smith *Administration* i 42.
9 *Iliad* 11.807, 16.387, 18.497.
10 Cf. Gernet *Droit* 9–18.
11 Bonner and Smith *Administration* i 31–41, H. J. Wolff in *Traditio* 4 (1946) 34–49, H. Hommel in *Politeia und Res Publica* (ed. P. Steinmetz, 1969) 11–38, A. Primmer in *Wiener Studien* 4 (1970) 5–13, Ø. Andersen in *Symbolae Osloenses* 51 (1976) 11–16, etc.

CHAPTER II

12 Cf. Hignett *Constitution* 38–46.
13 Cf. Ostwald *Nomos* 174–5.
14 *AP* 57.3, 60.2.
15 Pol. 8.125.
16 Hdt. 5.71, Th. 1.126, *AP* 1, Plu. *Solon* 12, schol. on Ar. *Knights* 445.
17 Plu. *Solon* 19.4, *AP* 8.4, 16.10.
18 Lysias 10.16, Dem. 24.105.
19 *IG* i² 39 (ML 52) 75, 63.14, *ATL* D14.II.7.
20 Bonner and Smith *Administration* i 152–7, Wade-Gery *Essays* 173–4, Hignett *Constitution* 97.
21 Bonner and Smith *Administration* i 159, ii 232–5, Wade-Gery *Essays* 173; cf. Harrison *Law* ii 72–4.
22 Wilamowitz *Aristoteles* i 60, Hignett *Constitution* 97–8, E. Ruschenbusch in *Historia* 14 (1965) 381–4.

23 Wade-Gery *Essays* 192–5.
24 *IG* i² 39 (ML 52) 74; cf. Bonner and Smith *Administration* ii 246–53, Meiggs *Empire* 224–5.
25 Plu. *Aristeides* 2.5; cf. Wade-Gery *Essays* 176–8.
26 *IG* i² 16 (ML 31); cf. Wade-Gery *Essays* 182–6, R. Sealey in *CP* 59 (1964) 17, Stroud *Drakon* 42–5.
27 Arist. *Politics* 1274a 8–9, *AP* 27. 3–4, Plu. *Perikles* 9.3–5; cf. Wade-Gery *Essays* 235–8, Hignett *Constitution* 342–3.
28 Ar.*Wasps* 662, *AP* 24.3, 27.4, 63.3.
29 Ar. *Wasps* 303–11, [Xen.] *Ath.* 3. 8, Dem. 24. 80.
30 Ar. *Knights* 51, 800, schol. on *Wasps* 88, 300; cf. J. J. Buchanan *Theorika* (1962) 14–21.
31 Ar. *Wasps* 1108–9, Ant. fr. 42, Dem. 59.52, etc.
32 *IG* i² 39 (ML 52) 75, Ant. 6.21, etc.; cf. MacDowell *Wasps* 273–5.
33 Ar.*Wasps* 1109, Dem. 59.52, *IG* ii² 1641. 28–30.
34 Ar. *Wasps* 120, 389, Ant. fr. 42, *FGrH* 324 F 59, Pausanias 1.28.8, Pol. 8.121, etc.; cf. Jacoby's commentary on *FGrH* 324 F 59, MacDowell *Wasps* 274–5.
35 Thompson and Wycherley *Agora* 56–72.
36 Ar. *Wasps* 242–4, 303–5.
37 *ATL* List 25.60–1 and A9.16, Lysias 13.35, Plu. *Perikles* 32.4.
38 Isok. 18.54; cf. MacDowell *Homicide* 53–4 and in *RIDA* 18 (1971) 267–73.
39 *AP* 27.5; cf. page 173.
40 Ar. *Wasps* 662, And. 1.17, *AP* 24.3, 63.4.
41 Isaios 5.20.
42 *Kleroteria* are described with diagrams by S. Dow in *Hesperia* Supp. 1 (1937) 198–215 and *HSCP* 50 (1939) 1–34; some modifications and additions are made by J. D. Bishop in *JHS* 90 (1970) 1–14. *Pinakia* are described by S.

Dow in *Bulletin de Correspondance Hellénique* 87 (1963) 653–87, and fully catalogued with photographs and discussion by J. H. Kroll *Athenian Bronze Allotment Plates* (1972).

43 Dem. 24. 9; cf. 24. 27.
44 Cf. G. M. Calhoun in *TAPA* 50 (1919) 191–2, Kroll *Athenian Bronze Allotment Plates* 5–7, 62–8, 87–90.
45 Dem. 21.223, Dein. 1.52, 1.107; cf. Pol. 8.53, 8.123.
46 Dem. 21.223, *AP* 53.3.
47 Dem. 25.27; cf. Lipsius *Recht* 142.
48 Dem. 59.52, *AP* 66.1.
49 Ar. *Clouds* 206–8, *Birds* 108–9.
50 And. 1.66, Lysias 13.10, Isaios 4.17, Dem. 43.72, etc.; cf. Ar. *Wasps* 917.

CHAPTER III

51 Cf. Stroud *Drakon* 65–75.
52 Lysias fr. 10 (Thalheim), Xen. *Oikonomikos* 14.4–5, and later authors; cf. Stroud *Drakon* 75–82.
53 Ant. 6.2, And. 1.81–3, Dem. 20. 158, 23.51, *AP* 7.1
54 Stroud *Drakon* (ML 86).
55 *AP* 7.1, Plu. *Solon* 25.1; cf. A. Andrewes in Φόρος, *Tribute to B. D. Meritt* (1974) 21–8, H. Hansen and W. F. Wyatt in *Philologus* 119 (1975) 39–47.
56 E. Ruschenbusch Σόλωνος νόμοι (1966).
57 Dem. 24.149–51; cf. Bonner and Smith *Administration* ii 152–5.
58 Dem. 20.118, 23.96, 39.40, 57.63, Ais. 3.6.
59 Cf. Ostwald *Nomos* 20–54.
60 Ostwald *Nomos* 137–73.
61 Cf. F. Quass *Nomos und Psephisma* (1971) 30–9.
62 *AP* 35.2, And. 1.116, Dem. 59.76.
63 Cf. Stroud *Drakon* 28–9.
64 Lysias 6.10.
65 *SEG* xv 114; cf. S. Dow in *Proceedings of the Massachusetts Historical*

Society 71 (1953–7) 3–36, *Historia* 9 (1960) 270–93, *Hesperia* 30 (1961) 58–73, Stroud *Drakon* 26.

66 And. 1.81–5; cf. MacDowell *Mysteries* 194–9.
67 And. 1. 85–7.
68 Lysias 30.4–5, 30.17–21; cf. S. Dow in *Historia* 9 (1960) 270–93, *Hesperia* 30 (1961) 58–73, MacDowell *Mysteries* 197–8.
69 Dem. 19.129, Ais. 3.187, etc.; cf. H. A. Thompson in *Hesperia* 6 (1937) 203–17, U. Kahrstedt in *Klio* 31 (1938) 25–32, A. R. W. Harrison in *JHS* 75 (1955) 27–9, Rhodes *Boule* 31.
70 For detailed discussion see MacDowell in *JHS* 95 (1975) 62–74.
71 Dem. 20.89–96.
72 Dem. 3.10, 20.91, 24.33.
73 Dem. 24.20–3.
74 Dem. 20.91, Ais. 3.38–9.
75 Antiphanes 196, Hyp. *Philippides* 11–12, Dem. 51.12, Plu. *Phokion* 26.3; cf. Harrison *Law* ii 176.
76 And. 1.17, Plu. *Ethika* 833d, Ant. fr. 8–14.
77 H. J. Wolff 'Normenkontrolle' und Gesetzesbegriff in der attischen Demokratie (Sitzungsberichte der Heidelberger Akademie der Wissenschaften, Philosophisch-historische Klasse, 1970), M. H. Hansen *The Sovereignty of the People's Court in Athens in the Fourth Century B.C. and the Public Action against Unconstitutional Proposals* (1974).
78 *AP* 59.2, Dem. 20.144 (with hypothesis 2.3).
79 Dem. 24.138.
80 Ais. 3.194, Dem. 18.251. 'Seventy-five' must be an exaggeration; cf. S.I. Oost in *CP* 72 (1977) 238–40.
81 Ais. 3.49.

CHAPTER IV

82 Plu. *Solon* 18.7.
83 G. M. Calhoun *The Growth of*

Criminal Law in Ancient Greece (1927) 6.
84 Dem. 24.20; cf. MacDowell in *JHS* 95 (1975) 66–7.
85 Cf. Ruschenbusch *Strafrecht* 53–64.
86 Cf. Hansen *Apagoge* 9–28.
87 Cf. H. Mummenthey *Zur Geschichte des Begriffs* βλάβη *im attischen Recht* (Dissertation, Freiburg im Breisgau, 1971) 3–34.
88 Ar. *Wasps* 691, *AP* 54.2.
89 Hyp. *Demosthenes* 38, Dein. 2.6, Plu. *Ethika* 833 f.
90 Dem. 59.16, 59.52.
91 Cf. J. O. Lofberg *Sycophancy in Athens* (1917) pp. vii-viii.
92 Ar. *Akharnians* 818–29, 899–958, *Birds* 1410–68, *Wasps* 1037–42.
93 And. 1.33, 1.76, Hyp. *Euxenippos* 34, Dem. 21.47, 26.9, 58.6, etc.; cf. Bonner and Smith *Administration* ii 56–7, Harrison *Law* ii 83, Hansen *Apagoge* 63–5.
94 Isaios 3.47, Hyp. *Lykophron* 12, Dem. 18.250, Pol. 8.53; cf. Harrison *Law* ii 51.
95 Ais. 2.93.
96 Lysias 7.37, Dem. 59. 121.
97 Dem. 20.145, 59.53, 59.68.
98 Dem. 58.43; cf. Bonner and Smith *Administration* ii 58–63.
99 Lysias 13.65, Ais. 2.145, *AP* 43.5.
100 Isok. 15.314, *AP* 59.3, Dem. 58. 11.

CHAPTER V

101 *AP* 26.4, Isaios 8.43, Dem. 57. 30, schol. on Ais. 1.39 (*FGrH* 77 F 2), Plu. *Perikles* 37, Athenaios 577a-b; cf. Hignett *Constitution* 343–7, Harrison *Law* i 25–6, Lacey *Family* 100–5.
102 *AP* 42.1, Plu. *Ethika* 834b, Isaios 3.45; cf. MacDowell in *CQ* 26 (1976) 88–91.
103 Cf. D. M. Lewis in *Historia* 12 (1963) 22–40, J. S. Traill *The Political*

Organization of Attica (*Hesperia* Supplement 14, 1975).
104 Dem. 57.10.
105 *IG* ii² 1194.3.
106 Lysias 21. 1, Dem. 30. 15.
107 Dem. 27.63, *AP* 42.1; cf. R. Sealey in *CR* 7 (1957) 195–7, Rhodes *Boule* 172.
108 Ar. *Wasps* 578, *AP* 42. 1–2; cf. Lacey *Family* 94–5, MacDowell *Wasps* 210.
109 Dem. 57.26.
110 Dem. 57 (with *hypothesis*), Ais. 1. 77 (with schol.), 1. 86, *FGrH* 324 F 52, DH *Isaios* 16, *Deinarkhos* 11; cf. A. W. Gomme *Essays in Greek History and Literature* (1937) 67–86.
111 Dem. 24.131 (with schol.), *Epistles* 3.29.
112 E.g. Dem. 57.54, 59.59; cf. Harrison *Law* i 64–5.
113 Plu. *Solon* 24.4.
114 Arist. *Politics* 1275b 36–7, *AP* 21. 4; cf. D. Kagan in *Historia* 12 (1963) 41–6.
115 Th. 3.55.3, 63.2, 68.5; cf. M. Amit *Great and Small Poleis* (1973) 75–8, W. Gawantka *Isopolitie* (1975) 174–8.
116 Dem. 59. 104–6, Isok. 12.94.
117 Th. 5.32-1, Pausanias 9.1.4.
118 Ar. *Frogs* 693–4 (cf. 33–4, 191), Hellanikos (*FGrH* 323a) F 25.
119 *IG* ii² 1 (Tod 96–7, ML 94); cf. W. Gawantka *Isopolitie* (1975) 178–97.
120 *AP* 40.2, Ais. 3.195, Plu. *Ethika* 835f–836a.
121 *IG* ii² 10 (Tod 100).
122 Hyp. *Athenogenes* 32.
123 Th. 2.29.5, 67.2, Ar. *Akharnians* 145.
124 *IG* i² 110 (ML 85), Lysias 13. 72.
125 Dem. 59.88–92; cf. M. J. Osborne in *BSA* 67 (1972) 129–58.
126 *IG* ii² 103 (Tod 133).
127 *IG* ii² 237 (Tod 178).
128 Hansen *Apagoge* 54–98.
129 Dem. 9.41–5; cf. Meiggs *Empire* 508–12.

130 And. 1.75–6, Lysias 16.3, 26.10.
131 Dem. 20.156, 24.22, 53.14; cf. Hansen *Apagoge* 11–17.
132 And. 1.2, 1.111, Dem. 24.105, *AP* 52.1; cf. Hansen *Apagoge* 20–1, 94–6.
133 Dem. 20.156, 24.105, 25.92, *AP* 63.3, etc.; cf. Hansen *Apagoge* 96–8.
134 Dem. 57.31–4.
135 Dem. 21.47, 59.16, etc.
136 Dem. 59.66; cf. Harrison *Law* i 195 n. 1.
137 Ar. *Wasps* 1042, Isok. 17.12, Dem. 32.9.
138 Dem. 25.57, DL 4.14, Harp. under μετοίκιον.
139 Hyp. *Athenogenes* 29, 33.
140 Ar. Byz. *Lexeis* fr. 38 (Nauck p. 193); cf. E. Stelzer *Untersuchungen zur Enktesis im attischen Recht* (Dissertation, München, 1971) 109–41, Gauthier *Symbola* 107–26.
141 E.g. ML 79.33.
142 Cf. Gauthier *Symbola* 126–36.
143 Cf. J. Pečírka *The Formula for the Grant of Enktesis in Attic Inscriptions* (1966), E. Stelzer *Untersuchungen zur Enktesis im attischen Recht* (Dissertation, München, 1971).
144 Cf. MacDowell *Homicide* 126.
145 Dem. 53.11.
146 Cf. Harrison *Law* i 164.
147 *AP* 52. 1, Isok. 15.90.
148 Lysias 23.9–12, Ais. 1.62, Dem. 58. 19, etc.
149 Lysias 23.9–12. Isok. 17.14, Dem. 58.21, 59.40, Harp. under ἐξαιρέσεως δίκη; cf. Harrison *Law* i 178–9, 221.
150 Hyp. *Athenogenes* 15.
151 Ar. *Wasps* 52, [Xen.] *Ath.* 1.11.
152 Cf. MacDowell *Homicide* 21–2, Harrison *Law* i 171–2.
153 Ar. *Wasps* 1309.
154 Ar. fr. 567, schol. on Ais. 3. 13.
155 [Xen.] *Ath.* 1. 10, Dem. 53. 16.
156 Plato *Gorgias* 483b, Dem. 47.70, 53.20; cf. MacDowell *Homicide* 20–1.

157 Dem. 37.21, 37.51, 53.20, 55. 31–2, Hyp. *Athenogenes* 22; cf. Harrison *Law* i 173–4.
158 Men. *Epitrepontes* 380.
159 Ais. 1.97.
160 Hyp. *Athenogenes*; cf. Gernet *Droit* 161–2.
161 Dem. 34.5; cf. Gernet *Droit* 159–64, Harrison *Law* i 174–6 (but I doubt their interpretation of Dem. 36. 14).
162 Harp. under ἀποστασίου, Pol. 3.83; cf. Gernet *Droit* 168–72, Harrison *Law* i 182–6.
163 Cf. Lipsius *Recht* 625.
164 Lysias 5.3–5, 7.16, And. 1.28 (the award of money to Andromakhos implies that he was no longer a slave). In Ant. 2c.4, 5.34 it is not clear whether liberation for information about homicide was a legal requirement.
165 Ais. 1.54, 1.62; cf. Harrison *Law* i 177–8.

CHAPTER VI

166 Men. *Aspis* 127–37; cf. Plautus *Trinummus* 573, 1156–8, E. Karabelias in *Revue Historique de Droit Français et Étranger* 48 (1970) 366–8.
167 Plato *Symposium* 192b, Dein. 1. 71, Plu. *Ethika* 493e, Pol. 8. 40.
168 Dem. 44.10, 47.38; cf. Lipsius *Recht* 341–2, Harrison *Law* i 19.
169 E.g. Men. *Dyskolos* 762, 842.
170 Cf. Harrison *Law* i 3–9.
171 Men. *Dyskolos* 784–7, *Georgos* 7–8, Dem. 40.4; cf. Harrison *Law* i 18.
172 Cf. Harrison *Law* i 21–4.
173 Plu. *Perikles* 37.
174 Dem. 59.16, 59.52; cf. Harrison *Law* i 26–8.
175 Men. *Dyskolos* 842–4, *Perikeiromene* 1013–15.
176 Dem. 30.7, 41.5–6.
177 On dowries cf. H. J. Wolff in *RE* under προίξ (1957), P. D. Dimakis

'Ο θεσμὸς τῆς προικὸς κατὰ τὸ ἀρχαῖον ἑλληνικὸν δίκαιον (1959), Harrison *Law* i 45–60, Lacey *Family* 109–10.

178 Dem. 59.87.

179 Dem. 41.4, Men. *Epitrepontes* 657–8, *Didot Papyrus* I (Menander, ed. Sandbach, pp. 328–30); cf. Paoli *Altri studi* 385–91.

180 Isaios 3.78, Dem. 30.17, 30.26, And. 4. 14, Plu. *Alkibiades* 8.5.

181 Plu. *Alkibiades* 8.6.

182 Isaios 2.9, 3.35–6, Dem. 59.52.

183 Isaios 3.36, Dem. 40.14, 40.50.

184 Isaios 3.8–9, 3.78, 8.8.

185 Dem. 42.27, 43.75.

186 Dem. 40.6; cf. H. L. Levy in *Mediterranean Countrymen* (ed. J. Pitt-Rivers, 1963) 142.

187 Isaios 3.8–9, 3.78, Dem. 27.17, 59. 52.

188 Isaios 8.8, Dem. 40.6–7.

189 Dem. 27.5, 45.28.

190 Dem. 23.53.

191 Eupolis 98 Kock (114 Edmonds), Plu. *Perikles* 24, 37.

192 Lysias 1.31–2, Dem. 23.53.

193 DL 2.26, Athenaios 556a, Gellius 15.20.6; cf. Harrison *Law* i 16–17.

194 Aristoxenos fr. 54a–b (Wehrli), DL 2.26, Plu. *Aristeides* 27.3–4, Athenaios 555d–556b; cf. J. W. Fitton in *CQ* 20 (1970) 55–66, L. Woodbury in *Phoenix* 27 (1973) 7–25.

195 Ar. *Birds* 922–3, Isaios 3.30, Dem. 39.22.

196 Dem. 39.2; cf. J. Rudhardt in *Museum Helveticum* 19 (1962) 39–64.

197 Dem. 39.39; cf. Harrison *Law* i 75–7.

198 Ar. *Clouds* 845, Xen. *Apom.* 1.2. 49, Ais. 3.251, *AP* 56.6; cf. Harrison *Law* i 80–1.

199 Lysias 13.91, Ais. 1.28, Dem. 24. 103–7, *AP* 56.6, Harp. under εἰσαγγελία.

200 Ais. 1.13, Plu. *Solon* 22.

201 Dem. 36.11, 48.12–13; cf. Har-

rison *Law* i 130–2, H. L. Levy in *TAPA* 87 (1956) 42–6, P. Walcot *Greek Peasants* (1970) 49–50.

202 Dem. 43.75, Ais. 1.158, etc.

203 Lysias 32, Dem. 27, Isaios 6. 36–7, *AP* 56.7; cf. Finley *Land* 38–44, Harrison *Law* i 104–8.

204 Dem. 38.23, Harp. under φάσις; cf. Harrison *Law* i 115–17.

205 Isaios 11.6 (cf. 3.46–7), Harp. under εἰσαγγελία; cf. Harrison *Law* i 117–19, Ruschenbusch *Strafrecht* 54–5.

206 Dem. 27–9, Lysias 32, etc.; cf. Harrison *Law* i 119–21, D. Becker in *ZSSR* 85 (1968) 30–93.

207 On *epikleroi* cf. Harrison *Law* i 132–8, Lacey *Family* 139–45, J. E. Karnezis 'Η ἐπίκληρος (1972), E. Karabelias in *Symposion 1971* (ed. H. J. Wolff, 1975) 215–54, D. Schaps in *CQ* 25 (1975) 53–7.

208 Men. *Aspis* 141–3, 185–7, 254–5.

209 Isaios 3.64, 10.19.

210 Isaios 1.39, Dem. 43.54, Terence *Phormio* 295–7, 407–10.

211 Cf. MacDowell in *Mnemosyne* 16 (1963) 131–3, A. W. H. Adkins in *CQ* 25 (1975) 217–18.

212 Plu. *Solon* 20.2–5; cf. Lipsius *Recht* 349 n. 35.

213 Isaios 3.46–7, Dem. 37.46.

214 Dem. 43.75.

215 For more detailed discussion of the order of succession see Harrison *Law* i 143–9.

216 Cf. Harrison *Law* i 138–42.

217 Men. *Aspis* 141.

218 Isaios 6.47, Dem. 43.51.

219 Ar. *Birds* 1649–68; cf. Harrison *Law* i 66–7.

220 Cf. Gernet *Droit* 121–49.

221 Isaios 3.45–51, Men. *Dyskolos* 729–39; cf. Paoli *Altri studi* 559–70.

222 Cf. Harrison *Law* i 82–96, Lacey *Family* 145–6.

223 Isaios 7.9, 11.8, 11.41.

224 Isaios 2.19, Dem. 46.14, 48.56.

225 Isaios 7.31, 11.49, Dem. 43.11–

15, 44.43; cf. Harrison *Law* i 90–3.
226 Harp. under νοθεῖα, schol. on
Ar. *Birds* 1656; cf. Harrison *Law* i 67.
227 Lysias 19.39–41, Dem. 27.44–5,
36.7–8, 45.28; cf. Harrison *Law* i
151–2, Lacey *Family* 131–7, G.E.M. de
Ste Croix in *CR* 20 (1970) 389–90.
228 *AP* 43.4.
229 Isaios 3.58, Dem. 43.16.
230 Cf. Wyse *Isaeus* 671–713, M.
Broadbent *Studies in Greek Genealogy*
(1968) 61–112, J. K. Davies *Athenian
Propertied Families* (1971) 77–89, W. E.
Thompson *De Hagniae Hereditate*
(1976).
231 Wyse *Isaeus* 673, Davies *Athenian
Propertied Families* 79.
232 Harrison *Law* i 143 n. 1 and in
CR 61 (1947) 41–3; cf. J. C. Miles in
Hermathena 75 (1950) 71–2, W. E.
Thompson in *Glotta* 48 (1970) 76–9.

CHAPTER VII

233 Dem. 43.62, Plu. *Solon* 21; cf.
D. C. Kurtz and J. Boardman *Greek
Burial Customs* (1971) 142–6, M. Alex-
iou *The Ritual Lament in Greek Tradition* (1974) 14–23.
234 Dem. 43.57–8.
235 Cf. MacDowell *Homicide* 1–5,
141–50.
236 Dem. 37.59.
237 Plato *Euthyphron* 4a–e, Dem. 47.
68–73; cf. MacDowell *Homicide* 12–19,
94–6, H. D. Evjen in *RIDA* 18 (1971)
255–65, S. Panagiotou in *Hermes* 102
(1974) 419–37, E. Grace in *Eirene* 13
(1975) 5–18.
238 Ant. 6.35, Dem. 20.157–8, 47.
69, *AP* 57. 2; cf. MacDowell *Homicide*
22–6, 144–5, M. Piérart in *L'Antiquité
Classique* 42 (1973) 427–35.
239 Dem. 24.105.
240 Dem. 23.82–5, Pol. 8.50–1, *Lex.
Rhet.* 213.30–214.2; cf. MacDowell
Homicide 27–31.

241 Dem. 23.53, *AP* 57.3, etc.; cf.
MacDowell *Homicide* 73–9.
242 Arist. *Ethika Nikomakheia* 1111b
18–19.
243 Dem. 21.43, 23.50, Arist. *Ethika
Megala* 1188b 29–38.
244 Dem. 54.25, 54.28; cf. W.T.
Loomis in *JHS* 92 (1972) 86–95.
245 Xen. *Apom.* 3.5.20, Ais. 1.92,
Lyk. *Leo.* 12, etc.
246 Cf. MacDowell *Homicide* 48–57,
Stroud *Drakon* 48–9.
247 Dem. 23.65–79, *AP* 57.3–4; cf.
MacDowell *Homicide* 58–84.
248 Dem. 23.76 (with Patmos schol.),
AP 57.4, Pol. 8. 120; cf. MacDowell
Homicide 85–9.
249 Ant. 5.11, *AP* 57.4.
250 Cf. MacDowell *Homicide* 90–109.
251 Ant. 5.13, Dem. 23.69; cf. Ant.
2b. 9, 4d. 1.
252 *IG* i² 115 (ML 86) 11–32, Dem.
23.28–52, 23.72, 37.59, 43.57, 50.59;
cf. MacDowell *Homicide* 117–25,
Stroud *Drakon* 50–4.
253 And. 1.94, Dem. 59.10, Lyk.
Leo. 65; cf. MacDowell *Homicide* 125–
7.
254 Cf. MacDowell *Homicide* 130–40;
different views on certain points are
taken by Hansen *Apagoge* 99–108, H.
D. Evjen in *Tijdschrift voor Rechts-
geschiedenis* 38 (1970) 403–15.

CHAPTER VIII

255 Dem. 47.45–7, 47.64, Isok. 20.19.
256 Lysias 3.41–2.
257 Lysias 6.15, Dem. 23.22, 40.32,
AP 57.3.
258 Ais. 2.93, 3.51, 3.212, Dem.
54.18; cf. Hansen *Apagoge* 108–10.
259 Lysias 3.38–48, 4.18, 6.15, Dem.
40.32.
260 Lysias 1.33.
261 Plu. *Solon* 23.1, Lysias 1.32,
Lex. Cant. under βιαίων δίκη.

262 Dem. 23. 53.

263 Lysias 1.49, Ar. *Clouds* 1083, *Wealth* 168; cf. K. J. Dover *Aristophanes: Clouds* (1968) 227.

264 Lysias 1.25, Dem. 59.65–6.

265 *AP* 59. 3; cf. Lipsius *Recht* 432.

266 Dem. 59. 87, Ais. 1. 183.

267 Ais. 1.14, 1.184, Plu. *Solon* 23.1.

268 Dem. 59.67, Lysias 10.19, Plu. *Solon* 23.1.

269 Lysias 1.32, Ais. 1.14, *Lex Cant.* under βιαίων δίκη.

270 Ais. 1.9–12.

271 Ais. 1.13, 1.19–20, 1.87, 1.195, And 1.100; cf. Harrison *Law* i 37–8, K. J. Dover *Greek Popular Morality* (1974) 213–16.

272 *IG* ii² 32.9–14, Pol. 6.153, *Lex. Cant.* under εἰργμοῦ δίκη.

273 Dem. 59.64–6.

274 Plu. *Solon* 21.1–2, Dem. 20.104, 40.49, Hyp. *Philippides* 3, *Lex. Cant.* under κακηγορίας δίκη.

275 Lysias 10.30, Dem. 23.50.

276 Isok. 20.3, Lysias 10.12, Dem. 21.88 (1000 drachmas, presumably for slandering two persons; cf. Lipsius *Recht* 651 n. 56).

277 Lysias 9.6–10, Dem. 21.32–3.

278 Schol. on Ar. *Akharnians* 67 and *Birds* 1297.

279 Ar. *Clouds* 353, *Wasps* 592, *Peace* 678, etc.; cf. MacDowell *Wasps* 130. Contrast Ar. *Birds* 290, 1473–81.

280 Cf. MacDowell in *Greece and Rome* 23 (1976) 14–31; for slightly different views, J. T. Hooker in *Archiv für Begriffsgeschichte* 19 (1975) 125–37, N. R. E. Fisher in *Greece and Rome* 23 (1976) 177–93.

281 Cf. E. Ruschenbusch in *ZSSR* 82 (1965) 302–9, MacDowell in *Greece and Rome* 23 (1976) 26–7.

CHAPTER IX

282 Cf. Kränzlein *Eigentum* 130–7, Harrison *Law* i 236–43.

283 Isaios 10. 10, Ar. *Ekklesiazousai* 1024–5.

284 Ais. 3.21.

285 *AP* 56.6, Plautus *Mercator* 451–7, Harp. under δατεῖσθαι, *Lex. Cant.* under εἰς δατητῶν αἵρεσιν.

286 Cf. E. Ruschenbusch in *Historia* 21 (1972) 753–5, M. I. Finley *The Use and Abuse of History* (1975) 153–60.

287 *AP* 60, Dem. 43.71; cf. Kränzlein *Eigentum* 56–7.

288 *SEG* iii 18; cf. R. Koerner in *Archiv für Papyrusforschung* 22 (1973) 182.

289 H. J. Wolff in *American Journal of Philology* 64 (1943) 316–24.

290 *AP* 47.2, Hyp. *Euxenippos* 34–6, Dem. 37.22, 40.52, etc.; cf. M. Crosby in *Hesperia* 19 (1950) 189–312, R. J. Hopper in *BSA* 48 (1953) 200–54, Harrison *Law* i 202–3, 315.

291 Dem. 37.2, 37.35–6, Hyp. *Euxenippos* 34–5, *AP* 59.5, Pol. 8.47, *Souda* α 345.

292 *Iliad* 23.702–5; cf. 7.472–5, *Odyssey* 1.431, etc.

293 Lyk. *Leo.* 23; cf. F. Pringsheim *The Greek Law of Sale* (1950) 245–6.

294 Isaios 8.23, Plautus *Mostellaria* 637–48, *Pseudolus* 342–6, 373–4, *Rudens* 45–6, 860–2, 1281–3.

295 Hyp. *Athenogenes* 14.

296 Theophrastos *Laws* fr. xcvii 1 (Wimmer); cf. Harrison *Law* i 305–8.

297 Hyp. *Athenogenes* 15.

298 Hyp. *Athenogenes* 13, Dem. 42. 12, 47.77, 56.2, Dein. 3.4, Plato *Symposium* 196c.

299 Cf. D. Behrend *Attische Pachturkunden* (1970) 40–9.

300 Examples in *IG* ii² 2490–2504.

301 Dem. 24.40, 43.58.

302 Lysias 8.10, 19.25–6, Dem. 27.24; cf. Harrison *Law* i 260–2.

303 Cf. Finley *Land* 28–37, 107–17, Fine *Horoi* 142–66, Harrison *Law* i 262–93, A. Biscardi in *ZSSR* 86 (1969) 146–68.

304 Isaios 6.36, *AP* 56.7, Harp. under ἀποτιμηταί; cf. Fine *Horoi* 96–115, Finley *Land* 38–44, Harrison *Law* i 293–6.

305 Dem. 30, 31, 41.5–10, Harp. under ἀποτιμηταί; cf. Finley *Land* 44–52, Wolff in *RE* under προίξ (1957) 159–62, Harrison *Law* i 296–303, L. R. F. Germain in *Symposion* 1971 (ed. H. J. Wolff, 1975) 333–46.

306 *Lex. Rhet.* 236.16–21.

307 Leist's view is presented and in large part accepted by Harrison *Law* i 214–17, rejected by Kränzlein *Eigentum* 141.

308 Dem. 39.25, 48.45, 52.14, Lysias fr. 1 and 27 (Thalheim), *AP* 52. 2, *Lex. Rhet.* 285.33–286.10.

309 Isaios 6.31.

310 DH *Isaios* 15.

311 Harp. under βεβαιώσεως, Pol. 8. 34; cf. Harrison *Law* i 210–14.

312 Ar. *Clouds* 499 (with schol.), Isaios 6. 42; cf. Wyse *Isaeus* 528–30.

313 Dem. 24.105, 24.114, Lysias 29. 11.

314 Dem. 21.44.

315 Ant. 5.9, Lysias 10.10, Isaios 4.28, Isok. 15.90, Ais. 1.91, Dem. 22.26, 24. 113–14, 35.47, *AP* 52.1; cf. Hansen *Apagoge* 36–53.

316 Ant. 2a. 6, Dem. 19.293.

317 Xen. *Hellenika* 1.7.22, *Apom.* 1.2.62, Isok. 20.6, Lyk. *Leo.* 65.

318 Philochoros (*FGrH* 328) F 121, Diodoros 12. 39. 1–2, Plu. *Perikles* 31; cf. G. Donnay in *L'Antiquité Classique* 37 (1968) 19–36.

319 Dem. 21.25.

320 Dem. 23.22, *AP* 57.3, Pol. 8. 40, Euripides *Andromakhe* 388–90; cf. Lipsius *Recht* 984.

321 *IG* ii² 2492.29–31.

322 ? Dem. 49.20.

323 Dem. 38.2.

324 Dem. 42.14.

325 Dem. 56 (if the title is trustworthy), 36.20.

326 Dem. 21.43.

327 Dem. 48.32.

328 Dem. 52.8–14.

329 Cf. Gernet *Droit* 216–22, Wolff in *ZSSR* 74 (1957) 26–72.

330 Dem. 21.35, 21.43, 23.50; cf. E. Ruschenbusch in *ZSSR* 82 (1965) 306, opposed by H. Mummenthey *Zur Geschichte des Begriffs* βλάβη *im attischen Recht* (Dissertation, Freiburg im Breisgau, 1971) 34–41.

331 Dem. 21.81, 52.16, Harp. under ἐξούλης.

332 Isaios 5.22–4.

333 Dem. 24.54, 37.19.

334 *Oxyrhynchus Papyri* 221 col. xiv 10–15, And. 1.73, Isaios 5.22–4, Dem. 21. 44.

335 Dem. 39.15.

336 Harrison *Law* i 217–20 gives references to many other discussions of the *dike exoules*.

CHAPTER X

337 Hdt. 2.177.2, Lysias fr. 10 (Thalheim); cf. Stroud *Drakon* 79–80.

338 Dem. 57. 32.

339 Isok. 7.46, Plu. *Solon* 22.3, Athenaios 168a.

340 Ais. 3.158.

341 Ant. 4c.5.

342 Ar. *Akharnians* 819–20, 910–17.

343 Th. 1.67.4, 1.139.1.

344 G. E. M. de Ste Croix *The Origins of the Peloponnesian War* (1972) 267–84.

345 Cf. Thompson and Wycherley *Agora* 117–19.

346 *AP* 51.1, Dem. 20.9, Hyp. *Athenogenes* 14, Harp. under κατὰ τὴν ἀγορὰν ἀψευδεῖν.

347 Xenarkhos 7.

348 Schol. on *Iliad* 21.203.

349 Ar. *Wasps* 1406–7, *Akharnians* 723–4.

350 *AP* 51.3, Lysias 22.1–5, 22.16;

cf. R. Seager in *Historia* 15 (1966) 172–84.

351 Dem. 35.28.

352 AP 51.4, Dem. 34.37, 35.50–1, Lyk. *Leo.* 27.

353 *AP* 51. 2.

354 Dem. 20.167, 24.212.

355 Cf. R. S. Stroud in *Hesperia* 43 (1974) 157–88.

356 Ar. *Akharnians* 819–27, 910–17, Dem. 35.51, 58.5–13, *Hesperia* 43 (1974) 158 lines 18–29.

357 *IG* ii² 412. 7–9, *Hesperia* 43 (1974) 158 line 29, Dem. 58.13.

358 *AP* 49.2, Lysias 14.8, 16.13, Xen. *Oikonomikos* 9.15; cf. Rhodes *Boule* 174–5.

359 Dem. 39.16, 59.27, Lysias 9.4.

360 Lysias 14.5–6, And. 1.74, Ais. 1.29, 3.175–6, Dem. 15.32, 21.103, 39.16–17, 59.27, etc.

361 Lysias 13.67, Xen. *Hellenika* 1.1. 15.

362 *AP* 61.2, Lysias 3.45, 9.5, Dem. 50.51.

363 Cf. J. K. Davies in *JHS* 87 (1967) 33–40.

364 Cf. B. Jordan *The Athenian Navy in the Classical Period* (1975) 61–93.

365 Cf. R. Thomsen *Eisphora* (1964) 206–26.

366 Lysias 32.24, Dem. 14.16, 20.8, 20.27, 21.155, 50.9, *AP* 56.3, 61.1, *IG* ii² 1629 (Tod 200) 204–17.

367 Dem. 42; cf. W. A. Goligher in *Hermathena* 14 (1907) 481–515, Harrison *Law* ii 236–8.

368 Dem. 21.79, 42.19, 42.27, Lysias 4.1.

369 [Xen.] *Ath.* 3.4, Dem. 28.17, Isok. 15.5.

370 Dem. 47.41–4, Ais. 3.19.

371 Dem. 18.107, 47.26, *IG* ii² 1629 (Tod 200) 251–8, 1613.202–6, 1631. 343–6, etc.; cf. Harrison *Law* ii 235–6, Rhodes *Boule* 153–8.

372 [Xen.] *Ath.* 3.4, *IG* i² 73.19, 74, ii² 1 (ML 94) 28–32, *Hesperia* 4

(1935) 5–19 no. 1; cf. B. Jordan *The Athenian Navy in the Classical Period* (1975) 30–46.

373 Dem. 37.37.

374 *AP* 47.3–48.1, 52.3, And. 1.77, Dem. 43.71, 58.48.

375 *AP* 59.3, Dem. 25.71–3, 58. 51–2, *IG* ii² 1631.394–5; cf. Lipsius *Recht* 410–12, 443–6.

376 And. 1.73, Dem. 58.48–9; cf. Harrison *Law* ii 172–5.

377 And. 1.73, Dem. 24.82, 59.7.

378 *AP* 43.4, 52.1, Dem. 40.20–2, 49.45–7, 53.1–2, 59.7, Lysias 17, Hyp. *Euxenippos* 34; cf. Harrison *Law* ii 180–1, 211–17.

379 And. 1.92–3, Dem. 24.135, 24. 144, *AP* 48.1; cf. Rhodes *Boule* 150–1.

380 And. 1.134, Dem. 24.40, 24. 144, *Hesperia* 5 (1936) 401–2 lines 118–53.

381 *AP* 7.4, 47.1.

382 *AP* 45.3, 55.2, Dem. 20.90; cf. Hignett *Constitution* 205–8, Harrison *Law* ii 201–3, Rhodes *Boule* 176–8.

383 *AP* 55.3–4, Dein. 2.17–18.

384 Xen. *Apom.* 1.2.35, *AP* 62.3, Lysias 26. 10.

385 *AP* 43.4, 61.; cf. Hansen *Eisangelia* 41–4.

386 Xen. *Hellenika* 1.7.1, Dem. 58.27.

387 Th. 2.65.3–4, Plu. *Perikles* 35. 4–5; cf. Gomme *Commentary on Thucydides* ii 183.

388 *AP* 48.3, Lysias 30.5.

389 *AP* 45.2, Ant. 6.35, 6.49, Dem. 47.41–3; cf. Rhodes *Boule* 147–62, Hansen *Eisangelia* 21–8, 49–50.

390 Ais. 3.14–21.

391 *AP* 54.2, Ais. 3.22–3, And. 1.74. Dem. 24.112, 24.127, etc.

392 *AP* 48.4–5, 59.2.

393 *IG* i² 91 (ML 58A) 7–9, 324 (ML 72) 1, *ATL* List 1.2, etc., And. 1.78; cf. M. Piérart in *L'Antiquité Classique* 40 (1971) 526–73.

394 *IG* i² 57 (ML 65) 38, 63 (ML 69) 15, 76 (ML 73) 20, etc., and especially i² 127.18–20, ii² 1629 (Tod 200) 233–42.

395 And. 1.74, Dem. 21.113, Ais. 3.232, *AP* 54.2, Dein. 1.60, 2.17.

396 Hyp. *Demosthenes*, Dein. 1, Plu. *Demosthenes* 26. 1–2.

397 *AP* 27.5, Isok. 8.50, Ais. 1.86–7.

398 Ais. 1.27–32, Dem. 19.283–7; cf. Harrison *Law* ii 204–5.

CHAPTER XI

399 Ar. *Wasps* 463–507, *Birds* 1072–5, Th. 6.53.3, etc.

400 And. 1.95, Dem. 20.159, Lyk. *Leo.* 124–7.

401 *SEG* xii 87; cf. B. D. Meritt in *Hesperia* 21 (1952) 355–9, M. Ostwald in *TAPA* 86 (1955) 103–28.

402 Th. 1.138.6, Idomeneus (*FGrH* 338) F 1, Plato *Gorgias* 516d.

403 Lyk. *Leo.* 117.

404 Lyk. *Leo.* 113–15, Krateros (*FGrH* 342) F 17, Plu. *Ethika* 834b; cf. Hansen *Eisangelia* 82–3.

405 Plu. *Ethika* 833d–834b, Th. 8.68.2.

406 Dem. 21.64 (with schol.), 49.9 Diodoros 13.64.6, Plu. *Coriolanus* 14.6, *Ethika* 836d.

407 Cf. Hansen *Eisangelia* 35.

408 Dem. 20.100, 20.135, Hdt. 6.136, Plato *Gorgias* 516d–e.

409 Hyp. *Euxenippos* 29–30, Dem. 19.116, Ais. 2.6.

410 Ar. *Ekklesiazousai* 1089–90 (with schol.).

411 Ant. 5.34, Lysias 5.5, 7.16.

412 Lysias 13.21–3, 13.30–5, 13.55–6.

413 And. 1.11–68.

414 Dem. 24.11, Dein. 1.95, Plu. *Perikles* 31.2.

415 And. 1.42–3, Lysias 13.56.

416 Harp. and *Lex. Cant.* under εἰσαγγελία.

417 Lyk. *Leo.* 53, Pol. 8.52, *Lex Cant.* under εἰσαγγελία.

418 Hansen *Eisangelia* 12–20 summarizes other views.

419 *AP* 43. 4, Hyp. *Lykophron* 12, Dem. 18.250, Pol. 8.53; cf. G. Colin *Hypéride: Discours* (1946) 120–5, Hansen *Eisangelia* 29–31.

420 Xen. *Hellenika* 1.7.5.

421 Xen. *Hellenika* 1.7.34, Plato *Apology* 32b.

422 Dem. 47.43.

423 *AP* 40.2.

424 *IG* ii² 111 (Tod 142) 37–9, Isok. 17. 42, Lysias 22.2.

425 Cf. R. Bogaert in *RIDA* 9 (1962) 157–67, Rhodes *Boule* 180, Hansen *Apagoge* 30–5.

426 Dein. 1.50–8; cf. Hansen *Eisangelia* 39–40.

427 Dem. 18.132–3, Dein. 1.63.

428 Dein. 1.56.

429 Dein. 1.58, 1.63.

430 Dein. 1.62, Ais. 3.252, Lyk. *Leo.* 52.

CHAPTER XII

431 Lysias 6.10, And. 1.115–16.

432 Plato *Euthyphron* 4c, Isaios 8.39, Dem. 47.68–71, Theophrastos *Characters* 16.6.

433 J. H. Oliver *The Athenian Expounders of the Sacred and Ancestral Law* (1950).

434 And. 1.28–9.

435 Lysias 6.10.

436 Dem. 21.8–11, 21.147, 21.175.

437 Dem. 59.116.

438 *IG* ii² 1635 (Tod 125) 134–40.

439 Dem. 25.79–80, Philokhoros (*FGrH* 328) F 60.

440 Dem. 19.281 (with schol.).

441 Dem. 22.2.

442 And. 1.71, Lysias 6.9–12.

443 Arist. *Ethika Nikomakheia* 1111a 9–10, Clement of Alexandria *Stromateis* 2.60.3, Aelian *Poikile Historia* 5.19.

444 And. 1.113.

445   And. 1.11–12, Plu *Alkibiades* 22.4.
446   Cf. J. Rudhardt in *Museum Helveticum* 17 (1960) 87–105.
447   Plu. *Perikles* 32.2.
448   Plu. *Nikias* 23.4, DL 2.12–14.
449   Arist. fr. 67 (Rose), Plu. *Nikias* 23.4, DL 9.52.
450   Cf. K. J. Dover in *Talanta* 7 (1976) 24–54.
451   Ar. *Birds* 1073 (with schol.), Diodoros 13.6.7; cf. L. Woodbury in *Phoenix* 19 (1965) 178–211.
452   DL 2.40–2, Plato *Apology* 35e–38b; cf. S. Erasmus in *Gymnasium* 71 (1964) 40–2.

CHAPTER XIII

453   And. 1.87–8.
454   Dem. 21.94; cf. Gernet *Droit* 104 n. 7.
455   Isaios 5.31–2, Dem. 34.18, 52. 30; cf. Harrison *Law* ii 66 n. 2.
456   *AP* 16.5, 26.3, 53.1; cf. Wilamowitz *Aristoteles* ii 168.
457   *AP* 48.5, 53.1, Lysias 23.2, etc.
458   *AP* 53.2, 58.2.
459   Cf. MacDowell in *RIDA* 18 (1971) 267–73.
460   Dem. 27.49–53, 29.58; cf. R. J. Bonner in *CP* 2 (1907) 413–15, Bonner and Smith *Administration* ii 102–7, Harrison *Law* ii 20.
461   *AP* 59.4, Isaios 12.9–12; cf. Bonner and Smith *Administration* ii 111–14, Gernet in *Mélanges offerts à A.-M. Desrousseaux* (1937) 171–80.
462   *AP* 53.4–5, *IG* ii² 1926; cf. D. M. Lewis in *BSA* 50 (1955) 28–9.
463   Dem. 40.11, 47.12, etc.
464   Dem. 21.84, 47.45, Pol. 8.60; cf. Wolff *Paragraphe* 8 n. 5.
465   Harp. under παράστασις, Pol. 8.39, 8.127, *Lex. Rhet.* 290.19–22.
466   *AP* 53.2–3, Dem. 39.17, 45.57–8, etc.
467   Lysias 32.2, Dem. 21.90, 39.38,

Pol. 8.60; cf. H. C. Harrell *Public Arbitration in Athenian Law* (University of Missouri Studies 11.1, 1936) 33–4.
468   *AP* 53.6, Dem. 21.86–7; cf. Harrell *Public Arbitration* 18.
469   For the deletion of a gloss here, cf. Lipsius *Recht* 232 n. 46.

CHAPTER XIV

470   Gernet *Droit* 83–102, originally published in *Revue Historique de Droit Français et Étranger* in 1927.
471   And. 1.90–1.
472   Cf. U. E. Paoli *Studi sul processo attico* (1933) 75–173, Wolff *Paragraphe* 17–86, Harrison *Law* ii 108–19.
473   Dem. 45.57–8; cf. Bonner and Smith *Administration* ii 93.
474   Cf. MacDowell in *RIDA* 18 (1971) 267–73.
475   Lysias 23.10; cf. Wolff *Paragraphe* 112.
476   Dem. 36.25, 37.1, etc.; cf. S. Isager and M. H. Hansen *Aspects of Athenian Society in the Fourth Century B.C.* (1975) 228–37.
477   Dem. 38.17–18.
478   Dem. 44.58; cf. Gernet *Droit* 87 n. 1.
479   Cf. G. M. Calhoun in *CP* 13 (1918) 179–85, Bonner and Smith *Administration* ii 80–4.

CHAPTER XV

480   *IG* ii² 46, 144; cf. A. G. Woodhead in *Hesperia* 26 (1957) 221–33, D. M. Lewis in *Hesperia* 28 (1959) 248–50, G. E. M. de Ste Croix in *CQ* 11 (1961) 109.
481   *IG* i² 16 (ML 31) 12–14, 60. 8–9, 116 (ML 87) 26, ii² 1 (ML 94) 18, *SEG* x 6.41–3; cf. Th. 1. 77.1, Ant. 5.78.
482   Dem. 7.9–13; cf. Harrison in *CQ* 10 (1960) 248–52, de Ste Croix in *CQ* 11 (1961) 111, opposed by Meiggs *Empire* 433.

483 *IG* i² 55.7, 152.4–5, 153.5–9,
SEG x 23.5, 108.23; cf. de Ste Croix
in *CQ* 11 (1961) 273–4.
484 *IG* i² 16 (ML 31); cf. de Ste Croix
in *CQ* 11 (1961) 100–8, R. Seager in
Historia 15 (1966) 509–10, Meiggs
Empire 231–2.
485 *IG* i² 342.38, 343.89; cf. Jacoby
FGrH IIIb (Supp.) ii 380–1 n. 29,
Cohen *Maritime Courts* 166–76.
486 Dem. 45.4, 59.16, 59.66.
487 *AP* 58.3; cf. Lipsius *Recht* 65 n.
48, with correction on page 979.
488 *IG* ii² 46, 144.
489 *IG* i² 60. 8–9, 116 (ML 87) 26, ii²
1 (ML 94) 18.
490 Th. 1.77.1; cf. E. G. Turner in
CR 60 (1946) 5–7, de Ste Croix in *CQ*
11 (1961) 96–100, Gauthier *Symbola*
163–4, Meiggs *Empire* 228–33.
491 [Xen.] *Ath.* 1.16, Isok. 4.113,
12.63–6.
492 *SEG* x 31 (ML 46) 31–43.
493 *IG* i² 65 (ML 68) 37–51.
494 *ATL* List 25.60–1 and A9 (ML
69) 7–16.
495 Ar. *Birds* 1454–60; cf. de Ste
Croix in *CQ* 11 (1961) 279–80.
496 *IG* i² 10 (ML 40) 26–9.
497 *IG* i² 39 (ML 52) 71–6; cf. de
Ste Croix in *CQ* 11 (1961) 271–2,
Meiggs *Empire* 224–5.
498 Miletos: *IG* i² 22. 27–33; cf.
D. W. Bradeen and M. F. McGregor
Studies in Fifth-century Attic Epigraphy
(1973) 24–70. Samos: *IG* i² 101.7–9;
cf. D. M. Lewis in *BSA* 49 (1954) 29–
31, de Ste Croix in *CQ* 11 (1961) 272.
499 [Xen.] *Ath.* 1.14.
500 Ant. 5.47; cf. de Ste Croix in
CQ 11 (1961) 271, Meiggs *Empire*
224–6.
501 *IG* i² 59.20–2, *SEG* x 76.5–6.
502 *SEG* x 23.7–13, 99.1–3, Ar.
Peace 164–72; cf. Meiggs in *CR* 63
(1949) 9–12, de Ste Croix in *CQ* 11
(1961) 268, MacDowell *Homicide* 127–
8, Meiggs *Empire* 227–8.

503 *IG* ii² 43 (Tod 123) 41–6 and 57–
63; cf. J. A. O. Larsen *Representative
Government in Greek and Roman History*
(1955) 61–4.
504 *IG* ii² 111 (Tod 142) 73–5.
505 *IG* i² 22.34–5.
506 *SEG* x 31 (ML 46) 67–8.
507 *IG* i² 41.1–6.
508 Ar. *Birds* 1046–7, fr. 278, Phile-
tairos 12.
509 *Lex. Rhet.* 283.3–4.
510 Lysias 17.5; cf. Cohen *Maritime
Courts* 164 n. 14.
511 Harp. and Hesykhios under
ναυτοδίκαι, Pol. 8.126; cf. A. W.
Gomme *Essays in Greek History and
Literature* (1937) 82 n. 1, U. Kahrstedt
in *Klio* 32 (1939) 151–2, Jacoby's commentary on *FGrH* 342 F 4, A. Andrewes in *JHS* 81 (1961) 13, Cohen
Maritime Courts 162–84.
512 *AP* 59.6.
513 Dem. 33.1, *AP* 59.5.
514 Cf. Cohen *Maritime Courts* 23–
59.
515 Dem. 32.1, 33.1–3, 34.3–4, 34.42;
cf. Cohen *Maritime Courts* 100–14.
516 Dem. 56.10.
517 Dem. 33.1, 35.46–7, 56.4.
518 Dem. 58.11.
519 Ar. *Clouds* 1131–6, 1179–80,
1222, Dem. 46.22; cf. *IG* i² 65 (ML
68) 47.
520 *AP* 52.3, Dem. 37.2.
521 *AP* 52. 2; cf. Gernet *Droit* 173–9.
522 Cf. Gernet *Droit* 189–200.
523 E.g. Dem. 35.10–13; cf. G. E.
M. de Ste Croix in *Debts, Credits,
Finance and Profits* (ed. H. Edey and
B. S. Yamey, 1974) 41–59.
524 Dem. 34.5; cf. U. E. Paoli
Studi di diritto attico (1930) 105–9, Gernet *Droit* 162–3.

CHAPTER XVI

525 Lysias 9. 6–9.
526 Ais. 1.35, Dem. 43.75.

527 Cf. Harrison *Law* ii 7–36.
528 Ar. *Clouds* 1218, *Wasps* 1408, 1416.
529 *Hesperia* 4 (1935) 15 no. 1 line 5, Dem. 40.28, 53.14.
530 Dem. 53.15–18, And. 1.74, AP 59.3.
531 Ar. *Wasps* 1406–8.
532 Ar. *Clouds* 1131–1200, Dem. 47. 64, Pol. 8.38, etc.
533 And. 1.120, *AP* 59.3.
534 Isok. 20. 2, Isaios 3. 47.
535 Isok. 17.12, Dem. 32.29.
536 Ar. *Clouds* 770, *Wasps* 349, Isok. 15.237, Dem. 21.103.
537 *AP* 52.3, 53.2.
538 Dem. 45.46.
539 Cf. Harrison *Law* ii 179–83.
540 Isok. 16.2, Isaios 3.6–7, 5.1–2, 9.1, Dem. 43.3; cf. Harrison *Law* ii 99–100.
541 Dem. 52.17–18.
542 Lysias 30.3, Dem. 26.24.
543 Ais. 3.200, Dem. 18.111.
544 Ar.*Wasps* 963–6, And. 1.14, 1.18, 1.69, etc.
545 Dem. 45.44; cf. G. M. Calhoun in *TAPA* 50 (1919) 177–93, Bonner and Smith *Administration* i 353–62.
546 Dem. 46.6–9, 57.4, Isaios 3.18–21, Ais. 2.19.
547 Dem. 21.95, 59.26–7.
548 Dem. 49.19; cf. Harrison *Law* ii 141–2.
549 Ais. 1.46–7, 1.67–9, Lyk. *Leo.* 20, Dem. 59.28, etc.; cf. Harrison *Law* ii 140.
550 And. 1.7, Lysias 19.4.
551 Ant. 5. 69–71.
552 *AP* 68.4, Dem. 48.45; cf. Harrison *Law* ii 192–3.
553 Dem. 24.131, 47.49, Isaios 11. 46, schol. on Plato *Laws* 937d; cf. D. Behrend in *Symposion* 1971 (ed. H. J. Wolff, 1975) 131–56.
554 Dem. 46.10.
555 Ant. 2d.7, And. 1.74, Hyp. *Philippides* 12.

556 Dem. 46.10, 47.1, 49.56.
557 Ant. 5.32, Arist. *Rhetoric* 1377a 1–5; cf. R. Turasiewicz *De servis testibus in Atheniensium iudiciis saec. V et IV a. Chr. n. per tormenta cruciatis* (1963).
558 Ar. *Frogs* 615–25, Ant. 1.10, Isok. 17.15, Dem. 37.40, 45.61, 59.124.
559 And. 1.64, Lyk. *Leo.* 112, *Oxyrhynchus Papyri* 2686.
560 Lysias 3.33; cf. E. W. Bushala in *GRBS* 9 (1968) 61–8, C. Lacombrade in *Pallas* 20 (1973) 19–23. Ant. 5.49 refers to torture in Mytilene, where Athenian law may not have been observed.
561 Ais. 2.155, Hyp. *Athenogenes* 33, Dem. 19.146, 25.62, 35.14, etc.; cf. Isok. 17.14.
562 Ant. 1.20, Ais. 3.224, Dem. 18. 133, Plu. *Nikias* 30. 3, *Ethika* 509b.
563 And. 1.43, Lysias 13.27, 13.59.
564 Dem. 49.65, 54.40, 55.27.
565 Dem. 37.44.
566 Dem. 20.165, 54.41.
567 *AP* 66.2–3, *Hesperia* 37 (1968) 370 lines 15–19.
568 Ar. *Wasps* 894, Ais. 1.2.
569 Dem. 48.25–6, 58.43, Hyp. fr. 202.
570 Dem. 32.27, Pol. 8.61.
571 Dem. 27–8, 30–1, 48.51, *AP* 67.2.
572 *AP* 67, Dem. 43.8, 53.17, Ais. 2.126, 3.197.
573 Cf. S. Young in *Hesperia* 8 (1939) 274–84, Thompson and Wycherley *Agora* 55.
574 *AP* 67.3.
575 Plato *Apology* 25c–d, Lysias 12. 25, 13.30–2, 22.5, Isaios 11.5, Dem. 46.10.
576 K. J. Dover *Lysias and the Corpus Lysiacum* (1968) 148–74, opposed by S. Usher in *GRBS* 17 (1976) 31–40.
577 Dem. 46.26.
578 Plu. *Ethika* 833f, Dein. 2.6.
579 Cf. MacDowell *Wasps* 198–9.
580 Ar. *Wasps* 568–74, 976–8, Plato

Apology 34c, Lysias 20.34, Dem. 21.99, 21.186–8.

581 Ar. *Wasps* 94–9, 349, 987–92, etc.; cf. MacDowell *Wasps* 142–3.

582 *AP* 68–9; cf. A. L. Boegehold in *Hesperia* 32 (1963) 366–74, E. S. Staveley *Greek and Roman Voting and Elections* (1972) 95–100, Thompson and Wycherley *Agora* 56.

583 Dem. 43.10.

584 Dem. 27.67, 28.18, 56.4, Isok. 18.12; cf. Harrison *Law* ii 183–5.

585 Dem. 19.290.

586 Ar. *Wasps* 106–8, 167, *AP* 69.2.

587 Plato *Phaidon* 58a–c.

588 Hdt. 7.133.1, Xen. *Hellenika* 1.7.20, Plato *Gorgias* 516d, Lyk. *Leo.* 121, Dein. 1.62; cf. E. Berneker in *Studi in onore di E. Volterra* (1971) i 87–97.

589 Lysias 13.56, 13.67–8, Dem. 8. 61, 19.137, 21.105; cf. Bonner and Smith *Administration* ii 279–87, Mac-Dowell *Homicide* 111–13.

590 Cf. C. Gill in *CQ* 23 (1973) 25–8.

591 Lysias 12.17, 18.24, And. 3.10, Xen. *Hellenika* 2.3.56.

592 Dem. 23.37, 23.44.

593 Plu. *Ethika* 834a, *Lex. Rhet.* 199. 4–8, 237.10–11; cf. Harrison *Law* ii 212–13.

594 Cf. G. D. Rocchi in *Acme* 28 (1975) 257–79.

595 Dem. 21.47, 24.105, 33.1, 35. 46–7, 56.4, Plato *Apology* 37c.

596 Dem. 24.92, 24.146, Plato *Apology* 37b–c, And. 4.4; cf. I. Barkan in *CP* 31 (1936) 338–41.

597 Dem. 20.147, 24.54.

598 And. 1.87, Dem. 24.56.

599 Th. 8.97.3.

600 Xen. *Hellenika* 1.5.19, Pausanias 6.7.4–5.

601 And. 1.73–80.

602 And. 1.87, Dem. 24.45, 24.59.

603 Plu. *Demosthenes* 27.6, *Ethika* 842e, Nepos *Timotheus* 4.1.

INDEX